THE NEW PASSOVER

Sue & Peter

With best wishes

Nigel

15 July 2019

THE NEW PASSOVER

Rethinking the Lord's Supper for Today

Nigel Scotland

CASCADE *Books* • Eugene, Oregon

THE NEW PASSOVER
Rethinking the Lord's Supper for Today

Cascade Books
An Imprint of Wipf and Stock Publishers
199 W. 8th Ave., Suite 3
Eugene, OR 97401

www.wipfandstock.com

PAPERBACK ISBN: 978-1-4982-1813-9
HARDCOVER ISBN: 978-1-4982-1815-3
EBOOK ISBN: 978-1-4982-1814-6

Cataloguing-in-Publication data:

Scotland, Nigel.
The new passover : rethinking the Lord's Supper for today / Nigel Scotland.
Eugene, OR: Cascade Books, 2016 | Includes bibliographical references.
Identifiers: ISBN 978-1-4982-1813-9 (paperback) | ISBN 978-1-4982-1815-3 (hardcover) | ISBN 978-1-4982-1814-6 (ebook)
Subjects: LCSH: 1. Lord's Supper. | 2. Early works. | 3. Passover.
Classification: BV825.5 S4 2016 | BV825.5 (ebook)

Manufactured in the USA.   08/02/16

For my lovely wife Anne,
who shares the views expressed in this book.

Contents

Preface

Earlier this year when my wife and I were on holiday in Europe, we attended the local English church for Sunday morning worship. The service was Holy Communion. It was one of the most gloomy and sad experiences we could remember. We were greeted by the chaplain who informed us that it was "Low Sunday"—Anglican speak for the Sunday after Easter Day. We were also told that the church was very short of money and that if we were British tax payers it would be helpful if we could sign a tax declaration form that would enable them to claim a rebate on what we put in the offertory. These were brought round during the singing of the first hymn! After some readings a sermon followed on "Doubting Thomas" and all the many things in the contemporary world that cause us to doubt God. Then came a rapid and perfunctory gallop through the liturgy of *Common Worship*, which reached a climax when the priest held up and broke a large wafer during which a small and very tinny sounding bell was rung. The host was then held aloft so that we could all gaze upon it. The congregation then queued in lines and a circlet of what looked like rice paper was thrust into our mouths or hands as we knelt at the Communion rail. The chaplain was followed by a tall lay assistant clad in a long white robe who had to stoop down and then do his best to push the Communion cup into our mouths. No wine actually reached my wife and I suspect the same was true for some of the others. After the final hymn we were ushered out into the hot sunshine without so much as "Thank you for coming," never mind a cold glass of white wine or even some cool fruit juice.

As we walked away we both thought is it any wonder, as Richard Dawkins has pointed out, that there is a loss of respect for religion in the Western world. It's this kind of mind-numbing, dull, esoteric ritual that challenges me because it seems so far from the Last Supper meal that Jesus instituted and shared with his disciples. It also underlined something I have known for a long time, and that is churches with this kind of Eucharist as their main Sunday worship are by and large not growing churches. This of course should not surprise us since Jesus never intended that his Supper should be for large numbers of people, many of whom are uncommitted or nominal Christian people.

This book contends that the Lord's Supper should be kept with ordinary bread and wine Passover style: that is, in the context of a celebration evening meal or shared food, in Christian households and in small groups. It is a great and vital source of spiritual strength that comes as Christian brothers and sisters eat and drink together in fellowship, remembrance, and thanksgiving. My hope is that as you read on you will be persuaded that the ways in which the great majority of contemporary churches keep the Lord's Supper need some radical and serious rethinking!

List of Abbreviations

BOOKS OF THE OLD AND NEW TESTAMENTS

Note: All biblical quotations are taken from the NIV version.

Acts	Acts of the Apostles	Luke	Luke
Chr	Chronicles	Mark	Mark
Cor	Corinthians	Matt	Matthew
Deut	Deuteronomy	Neh	Nehemiah
Eph	Ephesians	Pet	Peter
Exod	Exodus	Phil	Philippians
Gen	Genesis	Ps(s)	Psalm(s)
Heb	Hebrews	Rev	Revelation
John	John	Thess	Thessalonians
Jude	Jude	Tim	Timothy

TRACTATES OF THE TALMUD

Pes.   Pesaḥim

1

A Passover-Style Meal

The middle years of the sixteenth century saw the Roman Counter Reformation reach a zenith point during the papacy of Paul IV, who took office in 1555. The central aspect of the Western church's worship and spirituality at this point in time was the Mass. At the heart of this sacrament stood the priest, whose consecration prayer—which included the recitation of Jesus' words of institution at the Last Supper, the laying of his hands over the bread and wine, and an invocation of the Holy Spirit—was believed to change the elements into the very body and blood of Christ. These he then offered up at the altar, not as a remembrance of Christ's death but as the very body and blood of Christ for the sins of the living and the dead. This miracle of the Mass was depicted by Raphael in his celebrated painting entitled *The Dispute over the Holy Sacrament*, which he completed in 1509. In reality, as it has often been pointed out, the painting is really about "the adoration of the sacrament." This fact is made obvious by the monstrance, a small glass-fronted container that holds the reserved sacrament and stands in the center of the altar.

However, not all sixteenth-century painters of the period were quite as focused on the Roman Mass as Raphael. For example, Jacopo Bassano (1510–1592) in his painting of 1542 depicted the Last Supper as a rustic Passover-style meal. Bassano portrayed the disciples as barefooted rugged fishermen and tax collectors. On the table is the remains of the Passover lamb and the disciples are almost asleep and look as though they have had plenty to drink. Theophanes the Cretan (d.1559) went considerably further in his painting of the Last Supper that hangs in the refectory of the monastery at Stavronika. Completed in 1546, he also portrayed the Last Supper as a Passover. Each disciple has their own drinking vessel as they would have done at a first-century Passover Seder and on the table there are various Passover ingredients including the bitter herbs.

These paintings help us to recognize that the way in which contemporary Christian churches understand and practice the Lord's Supper is a long way removed from the simple Passover meal or, according to some scholars, a Passover-style meal or Jewish meal at Passover time that Jesus shared with his disciples in the Upper Room. From a simple meal around a domestic table the Lord's Supper developed over time into a lengthy theological and esoteric ritual in which bread and wine were and are believed to be transubstantiated into the body and blood of Christ. It's still called the Lord's Supper in many sections of the church but there is no longer any meal and little time for what should be the key ingredients of joyful celebration, remembrance, and fellowship. It is the purpose of this book that in view of these developments Christian people and churches need to have a radical rethinking of the Lord's Supper for today.

This first chapter examines the Passover context of the Last Supper and the Passover ethos of the early Christian Lord's Supper. In doing so it will be apparent that the ways in which many contemporary churches practice the Lord's Supper has moved a long way from the meal Jesus shared with his disciples in the Upper Room and which he intended to be the pattern for his subsequent followers.

THE PASSOVER IN THE OLD TESTAMENT

The Passover was the ritual which the people of Israel were instructed to carry out so that the Lord could spare or "pass over" their lives while at the same time destroying those Egyptians who were holding them captive in slavery. The Passover meal or Feast of Unleavened Bread is the annual ceremony that God commanded his people to keep in memory of this dramatic escape from bondage.

ESCAPE FROM EGYPT

In the book of Exodus, 12:1–13, 21–27, and 43–49 recounts what most scholars take to be Moses's account of the Passover. The word "Passover" is the English translation of the Hebrew *pesah*, which can also mean "to spare." The Passover took place in the month when the grain was ripening and which later came to be called Nisan. It was then made the first month of the Jewish year.[1] On the tenth day of the month Moses and Aaron were instructed to tell the whole company of Israel to take a lamb each for his family. If any household was too small for a whole lamb they were to share it with their nearest neighbor. The animals that were chosen had to be year-old males without any defect. They were to be cared for until the fourteenth day of the month, at which point the whole community was to slaughter them at twilight. This having been done, each family was to take a bunch of hyssop, dip it into the basin, and put some of the blood on the sides and tops of the doorframes of the houses where they were to eat the lambs. They were to eat the meat roasted over the fire together with bitter herbs and bread made without yeast. They were not to eat it raw or cooked with water but to roast it over the fire including the head, legs, and inner parts. Nothing was to be left over till the following morning. All the leftovers were to be burnt. They were to eat it in haste, which was why the bread was to be unleavened. No one was to leave the house until morning.

The blood on the door posts was the sign to the Lord to "pass over" when at midnight he struck down all the firstborn of Egypt from the house of Pharaoh to the prisoner who was in the dungeon. When this took place Pharaoh and all of his officials got up in the night amid loud wailing from every quarter and summoned Moses and Aaron to get up and leave the land as quickly as possible, taking their flocks and herds with them. So the Israelites moved rapidly, taking their dough with them before the yeast was added, carrying it on their shoulders in kneading troughs wrapped in clothing.

THE PASSOVER MEAL

Following the Israelites' escape from Pharaoh there are a number of Old Testament references to subsequent Passover celebrations. In Numbers 9:1–14 there is an account of the feast being kept in the desert of Sinai on

---

1. Exod 12:1.

the fourteenth day of the first month of the second year after the Exodus. Following the ceremony Moses petitioned the Lord regarding those who had not been able to take part on account of uncleanness through having come into contact with dead bodies. He was instructed to organize a second Passover on the fourteenth day of the second month for any such people and for those who had been away on a journey. The regulations for these second Passovers were to be the same including the instructions for the aliens and the native born.

In Joshua 5 there is a reference to the Israelites celebrating the Passover at Gilgal on the plains of Jericho. It was evidently a significant moment, for on the day following they ate some of the produce of the land, unleavened bread and roasted grain. The second book of Chronicles has a detailed account of the way in which the good King Josiah brought about a renewed commitment to the Passover celebrations in the eighteenth year of his reign. The people were instructed to prepare themselves for the feast in families in their respective divisions. Then, from his own resources, he provided 30,000 sheep and goats for all the households. The lambs were slaughtered and skinned by the priests and Levites, and then collected by each household and taken away to be roasted. The Chronicler noted that the Passover had not been kept in such a dedicated manner since the time of the prophet Samuel.[2] In the prophecy of Ezekiel 45:21–25 there is a brief reference to the Passover, which stated that the prince was required to play a public role on each of the seven days of the feast in providing seven bulls and seven rams without defect as burnt offerings to the Lord, a male goat for a sin offering and grain offerings to accompany each of the animal sacrifices.

It should be noted that by the time of Jesus' ministry a number of other developments had taken place in the Passover meal. Among them were the drinking of four cups of red wine and the eating of the *harosheth*, a mixture of figs, nuts, dates, pomegranates, apples, almonds, cinnamon, and ginger. When these were mixed together they produce a clayish-colored source that reminded those at the meal of how their ancestors had to make bricks in Egypt. The crushed cinnamon bark reminded them of the straw that had to be mixed with the clay.[3] The "sop" which the Lord gave to Judas was probably *harosheth*. It is generally believed that the four cups of wine were introduced into the Passover Seder at some point during the period of

2. 2 Chr 25:18.
3. Keith, *The Passover*, 34.

Roman rule. It was a frequent custom for Roman citizens to drink cups of wine at festive and celebratory occasions, and this may well have impacted the Jews, who felt they had more genuine reasons to celebrate. Add to this the fact that the Old Testament was clear that "wine made glad the heart of man" and that the rabbis asserted that "without wine there could be no celebration."

THE VIEW THAT THE LAST SUPPER WAS A PASSOVER MEAL

Possibly within a short space of time some developments took place in the way the Passover meal was kept by the Israelites. The regulations in Deuteronomy 16:1–8 show a number of differences from the Exodus narrative. These should not be seen as contradictions, but simply represent obvious developments as the ceremony changed in purpose from being one which produced deliverance to one which remembered that deliverance. The emphasis on the blood has disappeared. There seems to have been a greater choice in the animal chosen for the meal, which could be taken from either the flock or herd.[4] The unleavened bread is called in Deuteronomy "the bread of affliction" and appears to focus the thoughts of the participants so "that all the days of your life you may remember the time of your departure from Egypt."[5]

It seems clear that Jesus intended that his disciples and all his subsequent followers should understand and treat the Lord's Supper in the same or very similar ways that they understood and kept the Jewish Passover. In the first place, Jesus called the Last Supper a "Passover." Luke 22 records that he told his disciples, "I have eagerly desired to eat this Passover with you before I suffer."[6] The Last Supper can only have been held on the evening of 14th Nisan, as Mark 14:12 indicated, since only on that day would the Passover lambs have been slaughtered in the temple precincts and made available for that purpose.

Scholars are divided as to whether the Passover ritual as it was kept in New Testament times is preserved in the Passover or Pesaḥim tractate of the Mishnah, a collection of ancient Jewish traditions, which were compiled by Rabbi Yehudah HaNasi (c. 135–c. 217) between AD 180–220. The

4. Deut 16:2.

5. Deut 16:3.

6. Luke 22:15.

Mishnah, it should be noted, describes the celebration of the Passover as it was kept in the years after AD 70, at which time there were some changes, including the fact that it was no longer celebrated by the whole nation within the city of Jerusalem but in individual homes where the people lived.

The Last Supper meal did however take place in Jerusalem and the disciples would then have collected their lamb from the temple area and taken it to the Upper Room. At this time the Passover had to be eaten within the gates of Jerusalem and at night. This accords with the accounts in John 13:30 that "it was night" and 1 Corinthians 11:23 that "the Lord Jesus on the *night* he was betrayed took bread." The Passover, as has been noted above, began at sunset and lasted into the night.[7]

According to Matthew 26:20 and Mark 14:17 Jesus celebrated the Last Supper with his twelve disciples. This, according to the Mishnah, represented the average ideal number as it was assumed that a one-year-old lamb would provide enough food for about ten people.[8] The Passover normally included women and children[9] and there are many detailed instructions recounted in the Mishnah and elsewhere about keeping the children awake for the Passover meal.[10] Significantly, Jeremias pointed out that, "it is not possible to assume from the Last Supper narratives that the women mentioned in Mark 15:40, and Luke 23:49 and 55, were excluded."[11] It is reasonable, he suggested, that one or two of them could have reclined together at a separate smaller table.

At the time of Jesus' earthly ministry the ordinary people gathered in the outer court of the Jerusalem temple to slaughter the Passover lambs. The priests stood in two lines and each one held a silver basin in which to catch the blood from the sacrificial animal. The vessel was then passed down to the end of the line where the last priest ceremoniously dowsed the altar with it.[12] While this was being done the people sang the Hallel Psalms 113–18. This accords well with the account in Luke 22:7–8, which states that Jesus and his disciples prepared the Passover on the day of unleavened bread when the Passover lamb had to be sacrificed. The same information is recorded in Matthew 29:17 and Mark 14:12.

7. Exod 12:8.
8. Mishnah, Pes. 8:3.
9. Exod 12:26.
10. Mishnah, Pes. 10:9.
11. Jeremias, *The Eucharistic Words*, 46.
12. Mishnah, Pes. 3:6.

Despite there having been some developments with the passing of time the ritual and structure of the Passover remained relatively simple. It is necessary to briefly return to the three core ingredients of the Passover stressed by Rabbi Gamaliel, the teacher of the Apostle Paul, mentioned earlier. He said: "Whoever does not explain three things in the Passover has not fulfilled the duty incumbent on him. The *Passover Lamb* signified that God 'passed over' the blood-sprinkled houses of our fathers in Egypt; the *unleavened bread* testified that our fathers were delivered out of Egypt (in haste), and the *bitter herbs* were a reminder that the Egyptians made bitter the lives of our fathers in Egypt."[13] There are other instructions which deal with the arrangements for the meal. From the time of the evening sacrifice no food was to be eaten until the Paschal Supper, so that all might come to the feast with relish.[14] It is not altogether clear whether at the time of Jesus' ministry two or as at present three large cakes of unleavened bread were used in the meal. The Mishnah mentions several kinds of vegetables which could be used to represent "bitter herbs," namely lettuce, endive, succory, charchavina, and bitter coriander.[15] The bitter herbs appear to have been taken at two points during the meal, once dipped in salt water or vinegar and at a second occasion in a mixture of dates, raisins, and vinegar, though the Mishnah makes it plain that this second dipping is not obligatory.[16] Some of these may possibly have been among the items which Jesus told the disciples to attend to as they prepared the Passover room (Mark 14:12–16).

The Mishnah is manifestly clear that only red wine is to be used and always mixed with water.[17] Each of the four cups were required to contain at least the fourth quarter of a *hin*, which approximates to one gallon and two pints. There was to be no *Aphikomen* (after dish) or something akin to dessert after the end of the meal.

---

13. Mishnah, Pes. 10:1.

14. Ibid.

15. Ibid., Pes. 2:6 states, "And these are the herbs by [eating] which at the Passover a man fulfils his obligation: lettuce, chicory, pepperwort, snakeroot, and dandelion. He fulfils it whether they are fresh or dried, but not if they are pickled, stewed or cooked. And these may be included together to make up [the prescribed quantity of] an olive's bulk. He can fulfil his obligation if he eats but their stalks, or if they are *demai*-produce, or First Tithe from which the Heave-offering has been taken, or the Second Tithe or dedicated produce which have been redeemed."

16. Ibid., Pes. 10:3.

17. Ibid., Pes. 7:13.

All those who took part in the Passover meal were required to be ritually clean in the manner described in Numbers 19:19, "The person being cleansed must wash his clothes and bathe with water and that evening he will be clean." The Mishnah gave the following instruction on the matter of cleansing for the Passover meal.

> He that mourns his near kindred may, after he has *immersed* himself, eat the Passover-offering in the evening, but he may not eat [other] Hallowed Things. If a man heard of the death of one of his kindred or caused bones of his dead to be gathered together, he may, after he has immersed himself, eat Hallowed Things. The School of Shammai say: If a man became a proselyte on the day before Passover he may immerse himself and consume the Passover-offering in the evening. And the School of Hillel say: He that separates himself from his uncircumcision is as one that separates himself from a grave.[18]

Those who were not clean in this way were to be cut off from the community because they "had defiled the sanctuary of the Lord." There is a passing reference to this cleansing in John 11:55. The apostle recorded that "when it was almost time for the Jewish Passover, many went up from the country to Jerusalem for their ceremonial cleansing before the Passover." This is the point at which details of Jesus girding himself with a towel and washing the disciples' feet fits into the Passover narrative. When he came to wash Peter's feet he refused saying, "not just my feet but my hands and my head as well" (John 13:9). To this Jesus replied, reminding him that he was already ritually clean [for the Passover meal] since he had had a bath (John 13:10)! It was therefore only necessary at that point that he should have his feet washed in order that he should be visually reminded that he, like the other disciples, was called to a servant ministry.

A significant indicator that the last supper was intended to be the New Passover was the fact to which all the Synoptic Gospels bear witness (Matthew 26:20; Mark 14:18; Luke 22:14) that Jesus and his disciples "reclined" at the table at the Last Supper. Jeremias argued from rabbinical texts that first-century Jews *sat* when dining. "Wherever the gospels speak of reclining at meals," he wrote, "they mean either a meal in the open (feeding of the multitudes), or a party, or a feast, or a royal banquet, or a wedding feast, or the feast of salvation time."[19] Jeremias continued on from this point to state

---

18. Ibid., Pes. 8:8.

19. Jeremias, *The Eucharistic Words*, 48.

with emphasis that "It is *absolutely impossible* [his italics] that Jesus and his disciples should have *reclined* [his italics] at table for ordinary meals."[20] How is it then that they reclined at table in the case of the Last Supper? There could only be one answer, according to Jeremias: "it was a ritual duty to recline at table as a symbol of freedom, also, as it is expressly stated, for 'the poorest man in Israel.'"[21] Rabbi Levi (c. 300) said that people should recline to eat the Passover, "to signify that they have passed from slavery to freedom."[22]

Another fact which makes it plain that Jesus and his disciples were eating a Passover meal comes in both Mark and Matthew's accounts of the Supper where it is stated that "while they were eating" Jesus took the bread, gave thanks, broke it, and gave it to the disciples. Both Gospel writers were describing what was an unusual practice because ordinary Jewish meals began with the breaking of bread but here it is clear that the meal was already in progress.

FIRST CUP

In the Mishnah account of the Passover the service begins when the one who is presiding over the company takes the first cup of wine in his hand and gives thanks using the following words.

> Blessed art Thou, Lord our God, who has created the fruit of the vine! Blessed art Thou, Lord our God, King of the Universe, who has chosen us from among all people, and exalted us from among all languages, and sanctified us with Thy commandments! And Thou hast given us, O Lord our God, in love, the solemn days for joy, and the festivals and appointed seasons for gladness; and with this day of the feast of unleavened bread, the season of our freedom, a holy convocation, the memorial of our departure from Egypt. For us hast Thou chosen; and hast Thou sanctified from all nations, and Thy holy festivals with joy and gladness Thou hast caused us to inherit. Blessed art Thou, O Lord, who sanctifies Israel and the appointed seasons! Blessed art Thou, Lord, King of the Universe, who preserves us alive and sustained us and brought us to this season![23]

20. Mark 14:22; Matt 26:26.

21. Jeremias, *The Eucharistic Words*, 49.

22. Ibid., 49n2.

23. Mishnah, Pes. 10:2.

The first cup is then drunk and each person washes their hands by "dipping" them into the basin. It was quite possibly this first cup which Jesus took and was the first of the two which Luke 22:17 records.

Jeremias made much of the fact that Jesus and his disciples drank wine at the Last Supper. He points out that wine was drunk in most Jewish homes only on festive occasions and particularly on the three pilgrimage festivals of Passover, Pentecost, and Tabernacles. Drinking wine was a prescribed part of the Passover ritual and according to Pesaḥim 10.1 four cups should be the minimum. In everyday life water was drunk and the breakfast consisted of bread with salt and a large jar of water. At other times wine was mainly used for medicinal purposes, as in Luke 10:34 and 1 Timothy 5:23. Jeremias underlined the fact that there are only two occasions where it is explicitly stated that Jesus drank wine, the first being Matthew 11:16–19 where he is accused of being a wine drinker and the second being at the wedding in Cana in John 2:1–11. Jesus and his disciples would have drunk wine on festal occasions but apart from those occasions, according to Jeremias, they would have drunk water with their daily meals. Clearly Jesus and his disciples drank red wine at the Last Supper because of the comparison which he drew between the wine and his blood. Rabbi Judah (c. AD 150), representing an earlier tradition, laid it down that red wine must be drunk at the Passover.[24]

THE BREAD

After this first cup Luke recorded that Jesus took bread, gave thanks, and broke it and gave it to them saying, "This is my body given for you, do this in remembrance of me" (see also Mark 14:22). It was probably at this point that the reference to Judas dipping bread in the dish with Jesus fits into the accounts of Matthew 26:23 and Mark 14:20. John 13:29 records that after Judas had taken the bread from the hand of Jesus he went out into the night. Since he had charge of the group funds the other disciples could well have thought that Jesus was telling him to go and purchase something for the poor. This focus on the needy was manifest in the right to four cups of wine, "even from the pauper's dish [from charity]."[25] Jeremias cited the ancient Aramaic Passover saying which adds significance to this point, "Behold, this is the bread of affliction, which our fathers had to eat as they came out

24. Jeremias, *The Eucharistic Words*, 53.
25. Ibid., 54.

of Egypt. Whoever hungers, let him come and eat, and whoever is *in need*, let him come and keep Passover (with us)."[26]

DIPPING THE BREAD

Once the preliminaries of the first cup and the bread were completed the president of the feast invited those present to dip their bread into the salt water. The second cup was then filled but not yet drunk. Jeremias pointed out from the Mishnah that at every Passover the children ask the question, "How is it that on every evening we dip bread into the dish but on this evening we simply dip (without bread) into the dish"? He then commented, "This children's question shows conclusively that this was the Passover meal because it was the only meal in the year at which the serving of a dish (Mark 14:20) preceded the breaking of bread (Mark 14.22)."[27] The dipping of the herb directly in the salt water served as a reminder of the bitterness of the time of slavery in Egypt.

THE SON'S QUESTION

At this point in the meal a very significant question is asked of the Father or the one presiding by the son or else the youngest child present: "Why is this night distinguished from all other nights? For on all other nights we eat any kind of herbs, but on this night only bitter herbs? On all other nights we eat meat roasted, stewed, or boiled, but on this night only roasted? On all other nights we dip (the herbs) only once, but on this night twice"? The Mishnah adds: "then the father instructs his child according to the capacity of his knowledge, beginning with our disgrace and ending with our glory, and expounding to him from, 'A Syrian, ready to perish, was my father,' till he has explained all through, to the end of the whole section" (Deut 26:5–11).[28] What is intended here is that the father shall recount the national history beginning with Terah, Abraham's father, and then continuing with an account of Israel's deliverance from Egypt and the giving of the law.

When this history is completed the president takes up in succession the dish containing the Passover lamb, followed by the bitter herbs and

26. Ibid., 54.
27. Ibid., 50.
28. Mishnah, Pes. 10:4.

then that containing the unleavened bread, and briefly explains what the significance of each of them. According to Rabbi Gamaliel, "From generation to generation every man is bound to look upon himself not otherwise than if he had come forth out of Egypt. For so it is written (Exod 13:8), "And thou shalt show thy son that in that day, saying, 'This is done because of that which Jehovah did unto me when I came forth out of Egypt.'" Therefore, the Mishnah continues, citing the very words of the prayer used, "We are bound to thank, praise, laud, glorify, extol, honour, bless, exalt, and reverence Him, because He hath wrought for our fathers and for us all these miracles. He brought us forth from bondage into freedom, from sorrow into joy, from mourning to a festival, from darkness to a great light, and from slavery to redemption. Therefore let us sing before Him Hallelujah!"[29] This is then followed with the singing of the first part of the "Hallel" which consists of Psalms 113 and 114 ending with a short thanksgiving, "Blessed art Thou, O Lord our God, King of the Universe, who hast redeemed our fathers from Egypt."

At this point the second cup was drunk. Hands were again washed in the same manner and with the same prayer as before. One of the two unleavened cakes is broken and a thanksgiving is offered.

THE BREAKING OF THE BREAD

For Jeremias the most convincing proof of the paschal character of the Last Supper was the simple fact that the words of interpretation which Jesus spoke over the bread and wine precisely followed the structure of the interpretation of the Passover ritual. The Passover meal took place after the preliminary course and the mixing of the second of the four ritual cups of wine. Rabbi Gamaliel (c. AD 130) stated that "whoever did not mention in his interpretation the three essential things at Passover has failed in his obligation, these being the *Passover lamb*, the *unleavened bread*, and the *bitter herbs*."[30] The form of the interpretation was made clear in Exodus 20. The Passover lamb was because "God in his mercy 'passed over' the houses of our fathers in Egypt." The unleavened was bread because the dough of our fathers had not time to leaven when the Lord redeemed them. The bitter herbs spoke of the embittered lives of our fathers in Egypt.

29. Mishnah, Pes. 10:37.
30. Mishnah, Pes. 10:5.

Jesus who called himself "the bread of life" and "living bread" used the bread of the Passover to refer to himself as the spotless lamb who was about to be sacrificed for sin. This also finds support in 1 Corinthians 5:7b–8 where the Apostle Paul wrote of the unleavened loaves as representing Christ the Passover lamb who had been sacrificed for the people's sins. He made the point in these words that to be a Christian is to live in deliverance from sin. It meant throwing out the old leaven or yeast of the old life in order to live out the new life of the bread of sincerity and truth.

Jesus therefore followed the pattern of the Passover that commemorated a past deliverance by the sacrifice of a lamb and the sprinkling of its blood on the lintels of their houses. The differences were that the New Passover commemorated a greater deliverance from bondage to sin and selfishness and he himself was indeed the perfect sacrificial lamb. Clearly however after Jesus' crucifixion the Passover lamb could have no further meaning for his followers since he was himself to be "the perfect and spotless lamb of God."[31] It was for this reason that all future New Passovers or Lord's Suppers would be commemorations.

THE THIRD CUP

Immediately following the meal the third cup was drunk, a special blessing having been pronounced over it. According to Jeremias, there can be no reasonable doubting that this was the cup which Jesus connected with his own Supper and that symbolized his blood. This finds some support in the Apostle Paul's letter to the Corinthians, where he referred to the cup in the Lord's Supper as "the Cup of Blessing" (1 Corinthian 10:16). This can also be seen as fitting with the Last Supper narratives in both Luke and 1 Corinthians, which are in agreement that it was *after* supper that Jesus took the cup (Luke 22:20; 1 Cor 11:25).

THE FOURTH CUP

The Passover liturgy concludes with the fourth cup over which the second portion of the "Hallel" was sung that comprised of Psalms 115, 116, 117, and 118. The ceremony finally ended with what was called the "blessing of the song," which was formed of the following two prayers: "All Thy works

31. John 1:29.

shall praise Thee, Jehovah our God. And Thy saints, the righteous, who do Thy good pleasure, and all Thy people, the house of Israel, with joyous song let them praise, and bless, and magnify, and glorify, and exalt, and reverence, and sanctify, and ascribe the kingdom to Thy name, O our King! For it is good to praise Thee, and pleasure to sing praises unto Thy name, for from everlasting Thou art God."[32] This fits well with the Matthew and Mark's accounts, which both record that the Supper ended with the singing of a hymn (Matt 26:30 and Mark 14:26).

Matthew 26:30, Mark 14:26, and Luke 22:39 all record that Jesus left the Passover room and went out with his disciples to the Mount of Olives. Whilst this might seem to militate against the regulation that no person could leave Jerusalem on Passover night it was in fact permissible after the meal was over to spend the night anywhere in the greater Jerusalem district. The chronology of the Fourth Gospel appears to contradict this time frame. This is seen in John 18:28, which records that Jesus was led to the palace of the Roman governor in "the early morning" and in order to avoid ceremonial uncleanness, the Jews did not enter it because "they wanted to celebrate the Passover that evening." There are however traces of the chronology of the other three Gospels elsewhere in John. John 13:30 recorded that, as was always the case, the Passover meal was held at night and that it took place in Jerusalem (John 12:55). John also noted that at the meal those who took part "reclined" at the table (John 13:23). Furthermore he also recorded, as Passover regulations required, that the meal was taken in a state of ritual purity with the disciples clearly having bathed in preparation (John 13:10). John's gospel 11:55 reported that "when it was almost Passover many went up from the country to Jerusalem for their ceremonial cleansing before the Passover." What all this amounts to is that John's gospel provides several traces of evidence that suggest that the Last Supper was a Passover meal.

The Last Supper ended with the singing of a hymn (Mark 14:26 and Matt 26:30). This, according to Jeremias, can only be a reference to the second half of the Passover Hallel that in rabbinical literature is sometimes called *himnon*, a word derived from the Greek *humnos*, or "hymn." Jeremias concluded that "there is no point at which a contradiction between the description of the Last Supper and the Passover ritual of the earlier period can be demonstrated."[33]

---

32. Mishnah, Pes. 10.

33. Jeremias, *The Eucharistic Words*, 71.

THE VIEW THAT THE LORD'S SUPPER WAS NOT A PASSOVER MEAL

Down through the centuries however there have been a number of scholars who have not seen the Last Supper as a Passover meal. The most celebrated of the early supporters of this view was Melito (d. c. 190), Bishop of Sardis. Although he was strongly of the view that Jesus died on the evening of 14th when the Passover was being prepared, he nevertheless drew a number of clear parallels between the Jewish Passover and the Last Supper. In *Concerning the Passover* he wrote of Jesus as "the Passover of your salvation" and again, "This is the one who was taken from the flock, and was dragged to the sacrifice, and killed in the evening, and was buried at night . . . who rose from the dead and who raised up mankind from the grave."[34] Among more recent supporters of Melito's views were William Maxwell in the earlier years of the twentieth century and Jonathan Klawans. Maxwell (1938) maintained that the Last Supper was derived from a simple weekly meal shared by a group of male Jews, often a rabbi and his disciples, and known as a kiddush. The main purpose of the kiddush was to prepare for the Sabbath or a festival. Such meals were apparently popular in Messianic circles.[35] The substance of Maxwell's argument was that the kiddush was always observed by a group of male friends as opposed to the Passover, which was traditionally a family meal or festival. At the Passover a lamb would be offered and unleavened bread was used. There is, as Maxwell pointed out, no mention of a lamb in the Last Supper and the synoptic narratives all use the Greek word *artos*, meaning ordinary bread as opposed to unleavened bread. Maxwell pointed to the fact that several cups were used at the Passover whereas at the Last Supper and the kiddush only one cup was used. However, it should be pointed out that Luke mentions two cups. Again Maxwell noted that the Last Supper was celebrated frequently, the kiddush weekly but the Passover was held only once a year. The disciples, it seems, felt that Jesus intended them to celebrate the Lord's Supper frequently. This, Maxwell felt, would have been unlikely if the Passover were the background rather than the kiddush.[36]

---

34. Melito of Sardis, *Concerning the Passover*, secs. 5, 69, and 71.

35. Maxwell, *An Outline of Christian Worship*, 6.

36. Ibid.

Klawans underlined the fact that in John "the seven day Passover festival doesn't begin until after Jesus is crucified."[37] If John's dating is correct the Last Supper could not therefore have been a Passover meal. Klawans also argued that "we cannot know how the Jews celebrated the Passover at the time of Jesus."[38] His ground for this assertion is that the accounts of the Seder in the Mishnah only details the Passover as it was kept after the destruction of the temple in AD 70.[39] However it could be countered that there is nevertheless sufficient minimal information concerning the first-century Passover available from the biblical material. It is plain there was a lamb and that there was bread and wine and bitter herbs. It is also clear that it was a meal in homes for the believing community. Klawans went on to assert that in the Synoptic Gospels (Matthew, Mark, and Luke) "we don't really have three independent sources here at all. What we have, rather, is one testimony (probably Mark), which was then copied twice by Matthew and Luke."[40] However, he does not take full cognizance of the fact that Luke has some distinct differences from Matthew and Mark, and that Luke and the account of the Supper in 1 Corinthians appear to represent a separate tradition. To make such an assertion doesn't necessarily argue against Markan priority.[41]

Klawans is of the view that to follow the synoptics "would mean Jesus' trial and crucifixion took place during the week-long holiday," which would have been "either forbidden or certainly unseemly."[42] It could however be countered that there was much else in the whole proceedings against Jesus that was outside the bounds of justice. Klawans does acknowledge that John in writing his Gospel had a theological agenda for claiming that Jesus was executed on the day of preparation when the Passover lambs were being killed. It was in order to present Jesus to his readers as "the spotless lamb of God who takes away the sin of the world."[43] He could of course have added that John set the Eucharist in the context of the feeding of the five

37. Klawans, "Was Jesus' Last Supper a Seder?," 2.

38. Ibid., 2.

39. Ibid., 9. Klawans wrote, "Thus the Passover Seder as we know it developed after 70 c.e. I wish we could know more about how the Passover meal was celebrated before the temple was destroyed."

40. Ibid., 7.

41. For instance the words "this do in remembrance of me" only occur in Luke and Paul.

42. Klawans, "Was Jesus' Last Supper a Seder?," 8.

43. John 1:29.

thousand and drew parallels with the Exodus and the Israelites being fed in the desert. Something else that Klawans doesn't mention is that following John's chronology means that Jesus would have been raised on the fourth day rather than the third day, which clearly militates against a very strongly held early biblical and creedal tradition (1 Cor 15:4). There is still much to be said for following Luke, the accurate and careful historian, in preference to John the theologian who uses history to illustrate particular theological themes.

Other scholars have come at this issue from differing angles. Among them, Karl George Kuhn argued that the Gospel of Luke set the Lord's Supper in a Passover context "in order to convince Christians not to celebrate Passover."[44] An opposite view was posited by Bruce Chilton that "the identification of the Last Supper with a Passover Seder originated among Jewish Christians who were attempting to maintain the Jewish character of the early Easter celebrations."[45] This kind of "Passoverization," Klawans pointed out, can also be found in the second century and even in the Middle Ages.[46]

Notwithstanding the arguments of Klawans, Kuhn, and others, there are a number of New Testament scholars, among them Nolland[47] and Darrell Bock,[48] who remain of the opinion that the Last Supper was a Passover meal. Yet whether or not the Last Supper was a Passover or merely a Jewish meal at Passover time, the argument of this book remains that the Lord's Supper in most contemporary churches has moved a long way from an informal meal in homes and houses. Indeed, it is clear that the early Christians retained the practice of celebrating the Lord's Supper with a Passover-style meal in a domestic setting at least until the end of the second century and in some places in Egypt and elsewhere to the middle of the fourth century and beyond. Furthermore, many of the early church fathers thought and wrote about the Lord's Supper's links and parallels with the Passover, as will be seen in the chapters that follow and in the following brief citations. For example, Justin in his *Dialogue with Trypho* wrote of the Passover as "a type of Christ with whose blood, in proportion to their faith in Him, Christians anoint their houses, themselves who believe in him."[49] Hippolytus, in

44. Kuhn, "The Lord's Supper and the Communal Meal at Qumran."

45. Chilton, *A Feast of Meanings*, 93–108.

46. Klawans, "Was Jesus' Last Supper a Seder?," 21.

47. Nolland, *Luke*, 1055.

48. Bock, *Luke*, 349.

49. Justin, *Dialogue with Trypho*, XL.

Against all Heresies, wrote that Christ "did not eat the Passover of the law for he was the Passover that had been proclaimed."[50] Leo, Bishop of Rome, referred to Last Supper as "the Holy Passover" in a sermon he preached on February 25, 445.[51] In another address he spoke of Jesus "being sure of his resolution and fearless in the working out of his Father's plan" and "putting and end to the Old Testament and establishing the New Passover. When the disciples had reclined with him to eat . . . he himself established the sacrament of his body and blood."[52] A little later in time Chrysostom in his *Homily XX* referred to the Lord's Supper as "the Holy Passover."[53]

IMPLICATIONS

Whether or not the Last Supper is regarded as a Passover meal it is clear that on, or very close to the night before he was betrayed, Jesus ate a meal with his disciples in the upper room of a house in Jerusalem. While they were eating he broke bread and poured out wine for his disciples to eat and drink in remembrance of his death. This fact is abundantly clear from all four Gospels and 1 Corinthians 11.[54] If this is so, and there would appear to be little other alternative, then it must surely be because many of the contemporary Christian churches seriously wanted to rethink the ways in which they celebrated and kept the Lord's Supper. What Jesus intended to be a domestic home-based fellowship meal shared by Christian families and small groups of believers in homes and houses had almost everywhere by the mid-fourth century been transformed into a priestly and clerical-led esoteric theological and complicated public ritual to which uncommitted and nominal Christians are invited to partake.

The chapters that now follow argue that the Lord's Supper or "New Passover" would be far better practiced by present-day Christians in keeping with the spirit and manner of the Jewish Passover. In other words, the Lord's Supper should be in the context of an agape evening meal or at least shared in the context of ordinary food. It should consist of common bread and ordinary wine. It should be a fellowship meal for believers only and

50. Hippolytus, *Against All Heresies*, fragment 1.
51. Leo, "Sermon 43/4."
52. Ibid., "Sermon 58," 3.
53. Chrysostom, *Homily XX*, sec. 19.
54. Matt 26:21, Mark 14:22, Luke 22:20, John 13:2, 1 Cor 11:21.

based in homes and houses. It should also be a celebration, a sit-down sacramental meal for remembrance and thanksgiving!

2

An Agape Evening Meal

While they were *eating*, Jesus took bread . . .

MARK 14:22

In referring to the Lord's Supper in his First Letter to the Corinthians the Apostle Paul uses the Greek word *deipnon*, meaning "supper." In present-day culture supper is not always the main meal of the day. It was so however in the Roman Empire of the first century. In Greek culture, breakfast was often no more than a little bread dipped in wine. The midday meal was often taken away from home and eaten on a street or in a city square. The *deipnon*, however, was the main meal of the day when people sat down with no sense of hurry or rush. As Professor William Barclay put it, "The very word [*deipnon*] shows that the Christian meal ought to be a meal where people linger long in each other's company."[1] R. L Cole aptly concluded that "there is no doubt that at the Lord's Last Supper there was a common meal, which was generally looked on by the apostles as an agape."[2]

At these meals the early Christians not only satisfied their hunger but they lingered at the table and enjoyed one another's company. It was for this reason that early Christians always preferred whenever it was possible

1. Barclay, *Letters to the Corinthians*, 113.
2. Cole, *Love-Feasts*, 229.

to have held their Eucharists in the evening. It was after all a "supper" and, more than that, it was the New Passover Supper, and for these reasons in the early days it was therefore held in the evenings. After all, the Lord had made himself known in what was probably the very first Eucharist in the home of Cleopas in the evening of the first Easter day.[3] The account of Paul "breaking bread" on the Lord's Day at Troas seems to have been a Eucharist since "breaking of bread" came to be the term by which the early Christians described the Lord's Supper. The meeting was obviously an evening event since we're told that Paul went on speaking till midnight.[4]

It is significant that the Apostle Paul spoke of the breaking of bread as "the Lord's Supper"[5] and of the church "partaking of the table of the Lord." Both terms strongly reinforce the fact that this was not finger food or even an hors d'oeuvre. It was the main meal of the day! Just as the Passover could only be eaten at night, so in the early centuries the Lord's Supper was held in the evenings.[6]

A MEAL WITHIN A MEAL

From the earliest times the Lord's Supper continued to be a meal within a meal. It was obviously no longer within the Passover but was contained within an agape or fellowship meal. These were social occasions to which Christian men and women brought food and drink to share with others. These were times when the poor who had very little resources of their own were provided for by their more prosperous believing brothers and sisters.

Down to the close of the second century the majority of Christian congregations appear to have shared the bread and wine of Communion within the context of agape meals. But a commonly held view among scholars is that gradually after that time in many areas, particularly in the West, congregations began to separate the Lord's Supper from the meal. Indeed Dix believed it happened "after the writing of 1 Corinthians but before the writing of the gospels."[7] Some, it is believed, shared the sacrament after the meal while others ate the meal first and then went on almost immediately to take the bread and wine. In some places, on account of persecution,

3. Luke 24:30–31.

4. Acts 20:7 and 11.

5. 1 Cor 10:20.

6. Exod 12:18.

7. Dix, *The Shape of the Liturgy*, 58.

congregations took both the Eucharist and the fellowship meal very early in the day because it was safer to do so. Most churches probably kept to the evening, which was the time for supper, the main meal of the day. That said, Paul Bradshaw wisely cautioned that the evidence for the separation of the Eucharist from the meal, particularly at an early point, is insubstantial. He wrote:

> There is no actual evidence at all that the Eucharist and meal were ever distinguished in this way in primitive Christianity. On the contrary, it seems to be a pure product of the minds of modern scholars who find it impossible to imagine that early Christians might have viewed the whole meal as sacred—as 'the Eucharist.' Hence they assume that, like later Christians, those early believers would instead have wanted to draw a clear line between 'the sacramental rite' and 'ordinary food.' Similarly, while it is true that in places where the meal had been composed of a variety of foodstuffs, it would eventually have become necessary for everything except the bread and cup to be eliminated altogether or transferred to a different occasion, there are no real grounds for supposing this happened at an early date, nor would it have happened at all in those communities where bread, salt and water formed the complete meal.[8]

Very shortly after the death of Ignatius, Pliny the Younger (61–c.113), the governor of the province of Bythinia, penned a letter to the Roman Emperor, Trajan, about the year 112.[9] He wrote that he had been investigating the practices of the Christians in his area and found that they "met on a fixed day and sang responsively a hymn to Christ as God" and that they "bind themselves by oath (sacramento se obstingere)." "When this was over," he continued, "it was their custom to depart and to assemble again to partake of food, but *ordinary* and harmless food."[10] It seems probable from Pliny's observations that the early Christians in this particular locality were doing two things. They were holding a sacrament, following which they were sharing ordinary food. Most scholars take this to mean that they were sharing the Lord's Supper and then going on to have an agape meal consisting of "ordinary food."

An early manual of church practice known as the *Didache* or *The Teaching of the Twelve Apostles* probably dates from the earlier part of the

8. Bradshaw, *Eucharistic Origins*, 64–65.
9. Pliny's letter to Trajan is generally dated c. AD 112.
10. Pliny the Younger, "Letter to the Emperor Trajan."

second century.[11] Chapter 9 deals with the Eucharist and includes prayers to be said at the sharing of the wine and the bread. They are both simple expressions of thanksgiving, first concerning the cup: "We thank thee, our Father, for the holy vine of David, thy son . . . ." And concerning the broken bread: "We thank Thee, our Father, for the life and knowledge which thou didst make known to us through Jesus."[12] It also appears that the Eucharist was being kept in the context of an agape meal, for chapter 10 begins with the words "And, after you are filled, give thanks thus . . . . Thou, Almighty Lord, didst create all things for thy name's sake, and gavest meat and drink for men to enjoy, that they might give thanks unto thee, and didst vouchsafe spiritual meat and drink and eternal life, through thy son."[13] It is not clear that the reference here to "spiritual food" refers specifically to the bread and wine of the Lord's Supper since it comes in the section which deals with the meal.

In his *First Apology* dated around AD 150 Justin Martyr (c. 100–165) included a lengthy section on Sunday worship and the Eucharist in particular. Justin wrote,

> For not as common bread and common drink do we receive these; but just as Jesus Christ our Saviour, being made flesh through the word of God, had for our salvation both flesh and blood, so, also we are taught that food for which thanks are given by the word of prayer which is from Him, and from which by the conversion our flesh and blood are nourished, is the flesh and blood of that Jesus who was made flesh. For the Apostles in the memoirs composed by them, which are called Gospels, thus delivered what was commanded to them: that Jesus took bread and gave thanks and said, "This do in remembrance of Me, this is my body"; and that he likewise took the cup, and when he had given thanks, said, "This is my blood, and gave only to them."[14]

In this passage there is an early strong hint that the churches with which Justin was familiar had come to believe in some form of change in the bread and wine which Justin maintained provided "spiritual nourishment." That said, Justin nevertheless still called the Eucharist "food" though he goes on

---

11. Scholars have estimated the *Didache* variously from AD 50–120.

12. *Didache* 9:1–3.

13. Ibid., 10:1–3.

14. Justin, *First Apology*, 66.

to say that it is not received "as common bread and common drink."[15] There is no specific mention of an agape in this particular paragraph, however in the following chapter 67 Justin wrote that "we afterward always remind one another of these things, and those among us who are wealthy help all who are in want, and we always remain together. And for all the things we eat we bless the maker of all things through His son Jesus Christ and through the Holy Spirit."[16] Here there is a clear hint of a fellowship meal with the more prosperous providing for the less fortunate.

Tertullian (c. 160–c. 220) of Carthage wrote of the sacrament of the Eucharist "which the Lord commanded to be taken at meal times and by all. We take it before day-break and not at the hands of others than the presidents."[17] Tertullian was clearly aware of Jesus' intention that the Eucharist should be taken as part of a meal though it seems to have been the case that persecution in his part of North Africa necessitated receiving it separately or as "a breakfast" while the authorities were hopefully still sleeping. In chapter 39 Tertullian does however make mention of agape meals at which the poor are fed. The Epistle, written by an unknown author to Diognetus[18] at some point in later part of the second century, carries a description of the early Christian communities stating that "they have their meals in common." This gives us a hint that the author who may well have lived in Alexandria knows that Christians in his area were still sharing fellowship meals.

Significantly, Clement of Alexandria made a number of references to both agape meals and the Eucharist. For instance, writing of the former he urged that "we are to partake of what is set before us as becomes a Christian, out of respect to him who has invited us, by a harmless and moderate participation in the social meeting."[19] In a reference to the Eucharist in *Miscellanies* Clement warned against "eating the bread and drinking the cup unworthily, and being guilty of the body and blood of the Lord."[20] In writing of the Eucharist in *Paedagogus* he wrote that those who "by *faith*

---

15. Ibid., 66.

16. Ibid., 67.

17. Tertullian, *De Corona*, 3:3–4.

18. Diognetus was probably a pagan Roman official of some importance, since the writer begins addressing him as "most excellent Diognetus."

19. Clement, *Paedagogus*, 2:4.

20. Clement, *Miscellanies*, 1:5.

partake of it are sanctified both in body and soul."[21] Again in *Paedagogus* Clement wrote "he that eats unto the Lord, keeps the Eucharist unto God . . . so that a religious meal is a Eucharist."[22] Here there is a hint that the Eucharist and agape were conjoined at least on some occasions. At Charles Biggs in his Bampton Lecture expressed the view that in Clement's time the Eucharist and the agape were being separated in Asia, Carthage, and Europe, but that the situation in the area surrounding Alexandria was different and still united as in primitive days. He suggested that there were two forms of the agape in North Africa. First, there were public agapes which were generally held in the evenings and presided over by a bishop or presbyter.[23] Then second, there were private agapes which were little more than an ordinary house supper.[24] At the majority of these occasions no presbyter would have been present, with the spiritual lead being taken by the head of the family. Biggs summed up his view of the relationship of the agape and Eucharist in the following lines.

> All that Clement says on this subject is of the highest value for those who wish to recast for themselves a faithful image of the church life at the end of the second century. But of all his phrases the most important are those which assure us that the ordinary evening meal of the Christian household was in a real sense an agape. It was preceded by the same acts of worship, it was blessed by a thanksgiving. It was a true Eucharist. The house father is the house priest. The highest act of Christian devotion is at the same time the simplest and most natural. Husband, wife, and child, the domestic slave and the invited guest, gathered round the domestic board to enjoy with thankfulness the good gifts of God, uplifting their hearts in filial devotion, expanding them in brotherly love and kindness.[25]

The church historian Socrates (c. 380–450) observed a very similar practice in the same area. In a remarkable passage he wrote: "The Egyptians in the neighborhood of Thebais hold their religious assemblies on the Sabbath, but do not participate in the mysteries in the manner usual among Christians in general; they after having eaten and satisfied themselves with

21. Clement, *Paedagogus*, 2:2.

22. Ibid., 2:1.

23. Ibid., 2:1–12.

24. Ibid., 2:10 and *Stromateis* 7:7.

25. Biggs, *The Christian Platonists*, 102–6.

food of all kinds, in the evening they make their offerings, and they partake of the mysteries."[26] This statement, made as late as late AD 439 is, as J. F. Keating pointed out, remarkable since it comes two hundred years after Clement's time but evidently refers to the practice in the region close to Alexandria, though not the city itself. Significantly, the same information is repeated by the church historian, Salminius Sozomen (c. 400–c. 450),[27] who recorded that in a number of cities and villages in Egypt people met on Sabbath evenings "to partake of the mysteries after they have dined." Whilst it is the case that some of Sozomen's material was taken from the writings of Socrates it is known that he went back and checked Socrates's sources.

The *Canons of Hippolytus*, which most scholars take to be a late–fifth-century compilation, has a section giving directions for the celebration of a commemorative agape that states that "Before they sit down (to the agape) let them first partake of the Mysteries, not, however, on the first day of the week."[28] The meaning of this text appears to be that a memorial Eucharist must always begin with an agape except when it was held on a Sunday. This suggests that in some areas, and very possibly in Ethiopia and Egypt,[29] the Eucharist and the agape were still closely linked at least at weekday worship.

After the emperor Constantine's conversion in AD 312 and Christianity becoming the established religion of the Roman Empire under Theodosius in AD 381 the Lord's Supper was transformed from being a meal in which ordinary bread and wine were shared around a domestic table into a public ceremony. That said, agapes still featured in a number of churches particularly in the Eastern provinces although, in most cases, they were not shared in conjunction with the Eucharist. By the end of the fifth century the title "Lord's Supper" had become known by the name "Mass," a word which originally derived from the Latin *missio*, "to send." Ambrose (c. 339–397), for example, used the expression "*missam facere*," meaning "to perform the Mass." In this way the informality of a fellowship meal gradually became completely submerged with the development of lengthy liturgical theological recitations and esoteric rituals. In all of this there was a growing emphasis on the priest whose ministrations, it came to be believed, changed the ordinary bread and wine into the body and blood of Christ. Thus the

26. Socrates, *Ecclesiastical History*, 5:22.

27. Sozomen, *Ecclesiastical History*, 7:19.

28. *Canons of Hippolytus*, 169.

29. This surmise is based on the fact that the text of the *Canons of Hippolytus* has survived in both Arabic and Ethiopic versions of the Coptic translations.

teaching of Jesus that the Last Supper was both a meal and a sharing of ordinary bread and wine was almost totally lost for the greater part of the Middle Ages. It wasn't until the beginning of the sixteenth century that Martin Luther and the Protestant reformers began to recall the church back to rediscover the biblical simplicity of the teaching of Jesus and the Eucharistic practice of the early Christians.

AN EVENING MEAL

The Jewish Passover was and always is an evening meal, and so it comes as no surprise that the early Christians held the Lord's Supper in the context of an evening meal. It seems to have been the general practice where possible at least in the first and second centuries for churches to hold their Eucharists in the evenings. Where there were fears of being discovered by the Roman authorities the timing may well have been changed. Tertullian, however, related that in his church agape meals were still held in his home area in North Africa.[30] Such was also the case during Pliny the Younger's governorship of the province of Bythinia. Hippolytus wrote of agape meals, presumably in the areas in and around Rome, being held on the Lord's Day "at the time of lamp lighting" and of the deacon "rising up for the purpose of lighting."[31] Hans Achelis, commenting on the *Canons of Hippolytus,* wrote, "on the evening of the Lord's Day, but also on other evenings, the whole community came to Church. . . . The bishop then said the Eucharistic prayer . . . they received with the words, 'This is the Body of Christ' etc."[32]

There is an important passage in the writings of Cyprian, Bishop of Carthage, dating around about AD 253. Cyprian wrote to correct certain

30. Tertullian, *De Cultu Feminarum,* 2:11. Interestingly Tertullian does mention in *De Corona* 3 that "we take also in gatherings before day break and from the hand of none but the presidents the sacrament of the Eucharist, which was commanded by the Lord both (to be) at meal-times and (to be) taken by all." However Bradshaw, *Eucharistic Origins,* 100, suggests that this refers to a custom whereby the faithful were allowed to take the consecrated bread home and consume it on days when there was no Eucharistic celebration. This information is found in *Ad Uxorem,* 2:5. In other words, what this refers to is the act of receiving communion from elements which had been received at the preceding evening celebration.

31. Hippolytus, *Apostolic Constitutions,* 164.

32. Achelis, "The Canons of Hippolytus," 205; Cyprian, *Concerning the Unity of the Church,* 14.

abuses in the administration of the Eucharist and remarked in passing that ideally the Eucharist should be held in the evening. He wrote:

> It may be said it was not in the morning, but after supper that the Lord offered the mingled cup. Ought we not then to celebrate the Lord's feast after supper, that so by multiplying the Lord's Feasts we may offer the mingled cup. It was fitting for Christ to offer about the evening of the day, that the very hour of sacrifice might symbolise the setting, and the evening of the world; as it is written in Exodus, 'and all the people of the synagogue of the children of Israel shall kill it in the evening'. And again in the Psalms, 'let the lifting up of my hands be an evening sacrifice'. But we celebrate the Resurrection of the Lord in the morning.[33]

In view of the nature of this evidence Paul Bradshaw wrote, "It was not until the third century that we encounter any indications in literary sources that the Eucharist might have been celebrated in the morning rather than the evening."[34] That said, Bradshaw followed the suggestion of McGowan that Cyprian's moving the Eucharist from the evening to the morning was probably for the reason that the there were too many people to come together in one place in Carthage. Doubtless other smaller congregations were still able to gather in smaller homes elsewhere in the evenings.[35]

During the Middle Ages the Eucharist was gradually transformed into the Mass and was largely celebrated in the mornings. However, in the wake of the sixteenth-century Reformation a number of English Baptist congregations insisted on celebrating the Lord's Supper in the evenings. They maintained that in doing so they were following the original time when Jesus instituted the sacrament. In 1652, for example, the Fenstanton Baptists made the following declaration at their church meeting, "After consideration of the example of Christ, Luke xxii, 19, 20, and the words of the Apostle Paul, 1 Cor, xi, 24, 25, it was generally concluded from the rule of Scripture that we ought always to break bread after Supper."[36]

The same custom was adopted by the Baptist congregation at Horsleydown at a church meeting in 1700. Their resolution stated,

> The Lord's Supper, in which bread is blest, and broken; and Wine blest and pour'd forth, and receiv'd by the Church met, and sitting

---

33. Cyprian, *Concerning the Unity of the Church*, 14.

34. Bradshaw, *Eucharistic Origins*, 68.

35. Ibid., 109, citing A. McGowan, "Rethinking Agape and Eucharist."

36. *Fenstanton Records*, 35.

together in the Evening time, as a sign to all, that in the Evening
time of the World, Christ's Body was broken and his Blood shed
for the Remission of Sins: Sealing only to worthy Receivers their
saving interest therein.[37]

The Assembly of General Baptists ruled in 1693 and again in 1701 the
Lord's Supper was to be celebrated monthly in the evening.

THE DEMISE OF THE AGAPE

It is clear that Jesus intended the Eucharist to be held within a meal. Indeed,
he called it a Supper. For at least until the close of the second century the
majority of early Christian congregations held their Eucharists in this meal
context.[38] By the beginning of the third century, however, change was in
the air and the Eucharist began to be separated from the fellowship meal.
This gradual parting happened for a variety of reasons. In some areas
Christians began to feel that large social gatherings could be noisy and alert
the persecuting Roman authorities as to their whereabouts. Jungmanns
suggested the reason for separating the meal and the Eucharist was due to
increased number of converts who were too many to eat together. This was
particularly the case after Christianity became a privileged religion in the
Empire.[39] In some provinces the governors outlawed such meetings for fear
that they might contain the seed of rebellion against their authority. Occasionally even a Roman emperor ruled against them for similar reasons.
In other places it was clear that agapes got out of hand in much the same
way as happened in the early church at Corinth, and like the Apostle Paul
their leaders found it necessary to call a halt to proceedings which were
dishonoring to the Lord.

The result of these influences was that some congregations separated
their Eucharists from their fellowship meals, some having them beforehand
and others afterwards. A further factor in these changes was the growing
emphasis being placed on clergy as a separate order from the laity. By the
time of Hippolytus, "presidency," as it came to be called, was being confined

37. *The Covenant to be the Lord's People*, 9.

38. Among the scholars who subscribe to this view see Cole, *Love-Feasts*, 222: "About
that date [the end of the second century]—a little later in the East, a little earlier in the
West—the two ordinances were separated."

39. Jungmann, *The Early Liturgy*, 37.

to the clergy. This meant that it was no longer easy or in many instances, possible for lay people to organize an agape meal even in their own houses.

The conversion to Christ of the Emperor Constantine in AD 312 marked the beginning of the end of agape meals. No longer was it necessary for Christians to worship covertly as there was now freedom of worship for all and Christians were encouraged by the state to erect large buildings, many of which were capable of accommodating several hundred people. Initially agapes were moved into this public environment where they became much larger occasions, often with entertainments that were lacking in taste and Christian standards. It was this change in atmosphere and the loss of the sense of focus on the Lord which contributed to the ultimate demise of the agape. R. L. Cole observed that "there arose a growing recognition of the incongruity between the entertainment and often hilarity of the agape and the chastened solemnity of the Eucharist."[40] C. F. D. Moule similarly suggested that it was these flagrant misuses around the Eucharist that eventually led to the removal of the main meal of fellowship from the consecration of and distribution of the bread and wine.[41]

Thus the Council of Carthage in AD 397 enacted that no bishop, let alone more junior clergy, "should hold a love feast in a public church building . . . and that their flocks should also, as far as possible, be debarred from entertainments of this kind."[42] That said, the *Egyptian Canons,* which are contained in the mid-fourth century document entitled *Apostolic Constitutions,* suggest that the churches in Egypt were still sharing in fellowship meals and in the Eucharist. Section 50 refers to the manner in which the Lord's Supper is to be taken and then goes on to urge that the catechumens be allowed to be permitted to receive the bread, presumably of the agape, for the next section goes on to give instructions as to how food is to be given to the widows who have been invited. In the majority of cases the most likely explanation for the demise of the agape was simply the practical difficulties of organizing large scale meals in public buildings on a regular basis.

Significantly about this time John Chrysostom (c.347–407), who was for a while Bishop of Constantinople, made reference in his sermons to the Eucharists held by the early Christians in the book of Acts. In a homily based on 1 Corinthians he wrote:

40. Cole, *Love-Feasts,* 223 and 229.

41. Moule, *Worship in the New Testament,* 47.

42. Stutzman, *Recovering the Love Feast,* 119.

As in the case of the three thousand who believed in the beginning, all had eaten their meals in common, and had all things in common. Such was also the practice when the Apostle wrote this; not indeed exactly, but as it were a certain outflowing of communion abiding among them that came after. And because it came to pass that some were poor and others rich, they laid not down all their goods in the midst, but made the tables open on stated days, as was natural; and when the meeting was over, after the communion of mysteries, they all went to a common entertainment, the rich bringing their provisions with them, and the poor and destitute being invited by them and all feasting in common. But afterwards this custom also became corrupt.[43]

In his Homily XII Chrysostom reminded his hearers of the way in which the early Christians kept a close relationship between their Eucharists and their fellowship meals.

MIDDLE AGES

During the Middle Ages the Lord's Supper moved further and further away from the context of any sort of meal. By the thirteenth century in the vast majority of places of worship the "Eucharist," or "Mass" as it increasingly came to be called, was a largely spectator event. The congregation was allowed to watch but most often not deemed holy enough to participate. Thus for example Archbishop John Pecham (1279–1292) issued a statute for the Province of Canterbury that "in minor churches it is permitted only to the celebrant to take the Blood in the form of consecrated wine."[44] The laity were allowed to partake of the bread but Peckham required that they should be instructed "that having taken the sacrament in their mouth, they should not break it in their teeth, but should swallow it down as little broken as possible, lest any small part of it remain between their teeth or elsewhere."[45] The Eucharistic bread and wine were regarded by the majority not so much as food and drink to be consumed but rather as sacrificial elements to be offered up for the forgiveness of the sins of the living and the dead. This was particularly apparent in the large number of chapels and altars where chantry priests offered masses for the faithful departed, most notably to

43. Chrysostom, *Homily XXVII*.
44. Pecham, *Statutes of the Province of Canterbury*.
45. Ibid.

ease their journey through purgatory. It was also hoped that the presence of Christ in the sacred host on the altar would bring peace and harmony to the local parish community. Additionally, every year on Corpus Christi day the consecrated host was carried in a public procession through the lanes and streets of numerous towns and villages in the expectation that this would bring unity and order to the social body. In all of this the move was steadily away from receiving spiritual grace by subjective eating and drinking of the bread and wine to venerating and gazing on them in the belief that in them and from them effectual divine grace and power was released.[46]

THE PROTESTANT REFORMATION

The magisterial Protestant reformers recognized that what the medieval church understood as the ceremony of the Mass had originally been intended by Jesus to be a meal. They returned to the biblical focus of eating and drinking in remembrance of Jesus' death and restored the bread and wine to the people. For these reasons they preferred to use the term "Supper" rather than "the Mass." Archbishop Thomas Cranmer subtitled his first Prayer Book Communion published in 1549 with the words "commonly called the Mass." However, following his meetings with a number of other reformers he removed these words altogether from the title page of the Communion service of his second Prayer Book of 1552.

Luther, Calvin and Cranmer all recognized the early churches kept the Lord's Supper in the context of a shared meal. However, none of them made any attempt to set the Lord's Supper in the context of "a bring and share meal" or even in a "token meal," in which some food was taken preceded by "breaking and blessing bread" and ending with the blessing and sharing of wine. They clearly recognized that this isolation of the bread and wine of the Lord's Supper from a meal was unnatural. They were well aware that the Old Testament Passover involved a meal which satisfied the people's hunger, as was commanded in the Exodus. This has led some contemporary scholars to remark that "they stopped halfway." They were in reality trying to have a supper without a meal. Quite possibly they recognized that there is only so much change that people can cope with at any one time and that they had initiated great changes already. They were aware that to move the Lord's Supper into private homes was probably one step too far and one

46. Harper-Bill, *The Pre-Reformation Church*, 64–68.

which might have caused the Protestant princes and the ruling authorities of Europe to reject the Reformation break with Rome.

Significantly, Calvin's understanding of 1 Corinthians 11 led him to the view that Paul rejected the meal aspect as part of the Lord's Supper. As Calvin saw it, Paul "reproves the abuse that had crept in among the Corinthians as to the Lord's Supper, in respect of their mixing up profane banquets with the sacred and spiritual feast, and that to the contempt of the poor."[47] "The apostle," Calvin wrote, "condemns that profane admixture" and requires them "in no way mix up this spiritual banquet with common feasts."[48] "Everyone," he continued, "has his own house appointed him for eating and drinking, and hence that is an unseemly thing in a sacred assembly."[49] From this it is clear that Calvin, along with other reformers interpreted the text in a way that separated the "sacred," the Lord's Supper, from what he considered to be the "profane," namely the meal. Had Calvin been more mindful of the major part which fellowship meals played in the lives of godly Jews and in the lives of Jesus and the apostolic community he might have reached a different conclusion on the matter, and had he also taken notice of the Passover meal context of the Last Supper he would have been much less ready to discard the agape meal from the Eucharist. In going on to comment on verse 25 Calvin recognized that "there was some interval between the bread and the cup" and speculated that "it may be the Lord delivered in the meantime some address after distributing the bread, and before giving the cup." The more obvious reason for this gap was surely that the early Christians shared a Passover-style meal in the interim that included sharing food with the poor in a wholly loving and generous way.

In the wake of the Reformation there were some who attempted to recapture a more meal-based context in their practice of the Lord's Supper. Among them were the Anabaptists, led by Balthasar Hubmaier (c. 1485–1528), and the Moravians. Although both groups for the most part worshipped in homes and houses, theirs were still largely token meals rather than proper meals. Shortly before his trial and execution in Vienna, Hubmaier produced *A Form for the Supper of Christ* which, among other things, required that a table be prepared in a suitable place and laid with ordinary bread and wine.[50] There was an emphasis on informality with or-

47. Calvin, *First Epistle to the Corinthians*, 11:20.

48. Ibid., 21.

49. Ibid., 22.

50. Kreider, "The Lord's Supper," 1.

dinary cups and plates, discussion and participation. Nicholas Zinzendorf (1700–1760), the great Moravian leader, organized a monthly celebration of the Lord's Supper for his congregations which was held in conjunction with a love feast.[51]

The majority of Protestant churches, however, followed Calvin and the magisterial Reformers and kept the Lord's Supper as a token meal. Among those who were influential in this regard was Charles Hodge (1797–1878) of Princeton. He added weight to this practice in America by arguing that Paul's words in 1 Corinthians 11:23–26 "are specially designed to separate the Lord's Supper as a religious rite from the social element with which it was combined."[52] However, as has been made clear, what Hodge severed the early Christians viewed and practiced together. Paul did not condemn the sharing of the meal, rather what he rebuked was the way that the Corinthians were doing it. They were not eating together and they were failing to provide for the needs of the poor who were being treated with contempt.

CONCLUSION

It is clear from all of this that the early Christian Eucharist and its close connexion with fellowship meals resonated with Jesus' emphasis on eating and drinking as being an integral part of kingdom life and experience. It was said of Jesus that "the son of man came eating and drinking."[53] Luke's Gospel records more than ten fellowship meals at which Jesus was present. At one of them a guest remarked to Jesus, "Blessed is the man who will eat at the feast in the kingdom of God."[54] He told his disciples that he was conferring a kingdom on them "so that you may eat and drink at my table in my kingdom."[55] J. F. Keating aptly commented: "His fellowship with his disciples was, in a word, to a large extent a 'table fellowship.'"[56] His miraculous feeding of the five thousand provided the setting for his teaching on the significance of the Eucharistic bread and wine. On more than one

---

51. Wainwright and Tucker, *Oxford History of Christian Worship*, 408.

52. Hodge, *First Epistle to the Corinthians* 11:23–26.

53. Matt 11:19.

54. Luke 14:15.

55. Luke 22:30.

56. Keating, *The Agape*, 37.

occasion Jesus likened being a part of his kingdom to being a favored guest at a celebration supper.[57]

The book of Revelation recounts the vision which the Apostle John had of the risen Jesus on the island of Patmos. He glimpsed the Lord seeking to gain entrance into the church at Laodicea. He was gently and continuously knocking on the church door, wanting to be invited in and to share a supper with them.[58] John's vision of heaven culminated with the redeemed people of God enjoying "the wedding supper of the lamb."[59] Both Luke and John record resurrection appearances of Jesus in which he shared meals with his disciples. Luke recounted how Jesus made himself known to Cleopas and his companion when he broke bread at the meal in their home in the village of Emmaus.[60] John related how the risen Jesus welcomed Peter and some of the disciples to eat with him beside the sea of Tiberias.[61]

In view of the evidence which has been examined in this chapter it is clear that there was a great deal of variety in the way that the churches kept the Eucharist in both the New Testament and early Catholic periods. That stated, it is plainly obvious that by establishing the Eucharist in a Passover meal Jesus intended that it should be kept in the context of shared food and drink. Such was the pattern seen in the teaching of the Apostle Paul and in the writing of the prominent Christian leaders during the first two centuries. After this time many churches, for a variety of reasons, began to separate the agape meal from the Eucharist. However, it needs to be recognized that the misuse of agape meals was not a valid reason for giving them up altogether. The right response is not disuse but the proper use, as Jesus made plain. By changing what Jesus clearly intended to be a small group fellowship meal into an extended and often complicated public ritual, the Christian faith has been denied a vital aspect of joy and spiritual strength. It is the act of sharing a meal with other believers that creates a "bond," "fellowship," or "communion" in a way that large public esoteric ceremonies rarely do.

Contemporary Christian churches, particularly those which belong to the historic denominations, therefore need at the very least to begin actively encouraging their members to keep the Lord's Supper in their homes

57. Luke 14:16.
58. Rev 3:20.
59. Rev 19:9.
60. Luke 24:30.
61. John 21:12.

and in small midweek groups. This is important, not just for the sake and well-being of their own members, but also for the mission of the church. It is not easily possible to attract people to the Christian faith who are strangers to the Christian message by inviting them to come in and share in what is in reality an alien ceremony intended to committed believers which they would find excluding.

Perhaps the last words of this chapter should go to Douglas Jacobi in his article entitled "Putting 'Supper' Back into the Lord's Supper." He wrote as follows:

> Let's restore the New Testament love feast the real meal at which the Lord's death was remembered . . . . Make the meal awesome! If your congregation opts for an actual meal frame the meal by the Lord's Supper so that the breaking of bread and prayer begin the meal and taking of wine and prayer end it. . . . As with any other event in the kingdom planning and effort make the difference between the magnificent and the mediocre . . . . Don't rush the meal. The goal isn't to be finished in fifteen minutes. . . . Remove the current "communion service" from the Sunday meeting. Get rid of the "old yeast"! It will probably be logistically simpler if we meet for communion separate from our main service.[62]

62. Jacobi, "Putting 'Supper' Back in the Lord's Supper," 9.

3

A Meal of Ordinary Bread and Ordinary Wine

<hr>

THE PASSOVER BREAD AND WINE

The Passover meal, as has been noted, consisted of four things: bitter herbs, unleavened bread, a roasted lamb, and four cups of wine. It was a meal of ordinary food and ordinary wine which remained in their natural state but which recalled and symbolized the deep spiritual truth that the Lord had "passed over" his people when the angel of death struck the homes of the Egyptians. No one for a moment believed the roasted lamb was anything other than lamb. No one entertained any notion that the lamb had changed into the substance of Yahweh. In the same way, in the New Passover Jesus took ordinary bread and ordinary wine to symbolize the events of his saving death, through which he delivered his people from slavery to their sin and selfishness. It is of course a fact that Jesus would have used unleavened bread (Greek *alums*) at the Last Supper in conformity with Passover rules, although interestingly Luke 22:19 uses the Greek word *artos* which generally means ordinary bread as opposed to unleavened bread.[1] Significantly, the matter of whether unleavened or leavened bread should be used at Communion was one of the issues which contributed to the split

1. Matt 26:26; Mark 14:22; 1 Cor 11:23.

37

between the Eastern and Western churches which ultimately became the Great Schism.[2] In 1 Corinthians 10:16–17 the Apostle Paul referred to the unity which the Lord's Supper should create among believers and reminded them that because they all shared the one loaf they ought to live and act as one united body. He used the word *artos*, meaning ordinary bread. In Acts 2:42 it seems that the early Christians referred to the Lord's Supper as "the breaking of bread" (*artos*). The main reason, of course, for asserting that "breaking of bread" referred to the Lord's Supper was simply the fact that it is impossible to imagine that it would not have been one of the four essential aspects of early Christian spirituality listed in Acts 2:42. After all, it was the only and very recent specific instruction that Jesus had given to his followers about worship.

JESUS REGARDED THE ELEMENTS AS ORDINARY BREAD AND ORDINARY WINE

The Lord's Supper at its inception, as was made clear in the previous chapter, was a meal within a meal. The Eucharistic bread and wine eaten and drunk in remembrance of Jesus' death and passion were taken in the context of an agape supper. The bread and wine used by Jesus was *ordinary* bread and *ordinary* wine. This fact is borne out clearly enough by Jesus' own words spoken at the end of the Last Supper, "I will not drink again of *this fruit of the vine* until that day I drink it new with you in my Father's kingdom."[3] It is clear from this that even when the Supper was over Jesus still spoke of it

---

2. This was the so-called Azymite-Prozymite Conflict. The Eastern churches used leavened bread and accused the Western church of being *azymite*. Many Westerners asserted that it was right to use unleavened bread because there were clear warnings about "leaven" in Matthew 16:11–12 and 1 Corinthians 5:6–8. Moreover, they followed the Synoptic Gospels, which held the Last Supper to be the Passover Meal. There were also practical issues, such as the fact that unleavened bread lasted longer and could therefore be kept aside for the needs of the sick. Furthermore, there were no crumbs to be dealt with. In the East the ordinary baker made everyday bread for Communion. In contrast to the West, the Eastern churches maintained that unleavened bread was "judaizing" whereas leavened bread was biblical, as in Matthew 13:33. They interpreted the references in Matthew 16:11–12 and 1 Corinthians 5:5–6 in a different light in the Greek as compared to Western translation from the Latin. The Eastern church followed John's gospel's dating that the Last Supper took place before the Passover and that therefore Jesus would have used leavened bread. The Eastern churches also held that bread represented Jesus' humanity in the Eucharist and that dead bread (unleavened) did not bespeak Jesus' resurrection. The issue therefore also became a Christological one.

3. Matt 26:29; Mark 14:25 and Luke 22:18.

as *ordinary* wine. There is no hint in his words that the substance of it was anything other than the fruit or produce of the vine. Interestingly, in Luke's account Jesus is also recorded as having spoken similarly of the bread saying, "I will not eat it again until it finds fulfillment in the kingdom of God" (Luke 22:15). There is of course one obvious reason that prevents a crudely literal view of Jesus' words "This is my body," and that is the simple fact that when Jesus spoke them his body and the bread were two entirely different and separate things. It was the tragic failure to recognize this abundantly clear distinction that caused the church in the succeeding centuries and in the Middle Ages in particular to develop strange and extravagant theories about the bread and wine changing in substance.

EARLY BELIEFS ABOUT CHANGE IN THE BREAD AND WINE

Notwithstanding Jesus' teaching that the bread and wine were representations of his death and passion, the succeeding generations of his followers fairly soon afterwards began to develop notions that they were more than mere symbols. Over the process of time they were first accorded an elevated status and ultimately with the passing of the centuries they were believed to have changed in nature and to have become the very body and blood of Christ himself.

This development grew by a process of accretion over time. The first sign of change was noticeable near the beginning of the second century, when church leaders began to speak of the bread and wine as "sacred" or "holy" and sometimes even as "the medicine of eternal life." What seems to have lain behind this was the experience of the Holy Spirit. Since the day of Pentecost the early Christians had constantly invoked the Spirit's presence in their daily lives and, more importantly, in their worship. The simple petitions "Come Holy Spirit" and "Maranatha," meaning "Come Lord" were constantly on the lips of the early Christian believers. At first these prayers were used to call down the Spirit's presence on those who gathered to share the agape meal and the bread and wine of the Eucharist. It was only a short step to extend the scope of these prayers to include the food which had been brought to the meal. There thus developed, as Anne McGowan has helpfully and clearly explained, the emergence of the "epiclesis prayer."[4] The meaning of the Greek term she makes clear is "to call upon" or "invoke."

4. See McGowan, *Eucharistic Epicleses.*

"It came to describe a prayer calling the Holy Spirit on an object such as baptismal water or the bread and wine."[5] In most cases "epiclesis" referred to the person leading or presiding over the Lord's Supper, who asks God the Father to send the Holy Spirit to imbue the bread and wine in order "to realize the purpose for which Christians believe it was instituted."[6]

At the beginning of the first century, where epiclesis prayers were used they were often general in nature and invited the Spirit to come on both the gathered congregation and the bread and wine. At a later point in time the liturgical services began to draw a distinction between "communion" and "consecratory" epicleses. The latter came to be specifically focused on the bread and wine, and a widespread belief emerged that there was a specific moment when the bread and wine were changed in status or nature. This was generally believed to be when the presiding minster or priest placed his hands over them and prayed that the Holy Spirit would make them the body and blood of Christ. Bradshaw thus concluded, "We can see a gradual development in the theology of Eucharistic consecration. While the earliest invocations . . . may have simply asked for the divine presence on the assembly, the later texts link the invocation more directly with the Eucharistic elements."[7]

In his *First Apology* which he wrote about the year AD 150 Justin Martyr (c. 100–165) included a lengthy section on Sunday worship and the Eucharist in particular. Justin wrote,

> For not as common bread and common drink do we receive these; but just as Jesus Christ our Saviour, being made flesh through the word of God, had for our salvation both flesh and blood, so, also we are taught that food for which thanks are given by the word of prayer which is from Him, and from which by the conversion our flesh and blood are nourished, is the flesh and blood of that Jesus who was made flesh. For the Apostles in the memoirs composed by them, which are called Gospels, thus delivered what was commanded to them: that Jesus took bread and gave thanks and said, 'This do in remembrance of Me, this is my body; and that he likewise took the cup, and when he had given thanks, said, 'This is my blood,' and gave only to them.[8]

5. Ibid., 13.
6. Ibid., 13.
7. Bradshaw, *Eucharistic Origins*, 155–56.
8. Justin, *First Apology*, 66.

In this passage there is an early strong hint that the churches with which Justin was familiar had come to believe in some form of change "by conversion" in the bread and wine which he maintained provided "spiritual nourishment." That said, Justin still called the Eucharist "food," though he went on to say that it was not received "as common bread and common drink."[9] Nevertheless it was still "bread" and still "common drink." Interestingly, in his *Dialogue with Trypho* Justin wrote of the Eucharist in much less materialistic terms. He referred to "the *bread* of thanksgiving, which Jesus Christ our Lord commanded to be offered for a memorial of the Passion he suffered for those who are being cleansed from evil."[10] Again he wrote of "the bread of thanksgiving and also the cup of thanksgiving" and added that "Prayers and thanksgivings are the only perfect and well-pleasing sacrifices to God."[11]

In the writings of Irenaeus (c. 120–202) there are also similar hints of a belief that he held the bread and wine were in some degree changed in status through the prayers of the person presiding over the Eucharist. In one passage in his major work entitled *Against Heresies* he wrote, "For as the bread which is produced from the earth when it receives the invocation of God is no longer common bread, but the Eucharist, consisting of two realities, earthly and heavenly, so, also, our bodies, when they receive the Eucharist, are no longer corruptible, having the hope of resurrection unto eternity."[12] This and one or two other passing remarks lend weight to E. H. Gifford's opinion that Irenaeus is apparently the earliest writer who represents the invocation of the Holy Spirit activating a change in the bread and wine.[13]

Although Irenaeus wrote of "change" in that the consecrated bread "is no longer common bread," it has to be noted that he also still wrote of the consecrated bread as "bread"! Nevertheless, his writings represent the beginnings in the development of the idea that there is a change in the status of the consecrated bread and wine. This process was carried forward into the third century and was captured in the *Acts of Thomas*, a Gnostic

---

9. Ibid., 66.

10. Justin, *Dialogue with Trypho*, 41.

11. Ibid., 41.

12. Irenaeus, *Against Heresies*, 18:5.

13. Gifford, trans., *The Nicene and Post Nicene Fathers*, vol. 7, 28. On this point Mc-Gowan, *Eucharistic Epicleses*, 29, notes, "Irenaeus may deserve credit for introducing the Greek term epiclesis to the context of the Christian Eucharist."

document which can be dated with reasonable certainty in the first half of the century. Chapter 50 contains the following lines.

> And he began to say . . . come, she that manifesteth the hidden things plain, the holy dove . . . come and communicate with us in this Eucharist which we celebrate in thy name and in the love-feast wherein we are gathered together at thy calling. And having so said he marked out the cross on the bread and brake it and began to distribute it.[14]

As in the case of the development of other Christian doctrines the notion of change in the nature of bread and wine grew slowly over time by a process of accretion. There were a number of factors which served to stimulate this transformation, one of the most obvious being the growing importance and role of church leaders which increased considerably following the emergence of religious toleration. The latter development eventually resulted in Christianity becoming the official established religion of the Roman Empire in AD 381. Indeed, much earlier when Hippolytus produced his *Apostolic Constitutions* in the third century, instructions were clear that lay men and women were not permitted even to make the sign of the cross or recite the prayer on the agape bread.

Hippolytus (c. 155–235) was a bishop in Rome from about AD 220. His *Apostolic Tradition* which is a mine of information on liturgical matters was published soon after the accession of Callistus to the see of Rome in AD 217.[15] In Part II section 23 Hippolytus gave details regarding the "Paschal Mass" and used the significant word "eucharistise."

> And he (the bishop) shall eucharistise (eucharistein) first the bread into the representation, (which the Greek calls antitype) of the flesh (sarx) of Christ: and the cup mixed with wine for the antitype (which the Greek calls likeness), of the Blood which was shed for all who have believed in Him.[16]

G. Every suggested that these words represented the beginnings of the idea of transformation into the body and blood of Christ from outward forms of bread and wine.[17] It may be countered however that it is doubtful whether

---

14. *Acts of Thomas*, 50.

15. There has been some debate concerning the authorship of the *Apostolic Tradition*. See, for example, McGowan, *Eucharistic Epicleses*, 78.

16. Dix, *The Apostolic Tradition of St Hippolytus*, 7–8.

17. Every, *Basic Liturgy*, 78.

"eucharistein" is sufficiently strong to convey this idea. Furthermore, the word "representation" would not seem to indicate a change in the substance of the elements but rather a reference to the symbolic meaning of the bread and wine. In addition, it is clear that Hippolytus still referred to the elements as bread and wine. In section 4 of the *Apostolic Constitutions* there is a further prayer, in which Hippolytus appeared to suggest that we make the Eucharist by invoking the Holy Spirit to come down on the bread and wine.

Origen (184–253) gave a further insight into the Eucharistic practice of the Alexandrian Christians, demonstrating that he regarded the Eucharistic bread as being something more than ordinary bread and the wine more than ordinary wine. In a homily on Exodus 35 he wrote:

> You who are accustomed to attend the divine service mysteries know how, when you receive the body of the Lord, you keep it with all caution and reverence, lest any part of it fall . . . . [H]ow can you think it is less of a sin to have treated the word of God with negligence than to treat his body with negligence.[18]

This paragraph, while not suggesting that the consecrated bread and wine were changed in nature, indicates that there was a growing reverence for the consecrated bread and wine. Nevertheless, Origen did not believe that the underlying structure of the bread was in any way changed. This is clear from an interesting passage in his sermon on Matthew chapter 15 where he spoke of the bread as "typical and symbolical" of Christ's body.[19]

Cyprian (c. 200–258) became Bishop of Carthage in North Africa from 248. In his writings about the Eucharist he was mainly concerned with the role of the priest. In Epistle 62 he wrote of the Communion as "a commemoration of the Lord and of His Passion." However, in his 53rd Epistle he wrote in realist terms of communicants being "fortified with Christ's body and blood."[20] Cyprian clearly saw the Eucharist as a means of imparting both physical and spiritual strength and nourishment, but it is doubtful that he regarded the elements of bread and wine as anything more than symbols.

---

18. Origen, *Homily XIII on Exodus Chapter 35.*

19. Origen, *Homily XI on Matthew 15.*

20. Cyprian, *Epistle,* 53.

CHANGE IN THE SUBSTANCE OF THE BREAD AND WINE

Following the Emperor Constantine's conversion to Christ in 312 Christianity became a privileged religion. Public places of worship could now be built and Christianity freely practiced without fear of persecution. In consequence of this legislation many clergy then became officers of the state, with Constantine ruling that they should receive payment for their pastoral work. Some of the higher clergy subsequently carved out influential roles for themselves in both church and state. In the ecclesiastical sphere in many places bishops and priests came to be regarded as "Christ figures" who stood in his place at the Lord's table when they presided over the sacramental services. This may be one of the reasons why they adopted the practice of using one common cup for the celebration of the sacrament. They were taking and administering the one cup that Jesus had taken at the last supper and invited those who had gathered for worship to share it. By the time of Constantine the custom of the communicants sitting round a domestic table and sharing food and drinking from their own cups was gradually being replaced by designated officials, bishops, and priests, who, it came to be believed, could set apart the bread and wine in such a manner that they would become the body and blood of Christ.

It is significant that very soon after the beginning of Constantine's rule Christian leaders began to articulate more elaborate and complex theories of the bread and wine changing in nature. One of the earliest to do so was Serapion (d. after 360). A close friend of Athanasius, he became bishop of Thmuis in the Nile delta around the year 339. About the year 350 he published a *Sacramentary* which contained a miscellaneous collection of prayers intended for the use of the Bishop. One of these prayers which follows Jesus' words of institution carries with it a clear suggestion that the bread and wine are changed in nature.

> O God of truth, let Thy holy word come upon (epidemesato) this bread that the bread may become Body of the word, and upon this cup that the cup may become Blood of Truth; and make all who partake to receive a medicine (lit. drug) of life, for the healing of every sickness and for the strengthening of all advancement and virtue, not for condemnation, O God of truth and not for censure and reproach, for we have called upon Thy Name, O Uncreated, through the Only-begotten in the Holy Spirit.[21]

21. Dix, *The Shape of the Liturgy*, 164.

The significance of Serapion's prayer is that it explicitly prays that the bread and wine may *become* the "body of the word" and the cup the "blood of truth." The wording suggests that consecration was understood to take place as a result of the invocation rather than from the recitation of the words of institution. The closing lines of the invocation pray that the communicants may receive "a medicine of life for the healing of every sickness. . . . for we have invoked Thee, the uncreated, through the only-begotten in the Holy Spirit." Dix commented: "Even in so early a specimen as that of Serapion, the prayer is definitely 'consecratory' in form, and thus prepares the way for the conception of 'a moment of consecration' within the eucharistic prayer as a whole."[22] Such a moment of consecration eventually gained acceptance in both East and West, though they contended for "different moments."

Athanasius (c. 296–373), who was bishop of Alexandria for several periods beginning in 328, made a number of references to the Eucharist. His writing is of particular interest since he was a friend of Serapion, but nevertheless held different views. In one passage, he connected consecration with the operations of the Logos, and declared: "When the great prayers and holy supplications have been sent up, the Word comes down into the bread and the cup, and they become his Body and his Blood."[23] He seems to have believed that consecration was effected by the Word "coming down" into the bread and the cup and they "become his Body and his Blood." As with Serapion his writings contain no explicit invocation of the Spirit onto the elements.

The writings of Cyril (*c.* 315–386), who was Bishop of Jerusalem from c. 346–386, give us a clear and detailed picture of the fourth-century Eucharist in his city. In his *Catechetical Lectures* that were given to baptismal candidates he gave a detailed commentary on each section of the liturgy. His comments on the consecration prayer show that it included a strong invocation.

> Then when we have sanctified ourselves with these spiritual hymns, we beseech the loving God to send forth His Holy Spirit upon the gifts lying before us, that He may make the bread the body of Christ, and the wine the blood of Christ. For whatsoever the Holy Spirit touches is sanctified and changed.[24]

---

22. Ibid.

23. Athanasius, *To the Newly Baptized*, 24.

24. Cyril, *Catechetical Lectures*, 2:7.

This is an unequivocal prayer for the descent of the Holy Spirit on to the elements, bringing about their "transformation" or "conversion." As has been noted, this was no sudden new or revolutionary idea. Indeed it had been gradually emerging ever since the second century. Earlier writers such as Justin, Irenaeus, and Hippolytus had spoken of the bread and wine as being "spiritual food" or "healing medicine." The importance of Cyril is that his prayer now gave the church a theory about the effects of consecration and opened the way for the development of the idea of a moment of consecration. This was ultimately to lead on to the classic metaphysical explanation of transubstantiation. Dix pointed out that from Cyril's time forward Christ began to assume a purely passive part in the Eucharist.[25]

The writings of the Cappadocian Fathers give added evidence of a growing belief that through the Eucharistic prayer the bread and wine were changed in nature into the body and blood of Christ. In his *Moralia* Basil (330–379), Bishop of Caesarea, described the epiclesis that formed part of his liturgy. "We pray," he wrote, "that the Holy Spirit may come upon . . . the gifts . . . that He may make them most holy, that He may make the bread the holy body of our very Lord God and Saviour, Jesus Christ, for the remission of sins and for life everlasting to all who partake."[26] Basil's brother, Gregory of Nyssa (c. 335–c. 395), made a number of references in his teaching and preaching to the concept of change in the bread and wine. In the course of a *Sermon for the Day of Lights* entitled "On the Baptism of Christ" he commented: "The bread again is at first common bread, but when the sacramental action consecrates it, it is called, and becomes, 'the body of Christ.'"[27]

Perhaps the most significant figure in the Byzantine tradition was John Chrysostom who was Bishop of Constantinople from 398–404. The consecration prayer in his liturgy is explicit in the matter of change.

> Again, we offer you this spiritual and unbloody worship and we call upon you, pray you, beseech you, to send your Holy Spirit upon us and upon these gifts presented, and to make this bread the precious body of your Christ, changing (metaballon) it by your Holy Spirit . . . so that they may be for those who partake . . . the remission of sins.[28]

25. Dix, *The Shape of the Liturgy*, 278.

26. Every, *Basic Liturgy*, 82.

27. Gregory of Nyssa, *Sermon for the Day of Lights*.

28. Chrysostom, *Liturgy of Chrysostom*.

This prayer asks the Holy Spirit to "make" the bread and wine "his body and his blood." The use of the word *metaballon* carries the idea of changing matter into something else.

The fourth century was the time when the epiclesis came to hold a central importance in the liturgies of the Eastern churches. It was in this same period that the notion of a specific moment of change gained widespread acceptance. By contrast the Western church was slower to articulate this notion of a moment of consecration. Ambrose (c. 339–397), who became Bishop of Milan about the year 397, wrote in *On the Sacraments*, "You see how effective is the word of Christ . . . . He spoke and they were made, He commanded and they were created (Psalm 148:5). Therefore, to answer you, it was not the body of Christ before consecration; but after the consecration, I tell you, it is then the body of Christ. He spoke and it was made, He commanded and it was created."[29] Again he wrote:

> Before it is consecrated, it is bread, but when the words of Christ have been added, it is the body of Christ. . . . And before *the words of Christ* it is a cup full of wine and water; when the words of Christ have operated *then and there* it is made to be the blood of Christ which redeemed people.[30]

Ambrose was clearly echoing the teaching of Cyril for the Western church and following him he articulated a moment when consecration was effected. At this stage, however, Ambrose put the emphasis on the elements being changed by the words of Christ being spoken over them rather than through an invocation of the Holy Spirit. With the passing of the centuries, however, the epiclesis found its way into Western liturgies. Consecration then included both the recitation of Jesus' words of institution together with the invocation of the Holy Spirit.

REASONS FOR THESE EARLY CHANGING BELIEFS CONCERNING THE NATURE OF THE BREAD AND WINE

There were several reasons why the early Christians moved away from the simplicity of Jesus' Last Supper as a Passover meal consisting of ordinary bread and ordinary wine. One of these was the impact of Marcion and the Gnostics. In an effort to confront their views that matter is evil, early

---

29. Ambrose, *On the Sacraments*, bk. 4:5, 15–16.
30. Ibid., bk. 4, ch. 5:22.

Christian leaders began to emphasize that Jesus "lived in the flesh" and to speak of the Supper in a materialistic way as "the body and blood of Christ." For the same reason, in opposition to Marcion, the early Christians also held firm to the Old Testament since it stressed the goodness of the material world in its creation stories and elsewhere. The language of the Old Testament was of course sacrificial language and this imagery carried over into the way in which sections of the church started to think about the Eucharist. Some early liturgies therefore began to speak of the Eucharist as a sacrifice.

In addition to this, early Christian life and worship was powerfully impacted by the cults and mystery sects of the Roman pantheon of the gods. In particular, as a number of scholars have pointed out, Mithraism, a religion of Persian origin, strongly influenced early eucharistic doctrine. Mithraism reached Rome by 67 BC and was fully embraced as an imperial cult in the first century. All creatures were supposed to be sprung from the bull that Mithras overcame and sacrificed before he ascended into heaven, where he guaranteed eternal life to all those who had been initiated as his followers. At the heart of its ritual was the sacred meal which had similarities to the Eucharist, including the use of bread and wine. The participants shared bread and wine and believed that as they did so they received the divine presence of Mithras. Tertullian was so struck by the similarities between Mithraism and Christianity that he sought to explain it by attributing Mithraism to the work of the devil.[31] The influence of Mithraic sacrifices may help to account for Irenaeus referring to the bread and wine as *"the new oblation of the new covenant"* and emphasizing the "Word of God" as "making the body and blood of Christ."[32] Later, probably for the same or similar reasons, John Chrysostom referred to the Eucharist in vivid sacrificial terms when he wrote "the sacrifice is brought forth, and Christ, the Lord's sheep is sacrificed."[33] In addition to these influences the daily sacrifices offered to the many Roman deities and the practice of sacrificial emperor worship must also have permeated Christian belief and practice.

Even after the Emperor Constantine was converted to Christ and Christianity was openly and freely practiced in elaborate and now legalized public buildings the church was unable to shake off the dust of the previous

---

31. Cross and Livingstone, eds., "Mithraism," *Oxford Dictionary of the Christian Church,* 909.

32. Ibid., 274. Italics mine.

33. Chrysostom, *Homily III on Ephesians.*

centuries of pagan practice. L. Wyatt made this point strongly in the following lines:

> Mithraism continued to shape the Roman interpretation of Christianity long into the 4th century a.d. . . . Their special buildings, the Mithraea, in which Mithraic rituals were enacted, became the model for the first Christian churches. These were small narrow buildings with a central aisle and seats for 20–25 on either side. At the end was an altar block with a carving of Mithras slaying the bull on one side.[34]

Regardless of how we understand and explain these changes in early Eucharistic teaching and practice, it is clear that the building blocks which were later going to form the basis of the medieval doctrine of transubstantiation had already been well laid in these early centuries.

THE MIDDLE AGES, THE MASS, AND TRANSUBSTANTIATION

During the centuries that followed Ambrose's time the notion that the bread and wine of the Eucharist were changed in substance into the body and blood of Christ continued to develop. John of Damascus (c. 676–756), who was born into a prominent Christian family and was ordained a priest some time before 715, spent his life in the monastery of St. Saba near Jerusalem expounding and defending the Christian faith. In his writing about the Eucharist he was concerned over a number of issues. One of these was whether the consecrated bread was the same body that came from the virgin and if so, was it still liable to the same injuries to which it was liable when Christ was on earth? John's answer was it was corruptible and liable to all accidents before it was eaten but once eaten it goes into the soul and became meat for the soul alone.[35] In his *An Accurate Exposition of the Orthodox Faith* he wrote: "The bread and wine are not merely types of the body and blood of Christ, not at all, but the deified body of the Lord itself. For the Lord has said, 'This is my body' and 'This is my blood,' not 'This is a type of my body' and not 'This is a type of my blood.'" And on a previous occasion he reminded the Jews "unless you eat the flesh of the Son of man, you do not have life in you." In a subsequent paragraph John added, "It is

---

34. Wyatt, *Approaching Chaos*, 265.
35. Herbert, *The Lord's Supper*, vol. 1, 554–63.

called communion, and it truly is, because through it we have communion with Christ and share in his flesh and divinity."[36]

Innocent III (1161–1216), who became Pope in 1198, convened the *Fourth Lateran Council* in 1215 and used the term "transubstantiation" to describe the change which took place when the priest consecrated the bread and wine. The following prayer from his *Order of the Mass* revealed the extent to which the doctrine of consecration had developed.

> Then, at the middle of the altar, the Nicene Creed . . . . Offering the host on the paten, "Receive, holy Father, this immaculate host, which I thine unworthy servant offer to Thee my living and true God for my innumerable sins and offences and my neglects and for all who are standing around and for all faithful Christians living and dead, that is may profit them unto eternal life, Amen."[37]

Innocent's teaching became enshrined in the Council's decree on transubstantiation which read as follows:

> But the universal church of the faithful is one, outside which there is no salvation. And in this Jesus Christ is the same Himself priest and sacrifice: and His body and blood are truly contained under the appearance of bread and wine in the sacrament of the altar, being transubstantiated, the bread into the body, the wine into the blood, by the Divine power, in order that to complete the mystery of unity we may ourselves receive from what is His own that which He received from what is ours. And also no one can fulfil or "make" this sacrament but a priest, who shall have been rightly ordained according to the keys of the church which Jesus Christ Himself gave up to the apostles and their successors.[38]

The key sentence was "His body and blood are truly contained in the sacrament of the altar under the forms of bread and wine, the bread and wine having been transubstantiated, by God's power, into his body and blood."[39] This was the first mention of the term "transubstantiation," a term which was later reiterated by the Council of Trent in its thirteenth session in October 1551 in opposition the views of Martin Luther and other Protestant Reformers. The Council's declaration was as follows:

36. John of Damascus, *An Accurate Exposition of the Orthodox Faith*, bk. 4, 82.
37. Innocent III, *The Order of the Mass*, 126.
38. Reardon, *Religious Thought*, 315.
39. Bettenson, *Documents of the Christian Church*, 148.

And because that Christ, our Redeemer, declared that which He offered under the species of bread to be truly His own body, therefore has it ever been a firm belief in the Church of God, and this holy Synod doth now declare it anew, that, by the consecration of the bread and of the wine, a conversion is made of *the whole substance* of the bread into the substance of the body of Christ our Lord, and of the whole substance of the wine into the substance of His blood; which conversion is, by the holy Catholic Church, suitably and properly called Transubstantiation.[40]

The priest in medieval times thus became a miracle figure who could turn bread into God through his prayers at the altar. In consequence, some jibed at him as a "hocus pocus" man, the term being a shortened form of the Latin *hoc est corpus meum*, meaning "this is my body." Now, instead of inviting the congregation to share bread and wine at a table in remembrance of Jesus who offered his own body in sacrifice for the sins of the world, the priest offered up the very body of Jesus under the substance of bread and wine as a sacrifice for the sins of the living and the dead. From having been a remembrance of Jesus' body once offered on the cross the Eucharist now became that offering. No longer was it a remembrance of Jesus, it was Jesus being offered here and now! The average peasant in the Western church did not understand the Latin language of the Mass and so it became customary for the priest to ring a bell when it came to that vital climactic moment when he was going to make the consecration prayer and transform bread and wine into the body and blood of Christ. This was a call for everyone to stop talking and kneel or stand in awe and reverence. In the later medieval years that followed it came to be believed that it was no longer even necessary to eat the consecrated bread to commune with Jesus. This could be achieved simply by standing in silence after the bell had been rung and gazing upon the elevated body of Christ that the priest held aloft at the completion of the prayer of consecration.

THE PROTESTANT REFORMERS AND THE RETURN TO THE NEW PASSOVER

Martin Luther and the sixteenth-century Protestant Reformers cut back through the traditions and practice of the medieval church and the early Catholic period to the books of the New Testament. As a result, they were

40. Reardon, *Religious Thought*, 264. Italics mine.

soon convinced that the Passover meal which Jesus shared with his disciples in the Upper Room consisted of ordinary bread and ordinary wine. It was clear to them that just as no Jewish household believed the Passover lamb that they had prepared and eaten at the festival ever became anything other than lamb, so no early Christians ever believed that the bread of the New Passover or Eucharist became anything other than bread. They saw clearly that after Jesus had distributed the bread and wine he still spoke of it as "bread and wine." Calvin, Zwingli, Martyr, Cranmer, and most other reformers were so convinced that the Eucharist was to be understood as a meal of ordinary bread and ordinary wine that they changed its title from "Mass" to "the Lord's Supper." They stood in strong and total opposition to any notion of change in the substance of the consecrated bread and wine. Zwingli even pointed out that Papists were divided among themselves as into which body the bread was transubstantiated. Some argued that communicants "take the body and blood of Christ as they hung on the cross and others that we take the resurrection body."[41]

Cranmer labored the point in both his Prayer Book liturgy and in his major theological work entitled *A Defence of the True and Catholic Doctrine of the Sacrament*. When it came to the doctrine of transubstantiation Cranmer was adamant that it was ordinary bread and wine at the start of the Communion service and it was ordinary bread and wine when the service came to a close. He added a rubric at the end of his 1552 Prayer Book Communion service that "to take away any superstition, which any person hathe, or myghte have in the bread and wyne, it shall suffyse that the bread bee such as is usuall to bee eaten at the Table with other meates, but the best and puest wheate bread, that conveniently be gotten." Indeed there was a further sentence to the effect that if any bread was left over at the end of the service "the curate shall have it to hys owne use."[42]

THE REFORMERS' ARGUMENTS AGAINST TRANSUBSTANTIATION

The view that after the consecration no bread or wine remained on the altar had led the medieval church into a number of other unbiblical doctrines and practices, the most significant being that the consecrated bread and wine which were now believed to be the body and blood of Christ were to

41. Zwingli, *On the Lord's Supper*, 185.
42. Post-Communion rubric in *Book of Common Prayer*, 1552.

be offered up at the altar by the parish priest for the sins of the living and the dead. The actual words of the Sarum Mass, a commonly used liturgy in medieval England, were as follows: "We offer this sacrifice for the sins of the living and the dead." In consequence of this, Cranmer asserted that the mass in which the priests made such a propitiatory sacrifice for the quick and the dead was "the greatest blasphemy and injury that can be against Christ."[43] Cranmer therefore devoted the whole of the second book of his celebrated *Defence of the True and Catholic Doctrine of the Sacrament* to this matter. He titled it "The Second Book Against the Error of Transubstantiation." Likewise, John Calvin devoted the greater part of chapter 17 of book four of *Institutes of the Christian Religion* to the same issue. Calvin called transubstantiation "this monstrous fiction not only against Scripture, but against the consent of the ancient church."[44] Regarding the presence of Christ in the Supper, Calvin very wisely wrote: "The presence of Christ in the Supper we must hold to be such as neither affixes him to the element of the bread, nor encloses him in the bread, nor circumscribes him in any way . . . and it must, moreover, be such as neither divests him of his dimension, nor dissevers him by differences of place, nor assigns to him a body of boundless dimension, diffused through heaven and earth."[45]

JESUS SPOKE THE WORDS OF INSTITUTION AFTER HE HAD GIVEN THE ELEMENTS

Cranmer was clear that it was *after* Jesus had given the bread and said "take and eat" that he then spoke the words "this is my body."[46] Likewise it was "before the words of consecration" that Jesus took the cup of wine, and gave it to his disciples, and only then that he uttered the words, "Drink you all of this."[47] In other words, the bread and wine were not consecrated until they were eaten and drunk.

---

43. Cranmer, *Defence*, bk. 5, ch. 1, 215.
44. Calvin, *Institutes*, 4:17.14.
45. Ibid., 4:17.19.
46. Cranmer, *Defence*, bk. 2, ch. 2, 82.
47. Ibid., bk. 2, ch. 2, 83.

JESUS STILL CALLED IT "THIS WINE" EVEN AFTER THE SUPPER WAS ENDED

Cranmer made the point that when the supper was ended Jesus told the apostles that he would not drink "this fruit of the vine, until that day that I shall drink it new with you in my Father's kingdom." These words, Cranmer urged, made it clear that it was the "very wine that the apostles drank at that godly supper."[48] Cranmer added to this argument with a reference taken from Paul's Letter to the Corinthians where the apostle spoke of "the bread which we break" being "a communion of Christ's body." This was clearly "consecrated bread" because the apostle spoke of it as "a communion of Christ's body" and yet he still spoke of it as "bread." Added to this, he immediately says that the communicants are "partakers of one bread and one cup."[49]

THE ARGUMENT FROM NATURAL DECAY

Cranmer pursued the view that the bread and wine do not change in substance after the consecration prayer with an argument from natural decay. "The wine, though it be consecrated, yet it will turn to vinegar, and the bread will mould, which then will be nothing else but sour wine and moulded bread, which could not wax sour nor mouldy, if there were no bread or wine there at all."[50] John Hooper (d. 1555), who became bishop of Gloucester in 1550, went a little further with this line of approach and wrote: "Good proof hath been taken, that bread remaineth after the consecration; for by the sacrament there was an Emperor [Henry VI], and a Bishop of Rome [Victor III], poisoned. In what subject should the poison remain? . . . And when men say, the mould and rot of the bread is nothing, every man that hath his senses knoweth it is a manifest lie: for so long it may be kept, that it may run about the altar."[51]

---

48. Ibid., bk. 2, ch. 2, 84.

49. Ibid., bk. 2, ch. 2, 85. See also 1 Cor. 10:16–17.

50. Ibid., bk. 2, ch. 2, 85.

51. Smythe, *Cranmer and the Reformation*, 101.

IF CHRIST'S BODY AT THE LAST SUPPER WAS BREAD THEN CHRIST'S BODY AT THE CRUCIFIXION WAS BREAD

Cranmer advanced another argument against transubstantiation. He suggested that if Christ's body that was eaten at the Last Supper was made of bread, then Christ's body that was crucified must also have been made of bread. Then, by the same logic, he maintained that if the body of Christ in the sacrament was made of bread and wine, and the body of Christ in the Virgin's womb was not made of bread and wine then the sacramental body of Christ is not the same as the Christ who was conceived in the Virgin's womb.[52]

CHRIST'S BODY IS IN HEAVEN AND CANNOT BE ON EARTH

Most of the Protestant Reformers argued that it was not possible for Christ to be bodily, physically, or materially in the bread and wine since he had ascended bodily in heaven. Calvin made much of the fact that Jesus told the disciples "he would not always be with them" and that "He is not here, for he sits at the right hand of the Father."[53] All bodies, Calvin pointed out, must of necessity have one particular locality."[54] John Lambert (d. 1538), a friend and associate of William Tyndale, devoted a lengthy section of his *Treatise to King Henry VIII* to showing that the Lord's body could not be in two places at once without contradicting Scripture and destroying the reality of our Lord's manhood. He underlined the fact that the Scriptures, the early church Fathers, and the Creeds are all in agreement that Christ's body is in heaven and coming again at the end of the world. If it is asserted that it is still in the world in the sacrament, "It should then be both to come and already come, which is a contradiction and a variant of his manhood."[55] John Calvin also denounced any local presence in the bread and wine on the ground that Jesus' humanity is in heaven. "To wish to establish such a presence as is to enclose the body within the sign or to be joined to it locally is not only a reverie but a damnable error. As our Lord took our

52. Cranmer, *Defence*, bk. 2, ch. 8, 103–4.

53. Calvin, *Institutes*, 4:17.26.

54. Ibid., 4:17.

55. Lambert, *A Treatise made by John Lambert unto King Henry VIII*, fo. 23.

humanity, so he is exalted in heaven, withdrawing from mortal condition but not changing in nature."[56] Yet he wrote "their vain bosters . . . fabricate a monster in their brains . . . that the body of Christ is visible in heaven, and yet lurks invisible on earthe under innumerable bits of bread."[57] Cranmer also tackled those "Papists" who "say that Christ is corporally present in as many places as there be hosts consecrated."[58] His argument was that Jesus' body and humanity are in heaven and will remain there "until he come at the last judgement." Such a conviction he stressed "hath been ever the catholic faith of Christian people."[59]

CHRIST'S BODY MUST BE VERY SMALL TO BE IN SO MANY BODIES AND BE ON MANY ALTARS

John Bradford (1510–1555), a Fellow of Pembroke College and chaplain to Bishop Nicholas Ridley, argued that Christ's body must be very small if it can lie in so little room [the confines of the stomach]. "Is it right," he asked, "that Christ should be kept in such a prison"? Bradford also raised the question of whether Christ has more than one body. "If a priest give the bread to a hundred communicants can he really be giving one hundred separate bodies of Christ into their mouths?"[60]

THE USE OF LOGIC AND COMMON SENSE

At the very outset, it should be said that the Reformers were clear that when Jesus said, "This is my body," nothing was more obvious than that his body and the bread he referred to were two entirely different and separate things. Hooper argued that "the very words, 'hoc est corpus meum' [this is my body] proveth that the bread is already the body, before the words be spoken, or else they misname the thing, and call bread flesh."[61] Using the same literalism as the papists did, Hooper contended that "If 'hic est corpus meum' [this is my body] can alter the substance of the bread, then can 'hic

56. Calvin, "Short Treatise on the Holy Supper."
57. Calvin, *Institutes*, 14:17.25.
58. Cranmer, *Defence,* bk. 3, ch. 2, 126.
59. Ibid., bk. 3, ch. 3, 127.
60. Bradford, "Sermon on the Lord's Supper," 90.
61. Smythe, *Cranmer and the Reformation*, 100–1.

calix est novatum testamentum' [this cup is the New Testament] alter the substance of the chalice, and thus, as they eat the bread, they should drink also the chalice."[62] Calvin also underlined the fact that Paul in his First Letter to the Corinthians declared that "the rock which Moses struck in the desert was Christ." Clearly, Calvin asserted, the apostle was speaking "figuratively." "Scripture," he continued, "calls God a man of war" and Calvin had no doubts that the advocates of transubstantiation would interpret this as "a similitude taken from man."[63] Peter Martyr Vermigli (1500–1562), who was for a while the Regius Professor of Divinity at Oxford, wrote in his *Treatise on the Eucharist* that "it does not properly suit the body of Christ to be eaten, since what we eat we crush and grind with our teeth, and passing down into the stomach they are digested and converted into our substance; this is a grave error when speaking properly of the body of Christ."[64]

REFORMERS WHO BELIEVED NO CHANGE IN THE ELEMENTS WAS EFFECTED BY A CONSECRATION PRAYER

In view of these kinds of argument it is not surprising that a number of Protestant Reformers objected to any idea of there being a single moment of consecration. In fact Calvin "did not have a prayer of Consecration in his Sunday Communion liturgy."[65] The cause of "this brutish imagination," he asserted, was that consecration became a "magical incantation." He went on to assert that "in the earthly elements when employed for spiritual use, no other conversion takes place."[66]

In this Calvin's views resonated with those of Thomas Cranmer who also asserted that what consecrated bread and wine was their change of use. Cranmer recognized that the major issue was who or what consecrated the bread and wine. Was it the priest reciting Jesus' words of institution over the bread and wine, or was it the manual acts of the priest laying his hands on the paten and the chalice, or was it the calling down of the Holy Spirit (epiclesis) on the bread and wine that changed them into the body and blood of Christ? With the passing of time it was clear that Cranmer did

62. Ibid.

63. Calvin, *Institutes*, 4:17.22.

64. Vermigli, *The Oxford Treatise*, 210.

65. Mayor, *The Lord's Supper*, 6.

66. Calvin, *Institutes*, 4:14–15.

not hold to any of those views. For him, "consecration is the separation of any thing from a profane and worldly use unto a spiritual use."[67] Indeed, to make the point explicit, Cranmer removed the words "consecrate," "bless," and "sanctify" from his 1549 Prayer Book liturgy. He pointed out that in baptism ordinary water is taken from other ordinary uses, and put to use for baptism. In the same way, "ordinary bread and wine is taken and severed from other bread and wine, to the use of Holy Communion," although it remains the same substance as that from which it was severed.[68] Cranmer went on to argue in this same section that "the bread and wine have no holiness in them."[69] It is for this reason that the sacrament is not to "be worshipped and adored, as the papists term it, which is plainly idolatry."[70] Cranmer made this explicitly clear in Article XXV, which stated, "The sacraments were not ordained of Christ to be gazed upon, or carried about, but that we should duly use them."

The Roman church's view was that good Christian men and women only ate the body and blood "at that time when they receive the sacrament." In contrast, Cranmer did not believe there was a single moment when the bread and wine were consecrated and so became the body and blood of Christ. It was for this reason that in his 1552 Prayer Book the consecration prayer contained no epiclesis or calling down the Holy Spirit on the bread and wine. Nor was the priest required to engage in any manual act by laying his hands on the cup or the paten, as later became the case in the revised 1662 Communion liturgy. What enabled a person to receive the spiritual presence of Christ into their lives was simply eating and drinking with faith in him. The only point in Cranmer's 1552 consecration prayer where it is suggested that the communicants may be "partakers of the body and blood of Christ" is as they are "receiving these thy creatures of bread and wine, according to thy son our saviour Jesus Christ's holy institution."[71]

67. Cranmer, *Defence*, bk. 3, ch. 15, 181.
68. Ibid., bk. 3, ch. 15, 181.
69. Ibid., bk. 3, ch. 15, 181.
70. Ibid., bk. 3, ch. 15, 191.
71. Gibson, *First and Second Prayer Books*, 389.

SUMMARY OF THE REFORMERS AGAINST TRANSUBSTANTIATION

Calvin wrote of "fictitious transubstantiation" and called the doctrine a "brutish imagination" brought about by "magical incantation."[72] Cranmer was particularly strong in his denunciation of his fellow English churchmen who in the matter of transubstantiation "speak more grossly herein than the Pope himself," many of them "affirming that the natural body of Christ is naturally in the bread and wine." Indeed, Cranmer was far from being charitable when discussing the doctrine of transubstantiation as taught by the Church of Rome, which he described as "although in name most holy, yet indeed it is the most stinking dunghill of all wickedness that is under heaven, and the very synagogue of the devil, which whosoever followeth cannot but stumble, and fall into a pit of errors."[73] The magisterial Reformers were clear that the sign or outward symbol of bread and wine and the thing signified, namely Jesus' body and blood, cannot be one and the same. If they were, they would no longer be signs but the reality.

THE PRESENCE OF CHRIST IN POST-REFORMATION EUCHARIST

In the centuries that followed the Reformation there were still many, most notably those who were Roman Catholics, who continued to maintain the teachings of the Council of Trent and uphold the doctrine of transubstantiation in particular. In the Anglican Church in both England and the American colonies High Churchmen followed the teachings of Archbishop William Laud (1573–1645), who asserted that there is a "real presence" in the Eucharist, though not materially contained in the actual elements of bread and wine. Indeed, Laud himself declared: "For the Church of England nothing is more plain than that it believes and teaches the real presence of Christ in the Eucharist."[74] For Laud this presence was conveyed to the believer through the complete action of consecration and reception. It was largely the Laudian emphasis which led the restoration compilers of the 1662 English Prayer Book to insert the requirement that the priest should place his hands over the bread and wine during the consecration prayer. In-

---

72. Calvin, *Insitutes*, 4:17.14–15.

73. Ibid., bk. 2, ch. 7, 102.

74. Hutton, *William Laud*, 150.

struction was also added in the rubric at the end of the service that if there was any consecrated bread or wine left over after all the congregation had communicated it should be reverently consumed by the priest, suggesting of course that it was no longer "ordinary bread" or "ordinary wine."

Until the nineteenth century most Church of England parishes held Communion services only three or four times in a year, usually at Christmas, Easter, and at one or two other major Christian festivals. This began to change during the mid-Victorian years, partly through Evangelical clergy starting to hold monthly evening Communions, and also as a result of the teaching of the leaders of the Oxford Movement. In their search for a church that was neither subject to Rome on the one hand or Geneva on the other, they read and studied the Fathers of the fourth century and they not only rediscovered the central place they accorded to the Eucharist but also their contention that the bread and wine changed in status and substance. The Oxford leaders published a Tract on "The Necessity and Advantage of Frequent Communion."[75] Not only did they believe in a real presence of Christ in the sacrament, the Tractarians, as the Oxford Movement came to be called, began the practices of "Reservation" and "Eucharistic Adoration." Reservation involved retaining some of the consecrated elements in a small locked container or tabernacle on or near the altar. This meant that worshippers could commune with Christ by praying close to the consecrated bread and wine. It also enabled the clergy to carry the bread and wine to those who were sick. During the main Sunday Eucharist the reserved sacrament of the previous week was consumed and then replaced with some newly consecrated bread and wine.

Notwithstanding these developments, the Reformation emphasis on the authority of Scripture had brought about a huge change in the worldwide church's understanding of the Lord's Supper. Protestant Nonconformist churches in England and America returned to thinking of the Eucharist as a Passover supper with bread and wine shared at a table. That said, although they rejected the sacrifice of the Mass, the great majority of Protestant churches have continued to keep a very passive understanding with the Eucharist still dominated and controlled by an up-front minister leading, presiding, and serving the elements in place of a priest offering up a consecrated bread and wine for the sins of the living and the dead.

---

75. "The Necessity and Advantage of Frequent Communion."

CONCLUSION

In summary, there can be no doubting that the biblical understanding is that the ordinary bread and wine which Jesus shared at the Last Supper were still ordinary bread and wine at the end of the Last Supper. This, as has been shown in this chapter, is abundantly clear from Jesus' actions and teaching at the Last Supper. When Jesus took the bread and said "This is my body," he clearly meant "already is" my body and not will become my body. It is an obvious fact that when Jesus said of the bread, "this is my body," he was one thing and the bread was another so that there could not have been two bodies of Christ. There is also the fact that even after the Supper was ended Jesus still referred to the bread as "bread" and to the wine as "wine." To this must be added the fact that if the consecrated bread and wine in the hand of the priest really is in truth the body and blood of Christ then the Eucharist can't be a remembrance of Jesus' death since, as in the case of the Jewish Passover, it only possible to remember what is already past.

In keeping the Supper surely it is best to use "ordinary wheaten bread of the best that can be had" and ordinary red wine. The use of nonalcoholic juice[76] instead of wine and unleavened wafer circles in place of ordinary bread is regrettable. It loses the connection between the Lord's Supper and everyday life. The use of common bread at Communion underlines the fact that, just as Christian believers always need material bread every day, so they also need Jesus, the divine and living bread, in their lives every day. It's clear that in the New Testament and early times it was a frequent practice for small house-based congregations to share one loaf of bread as a way of symbolizing their unity as the people of God.[77] The use of red wine reflected the red wine of the Passover as well as being a biblical symbol of Jesus' shed blood and the joy and celebration of his royal presence.

The use of unleavened wafers arose from the belief that the bread had changed in substance and there were concerns about dropping crumbs on the floor that could not be easily recovered. The use of common bread links the New Passover with the Old and with Jesus' claim to be "the bread of life" and "living bread."

The aim of this chapter has been to indicate that the best and most obvious way to celebrate the New Passover is with ordinary bread and ordinary wine with people gathered in small groups around a domestic table.

---

76. This is particularly regrettable on health grounds where a common cup is used.

77. 1 Cor 10:16–17.

Christian people should be taught that the bread and wine remain bread and wine and that there can be no change in their nature, and that no presence of Jesus is anywhere contained in them and for that reason they cannot and should nor be worshipped, gazed upon, or venerated in any way. They are and remain symbols or visual representations that prompt those sharing the meal to receive a fresh experience of the Holy Spirit presence of Jesus.

4

A Fellowship Meal

FELLOWSHIP

The word "fellowship"—koinonia—occurs eighteen times in the New Testament and means "participation" or "sharing." Fellowship is the relationship between Jesus and his followers. William Barclay pointed out that "koinonia" is "a sharing of friendship" and "keeping in the company of others."[1] It is a friendship based on common knowledge. The Apostle John (1 John 1:1–3) expressed it as follows: "that which we have seen and heard [namely the life and teaching of Jesus] we proclaim to you, so that you may have fellowship with us; and our fellowship is with the Father and with his son Jesus Christ." This fellowship or "communion" was worked out by the early Christians in practical ways. Chapter 2 of the book of Acts makes it plain that the fellowship of the Jerusalem church included a form of communal living at least for a time. Their fellowship resulted in the pooling of their material resources and collections of money for the support of the poor. Paul used the word "fellowship" three times in connection with the money he collected for the poor Christians in Jerusalem. Oscar Cullman

---

1. Barclay, *New Testament Word Book*, 71–72.

noted that "koinonia" particularly referred to the table fellowship which the early Christians shared in with a common meal or agape.[2]

Significantly, this kind of fellowship was also part of the Passover tradition. As has been noted, it was customary for provision to be made for the poor at the time of the Passover. This was why the disciples were not overly concerned when Judas made a sudden exit from the Last Supper. According to John 13:29, some of the disciples imagined that he had gone out "to give something to the poor." This practice of providing something for the needy became an integral part of the Eucharist in churches all over the world. Alms were taken up during the Mass and later when Archbishop Cranmer produced his second English Prayer Book in 1552 he included a rubric after the sermon in which the priest was to "earnestly exhort" the congregation "to remember the poor, saying one or more of these sentences following." The sentences were particularly to the point and included, "Blessed be the man that provideth for the sicke and needy; the Lord shal deliver him, in the tyme of trouble. Psal. Xli," and "Whoso hath this world's goods, and seeth his brother have need, and shutteth up his compassion from him, how dwelleth the love of God in him"?[3]

The Protestant Reformers were aware that the Lord's Supper was intended to facilitate both this upward focus of fellowship with the Father and Son and the horizontal aspect of fellowship between the Christians who gather to receive the sacrament. Thus the Lord's Supper is to be a *Holy Communion*, the subtitle which Cranmer gave to the service, as well as a personal encounter between Christ and the believer. A meal table is a place of fellowship and encounter. Sharing food with another individual is a way of getting to know them in a personal way and establishing a bond of friendship. Above all else, the Reformers regarded the Lord's Supper as an intimate encounter in which first and foremost the worshippers experienced a deep personal encounter with Christ himself. As the closing words of the Prayer of Humble Access in Cranmer's Prayer Books put it, Christians come the Lord's table in order "that we may evermore dwell in him, and he in us."[4]

2. Cullman, *Early Christian Worship*, 12.

3. Cranmer, "Rubric Following the Sermon," *Second Prayer Book of Edward VI*.

4. Gibson, *First and Second Prayer Books*, 225 and 386.

BIBLICAL FELLOWSHIP MEALS

The New Testament underlines a strong connetion between the breaking of bread or Lord's Supper and fellowship. The two are clearly linked in the book of Acts chapter 2, where Luke records that the early Christians in Jerusalem gave themselves to the fellowship and the breaking of bread.[5] They came obviously from an inherited Jewish culture in which fellowship meals were a familiar part of their social interaction and friendship. In the Jewish tradition shared eating and drinking were seen as a means of cementing and agreement or covenant. In Genesis 6, for example, Isaac and the Philistine King Abimelech got into a dispute regarding the use of wells. When they finally reached an agreement over the matter they sealed the oath they had taken by sharing a covenant meal.[6] Another obvious example was the occasion in Exodus 24, when God's covenant with the people of Israel was sealed. There we are told that Moses and Aaron met with God and "they ate and drank."[7] The eating and drinking was a very important part of sealing the covenant. As will be observed in what follows, it is clear that the Lord's Supper was a means by which believers sealed their covenant relationship and commitment with Christ. In short, it is a covenant meal that is not greatly dissimilar from that of Exodus 24. Indeed, the language Jesus used in instituting the Lord's Supper in Matthew 28:28, "this blood of the New Covenant," is the very language Moses used in Exodus 24:8, "see the blood of the covenant that the Lord has made with you in accordance with all these words."

It is important to keep in mind that sharing meals and table fellowship was a very important part of Jesus' life. Luke recorded ten meals which Jesus shared with other people. These occasions were not simply for sustenance and socializing, they were meals with a theological or spiritual importance. Such was the case in the Upper Room when Jesus instituted the Lord's Supper. As has already been noted, the Lord's Supper was intended to be a supper in the full sense of the word. The practice of sharing the bread and wine in the context of a meal appears to have been widespread throughout the first century. As F. F. Bruce observed: "In apostolic times it is fairly clear that the Eucharist formed part of the fellowship meal."[8]

5. Acts 2:42.

6. Gen 26:28–31.

7. Exod 24:11.

8. Bruce, *Spreading Flame*, 198.

In some parts of the Roman Empire the practice continued well into the second century and beyond. Ignatius in his Letter to the Smyrneans wrote: "It is not lawful without a bishop either to baptise or make an agape."[9] *The Didache* or *Teaching of the Twelve Apostles* knows of no separation between the Eucharist and the agape. Section 9 "Concerning the Eucharist" gives thanks "both for food and drink to men for enjoyment" and that "you have given spiritual food and drink and life eternal." It is apparent, as has been fully stated in chapter 2, that in many places at least until the end of the second century the Lord's Supper was set in the context of fellowship meal called an agape or Love Feast.[10] Tertullian (c. 160–c. 220) of Carthage wrote of the sacrament of the Eucharist "which the Lord commanded to be taken at meal times and by all."[11] The fifth-century church historian Salminius Sozomen recorded that in a number of cities and villages in Egypt people met on Sabbath evenings "to partake of the mysteries" after they have dined.[12] Clearly Sozomen was aware of the fact at the time of writing that many congregations still retained the link between the Eucharist and sharing common food.

TRANSFORMING FELLOWSHIP

In his First Letter to the Corinthians the Apostle Paul drew a parallel between the old leaven which needed to be thrown out before the Passover festival began and the behavior which should be cast out of the lives of those who participated in the Lord's Supper. In 1 Corinthians 5:7–8 he wrote, "For Christ our Passover has been sacrificed. Therefore let us keep the Festival, not with old yeast, the yeast of malice and wickedness, but with the bread without yeast, the bread of sincerity and truth." He was saying in effect that just as the Jews banished the old leaven from their houses

9. Ignatius, *Letter to the Smyrneans*, 8.

10. 2 Pet. 2:13; Jude 12. Commenting on agape as it appears in Jude 12, Davids, *The Letters of 2 Peter and Jude*, 68–69 writes: "While some writers view these meals as something separate from the Lord's Supper or Eucharist, we are not convinced that the evidence supports that position. Instead, it appears to us that at least until a.d. 250, when the concepts of priest, sacrifice, and altar begin to appear with respect to the Eucharist, the Lord's Supper was a re-enactment of the Last Supper or the fellowship meals of Jesus and his disciples. That is, it was a pot luck meal with bread broken at the beginning and a cup of wine shared at the end."

11. Tertullian, *De Corona*, 3:3–4.

12. Sozomen, *Ecclesiastical History*, bk. 8:19.

A Fellowship Meal

before the Passover festival took place, so Christians are called to live out the New Passover by banishing old leaven-style behavior from their homes and lives. In other words, Paul was urging them to live in a manner that would make godly fellowship a reality.

INTERACTIVE FELLOWSHIP

Considering the strong parallels between the Jewish Passover and the Lord's Supper as the "New Passover," it is hard not to advocate celebrating communion in the home. The household or small group of believing friends is the one obvious relaxed informal and natural environment where heart to heart sharing can take place. At the Jewish Passover the family members and close friends who gathered "reclined" round the domestic table. It was literally a laid-back occasion with the children taking an active part in the proceedings. Indeed, the Mishnah makes it clear that the Passover was a joyful, interactive fellowship meal. The central aspect was of course eating and drinking while joyfully remembering the deliverance of the Lord's people from slavery in Egypt. It was no rushed affair that was all over in a minute at a Communion rail or the front end of the bread and wine queue. It was literally a time of relaxed convivial sharing and discussion. Bread was not doled out into the guests' hands or mouths in tiny crouton-sized pieces. Rather, each participant broke a piece from a loaf. Before and as they ate the bread they were reminded what it symbolized. It was the bread of affliction. Passover wine wasn't a quick sip from cuplet or having a tiny drop from a chalice thrust to the lips by a Eucharistic minister. In fact there were four cups of wine that each guest was expected to drink. Participants in the first-century Passover had their own individual cups that were filled for each occasion. It may well be that the cup which Jesus took at the Last Supper was his own individual cup. While those present drank their four cups of wine, prayers of blessing were spoken by the leader.

Of course, as has already been made clear, the central aspect of the Jewish Passover was a meal consisting of a Passover lamb, and this was a time for happy and affirming fellowship or communion both among the guests as well as with the Lord. In a parallel with the New Passover, the early Christians shared in an agape meal that would have commenced with the breaking of bread and ended with drinking of the cup of wine that probably corresponded to the third cup in the Jewish Passover, the cup of blessing. The early Christian agape Eucharist was undoubtedly a time of joy, fun, and interactive conversation. The entire Lord's Supper was a time in which the Lord's people got to really know each other better and were bonded together in friendship and love.

In the catacombs in Rome there are a number of frescoes depicting the Eucharist that suggest that it was this deep home-based intimate fellowship that sustained and strengthened the early Christians with courage during the periods of bitter persecution. It was this that enabled them to stand firm and refuse to comply with the magistrate's request when they were brought before him and told to declare "Caesar is Lord."

THE KISS OF PEACE THE SYMBOL OF FELLOWSHIP

Jesus urged that wherever there was a breakdown in fellowship it should be restored as soon as possible. If a person going to worship was suddenly to remember that a Christian brother or sister had something against them they were immediately to return and effect a reconciliation.[13] The *Didache* also laid stress on this necessity of living in loving fellowship and being reconciled with fellow Christian believers. The kiss of peace had long been a sign of respect and friendship among the ancient Jews dating back as far as Isaac's blessing of Jacob and Jacob's reconciliation with his brother Esau. It was also a courteous sign of welcome at the any special meal or ceremony. The kiss was, and indeed is, seen as a symbol of fellowship. It is therefore no surprise that at an early point in time the kiss became a feature in Eucharistic liturgies. Justin mentions that in some of the congregations in Rome in his time the kiss took place before the offertory. Significantly the kiss of peace came at the same point in the Roman liturgies with which Hippolytus was familiar. In the Eastern church at roughly this time there was a tradition whereby the deacon from beside the bishop's throne cried out aloud while the kiss was actually being exchanged, "Is there any man that keeps anything against his fellow?" If there were such individuals and their issues could not immediately be resolved the bishop might on occasion step in and make peace between them.[14] It's clear from the *Stowe Missal* which has been dated variously between the sixth and tenth centuries that the kiss of peace in the Celtic tradition came at the same point as in the Roman church.

13. Matt 5:23–24.

14. Dix, *The Shape of the Liturgy*, 106–7.

Regardless of how Christians from a whole variety of denominations and independent church groups regard the kiss of peace, it is a vital reminder that Christian brothers and sisters need to be a united loving fellowship. Above all, this needs to be in evidence when they gather together to share in the Eucharist which is after all the family meal.

UNITED FELLOWSHIP

The Eucharist was intended by Jesus to be a service of unity. In John's gospel Jesus rebuked the disciples at the Last Supper for discussing which of them was the greatest. Similarly, the Apostle Paul instructed the Corinthian church not to contemplate sharing in the bread and wine "when there are divisions among them." To do so, Paul wrote in 1 Corinthians 11:20–22 and 27–32, "is to despise the church of God," and is "to eat the bread and drink the cup of the Lord in an unworthy manner," and more even than that, it is "a failure to recognize the body" of Christian believers, which will result in "judgement" and "sickness." Just as the Old Testament fellowship meal served as a means of effecting peace and unity among the guests (Ps 23), so the Communion table was intended to provide the opportunity to re-establish a bond of peace with neighbors and fellow worshippers. In his *Book of Common Prayer* Cranmer deliberately focused on this passage in 1 Corinthians 11 at the beginning of the exhortation that precedes the "Invitation and the General Confession." He urged all that "mind to come to the Holy Communion . . . to consider what Paul writeth to the Corinthians." He reminded them "diligently to try and examine themselves, before they presume to eat of that bread, and drink of that cup." He went on to speak of the great danger if people receive unworthily. By so doing "we kindle God's wrath against us, we provoke him to plague us with divers diseases, and sundry kinds of death." His exhortations serve to warn all who are blasphemers, adulterers, or be in malice, envy or any other crime "to bewail their sins, and come not to thy holy table; lest after the taking of that holy sacrament, the devil enter into you, as he entered Judas, and fill you full of all iniquities, and bring you to destruction, both body and soul."[15]

Although Cranmer did not include the kiss of peace from the Sarum Mass in his Prayer Books he included an invitation to the table in the Exhortation that follows, to those "that do truly and earnestly repent you of

---

15. Gibson, *First and Second Prayer Books*, 385.

your sins and are in love and charity with your neighbours."[16] He continued the theme in the second prayer after the reception of the bread and wine where the communicants pray to "continue in that holy fellowship and do all such good works, as thou hast prepared for us to walk in."[17] The same emphasis is also found in the prayer for the church militant that comes at an earlier part of the service where petition is made that all that do confess thy holy name "may live in unity and godly love."

PRACTICAL CARING FELLOWSHIP

Fellowship in the New Testament was something which needed to be worked out in practical ways between believers. Acts 2:42–47 records what may have been a not altogether successful experiment in communal living in which the believers pooled their material resources and collections were taken to support the poor. Regardless of whether or not the Jerusalem church's sharing is seen by recent scholars in a positive light or not, it demonstrates the practical outworking of the New Testament understanding of fellowship. Cranmer clearly understood the need for this to be expressed in the Lord's Supper.

Concern that all members of the local body of Christ are loved and provided for was made explicit by Cranmer in the requirement of a collection for the poor in both of his two prayer books. The curate is required "to earnestly exhort the congregation to remember the poor."[18] Such a concern seems also to resonate with the instruction of the Jerusalem church leaders to Paul and Barnabas "that we should continue to remember the poor" (Gal 2:9–10).

This whole aspect of the fellowship is one that rarely features in most Communion services where, particularly in Roman Catholic and Anglican traditions, the focus is most often on individual's personal devotion and Communion kneeling or standing before the altar. And yet the importance of a loving and united fellowship was a marked aspect of New Testament social life and worship. Somehow there needs to be an opportunity within the Communion service to facilitate interaction between worshippers in such a manner as to strengthen their bonds of love and friendship.

---

16. Ibid., 386.

17. Eph 2:10.

18. Gibson, *First and Second Prayer Books*, 380.

This element of fellowship was obviously much easier to achieve in the first three Christian centuries when the Lord's Supper was shared by small groups in homes. Nevertheless there are ways in which this could be achieved in a larger context. For example, worshippers could be invited to get into small groups of three or four and discuss something they have just learned from the sermon or they could briefly introduce themselves to each other and share some encouragements from the past week, as happened in early Methodist gatherings. They could also identify social needs that they are aware of within their local community.

COVENANT FELLOWSHIP

The Greek understanding of the word *koinonia* meant more than just inter-action, it also denoted commitment. Indeed "koinonia" is sometimes used in Greek literature of people who have entered into contractual agreement or a business relationship. For this reason New Testament Christians would have found it hard to understand the ways in which contemporary Christian people frequently change from one church congregation to another. This deeper form of committed fellowship is made clear in all four New Testament accounts of the Lord's Supper, which record Jesus' words that the cup of wine is "the New *Covenant* in my blood" (Matt 26:28, Mark 10:24, Luke 22:20, 1 Cor 11:25). When Moses established the Old Covenant between the Lord and the people of Israel at Sinai, he read out all the Lord's words and laws and the people responded with one voice, "Everything the Lord has said we will do." Moses then sealed the covenant agreement by sprinkling the people with the blood of young bulls (Exod 24:1–8). Thus the old covenant which was based on words and laws (Exod 24:3) was sealed in blood. In a similar way the new covenant was sealed with the blood of Christ symbolized by the Communion cup of red wine. In the third exhortation of his *Book of Common Prayer* Cranmer emphasized and called Christian people to recognize that the Lord's Supper ("these holy mysteries") are "pledges of his love . . . to our great and endless comfort" and that they for their part need to continually submit themselves "wholly to his holy will and pleasure, and studying to serve him in true holiness and righteousness all our days."[19]

Fellowship is clearly a crucial aspect and intention of the Lord's Supper that frequently fails to receive the attention it should be given. It is not

19. Ibid., 386.

often that communicants are reminded that in their eating and drinking of the sacramental bread and wine that they are pledging their love and commitment to Christ and reminding themselves once more of "the exceeding great love of our Master." This covenantal commitment and fellowship with the Lord finds expression in a number of places in both Cranmer's 1552 Prayer Book and in the later 1662 liturgy. It comes at the end of the Prayer of Humble Access as those who draw near to the table pray that they "may evermore dwell in him, and he in us." It is there also in the second post-communion prayer which reminds those who have "duly received" the bread and wine of "thy favour and goodness towards us."[20]

In summary, it may be confidently stated that Jesus intended fellowship to be a fundamental aspect of the Lord's Supper. The Reformers endeavored to make this understanding clear by using of the title *The Holy Communion* or sometimes simply *Communion*. They were fully aware that the Eucharist had emerged out of the biblical context of Jewish fellowship meals. They knew perfectly well that Jesus had promised to break bread with his disciples in the kingdom and that the early Christians in the book of Acts "broke *bread*" in their homes. It was clear to them that the medieval church had changed the Communion from a fellowship meal to a passive ritualistic spectacle and that the congregation should be "sharing" (1 Cor 11:20, 33) a fellowship supper at a table (1 Cor 11:17–34). They fully appreciated that the Lord's Supper was the New Testament counterpart to the Passover meal and that Jesus had instituted it during the meal in the upstairs room of a house. This fact was emphasized in the Proper Preface for Easter Day in the Book of Common Prayer, which speaks of Jesus Christ as "the very glorious Paschal lambe which was offered for us."[21]

TIME FOR FELLOWSHIP

Fellowship or Communion only develops and grows as people give time to each other and interact with one another. An ordinary family only grows into a close loving unit as they sit, share, interact, and speak together around the meal table in a relaxed and convivial atmosphere. This needs time. Good meals don't happen in a rush. One of the dysfunctional features of many present-day Communion services is that they so often appear to be

20. Ibid., 388.

21. Proper Preface, *Second Prayer Book of Edward VI*. This Preface was not included in the 1662 Prayer Book.

in a rush. There is a set liturgy and ritual that the priest, president, or minister is required to follow. These, together with the recitation of a creed and lengthy theological pieces and set prayers, are felt to be essential to achieving a valid Eucharist. Sadly, many contemporary communion services fail to make any opportunity for communion or fellowship among the people who make up the congregation. Even in the so-called Free or Nonconformist churches there is often little or no time for the congregation to talk and share concerns, apart from perhaps exchanging a greeting of peace. What is even worse is that the central focal moment of the Lord's Supper when the bread and wine are taken happens so quickly. In some Anglican churches it is often all over in a minute or less as the priest or Eucharistic minister delivers bread and wine to the kneeling communicants at the altar rail. In many other places of worship people queue cafeteria style and receive a morsel of bread that is thrust into their hands or a tiny paper-thin wafer is popped into their mouth. They then join the wine line where the chalice is often pushed to their lips while they are still trying to digest the bread. This is hardly communion with anyone since each person takes the bread and wine in turn on their own. The situation in many nonconformist churches is often only slightly better in that a little more time is made available in which to eat the bread and drink the wine and the congregation do at least all partake or "commune" in that they all eat and drink at the same time.

That said, what is really still lacking in most church communion services is the opportunity for any table fellowship of the kind Jesus clearly intended by calling the Lord's Supper the New Passover. At the very least, time needs to be made for this in some kind of conversational interaction or sharing at every Communion service. This will mean that people will at least commune with each other as well as sharing the elements of bread and wine. But it would be far better in every way for Christians to return to the early church practice of having the Lord's Supper in small Passover-sized groups in people's homes and houses. This vital aspect, as has already been emphasized, was lost in the immediate aftermath of the Emperor Constantine's conversion when Christianity became the established religion of the Roman Empire. This resulted in church officials moving the agape Lord's Supper from domestic homes into newly built and legalized large official places of worship that all citizens were expected to attend.

Despite breaking away from the medieval Mass in which the priest offered up the transubstantiated bread and wine for the sins of the living and the dead, the Protestant form of the Lord Supper in many contemporary churches still puts all the focus on the performance of the service leader. He or she must do all the talking and follow the rubrics and liturgy of a service book, which leaves little or no time for the people to engage in any fellowship or interaction.

It is apparent that Jesus intended the Eucharist to reflect his delight in eating and drinking as being an integral part of kingdom life and experience. It was said of Jesus that "the son of man came eating and drinking."[22] At one meal a guest remarked to Jesus, "Blessed is the man who will eat at the feast in the kingdom of God."[23] Jesus told his disciples that he was conferring a kingdom on them "so that you may eat and drink at my table."[24] J. F. Keating aptly commented, "His fellowship with his disciples was, in a word, to a large extent a 'table fellowship.'"[25] His miraculous feeding of the five thousand provided the setting for his teaching on the significance of the Eucharistic bread and wine. On more than one occasion Jesus likened being a part of his kingdom to being a favored guest at a celebration supper.[26] The book of Revelation culminates with the redeemed people of God enjoying "the wedding supper of the lamb."[27] Both Luke and John record resurrection appearances of Jesus and the ways in which he ate and drank and shared fellowship meals with his disciples.

CONCLUSION

The word *fellowship* that means "Communion" is another name by which the Eucharist is frequently called. However the truth of the matter is that it is difficult to really have fellowship with people who are strangers or we hardly know apart from an occasional nod at a Sunday service. And even if we are well acquainted with people it is not easy to have fellowship with them standing in cafeteria-style queues for the bread and wine, and probably even less so kneeling in hushed silence at an altar rail. In order to have meaningful fellowship with people we need to follow Jesus' example and practice and share food and drink with them. As David Cairns rightly stated, "Eating and drinking together at a table is one of the great central

22. Matt 11:19.

23. Luke 14:15.

24. Luke 22:30.

25. Keating, *The Agape*, 37.

26. Luke 14:16.

27. Rev 19:9.

human symbols. It is, indeed, more than a symbol of fellowship; it creates fellowship between the host and those who sit with him at his table, and it binds them also to each other."[28] Such fellowship between Christ and his people must therefore be a vital aspect of Eucharistic worship. Indeed, it must never be forgotten that the risen Lord made himself known to his two followers on the evening of his resurrection as they shared a fellowship meal in their home in the village of Emmaus.

28. Cairns, *In Remembrance of Me*, 46.

5

A Home-Based Meal

THE PASSOVER IN HOMES

In the account of the Passover in the book of Exodus Moses was instructed by the Lord to command each man to take a lamb for his own *household* and that if the number of individuals was small they were to share one with their neighbors. The animals selected had to be year-old males without defect. They were to be taken care of until the fourteenth day of the month when they were to be slaughtered at twilight. Some of the blood of each lamb was then to be taken and put on the sides and tops of the door frame of their homes. Then, when the Lord saw the blood, he would pass over the household. That night they were to eat the meat roasted over the fire with bitter herbs, and bread made without yeast. For seven days (verse 15) they were to eat bread made without yeast *in their homes*. In verse 46 the people of God were given strict instruction that the Passover "must be eaten inside one house; take none of it outside the house." The point to note is that Passover was to be kept in small or extended family groups in the context of a *home*.

THE LORD'S SUPPER IN HOMES

When Jesus instituted the Lord's Supper he did it, as has been noted,[1] in the context of a Passover meal or Passover-style meal in the room of a house. He could so easily have decided on a larger and a more public venue such as a synagogue, after all he was a rabbi and had gathered large crowds on a number of occasions and fed five thousand people by the sea of Tiberias. But by his institution of the Supper, Jesus focused on the home or household as being the basic unit of society and in so doing made it plain that Christianity is rooted in the home and proceeds from the home. It seems very likely that when Jesus broke bread on the evening of the first Easter Day in the house of Cleopas and his companion he was in fact sharing the Lord's Supper with them. This is suggested by Luke's use of the same term "breaking bread" that he used in the book of Acts. In fact, the pattern of Jesus' administration of the bread followed the same structure that he used at the Last Supper; namely taking, thanking, breaking, distributing.[2]

For this reason it comes as no surprise that the churches in the book of Acts broke bread in their homes (Acts 2:46). The term "breaking of bread" must refer to the Eucharist since Luke records that it was one of four core elements of early Christian worship, the other three being the apostles' teaching, fellowship, and prayer (verse 2). It is impossible to imagine that the Eucharist that Jesus commanded to be kept often would not be one of the essentials of early Christian spirituality. Acts 20:7–12 records that the disciples gathered on the first day of the week in the upper room of a *house* at Troas to break bread. Clearly the words "break bread" must imply this was a gathering to share in the Lord's Supper, since it took place on the first day of the week.

It's clear from the pages of the New Testament that *houses* were a key location for both the worship and the evangelism of the early church. The risen Lord appeared to the disciples in a house (John 20:14–29). The power of the Holy Spirit which was poured out on the Day of Pentecost happened in a house (Acts 2). In the later parts of the New Testament we find mention of churches in a house in Philippi (Acts 16:40), Corinth (Acts 18:7), Rome (Romans 16), Ephesus (1 Cor 16:19), Laodicea (Col 4:15) and Colossae (Phlm 1–2). In Acts 17:5 we find Jason's house at Thessalonica was used as a basis for evangelism, as also was Titius Justus' home opposite the synagogue

---

1. See chapter 1.
2. Luke 24:30.

in Corinth (Acts 18:7). The fact that whole households were converted in the New Testament era is also testimony to the solidarity of the family unit in Jewish, Greek, and Roman society. Archaeological evidence suggests that early Christians decorated their homes in a way that might well have attracted comment and led to opportunities for discussion. Second- and third-century excavations in Rome have revealed mosaics showing Eucharistic loaves, a chalice and the fish motif. A house in Pompeii belonging to Paquius Proculus was hit by disaster when Mount Vesuvius erupted in AD 79. Recent excavations have unearthed rich mosaics and Rotas Sator palindrome, suggesting that this was a place of worship. What to all intents and purpose appears to be a cross has been discovered on the wall of a house in the city of Herculaneum. This may also have been a discreet place of Christian worship.

SOME SIGNIFICANT EARLY HOUSES USED FOR WORSHIP

Whilst it was the case that ordinary Christian homes were places where families and small groups worshipped, some came to have a more prominent role. It often happened that a room or rooms in larger dwellings were set aside specifically for worship. These would have been the homes of the more wealthy believers. Archaeologists have brought to light a number of early Christian homes that were clearly used for worship, including obviously the breaking of bread or Eucharist. There are second- and third-century examples of this at Ostia and Rome. In Ostia there are mosaics showing images of Eucharistic loaves, a chalice, and fishes. In Rome on the Caelian Hill there was a complex of three adjoining houses which now lie underneath the Church of St. John and St. Paul. At some time before the middle of the second century two of the houses were modified and joined together and used as a place of Christian worship. One of the two houses was found to have a remarkable fresco of an orante (a person with arms outstretched in prayer) on the wall of the dining room (triclinium). This figure makes it clear that the house was owned by Christians. The house evidently remained in Christian hands, because there is a strong tradition that John and Paul were actually beheaded there in AD 362 during the reign of Julian the Apostate, following their refusal to join the imperial army. What is almost certainly their tomb was discovered under the stairs.[3]

3. O'Grady, *The Victory of the Cross*, 24; Green, *Evangelism in the Early Church*, 216;

Other similar house churches have been found underneath the churches of St. Prudentia and St. Martin ai Monti, and St. Clement near the Colosseum.[4] The house of Clement is a remarkable building, standing two levels below the present twelfth-century Church of St. Clement. This building stands on top of the fourth-century church that in turn is built on top of the fourth-century house of Clement. The fourth-century structure has been excavated as has the house below and visitors can now go down steps to both levels. The house is named after Clement, the third successor to Peter as Bishop of Rome, who died about AD 100. There is very little information about this Clement though some second-century Christian leaders knew him. Clearly he was a significant Christian leader in the first city of the Empire. His Letter to the Corinthians, written in AD 96, is important because it is the first indication of the leader of the church at Rome addressing with authority a Christian church in another part of the empire.[5] For the present purpose it is significant to note that the leader of church in Rome clearly also pastored one of the city's several congregations which met in his own substantial house.

One other very early extant house church was that at Dura Europos, close to the banks of the river Euphrates. Not only was this residence a place of worship where the Eucharist was regularly kept but it had an immersion baptistery which is believed to have been constructed about the year AD 232. There are frescoes on the walls on the theme of water which depict Jesus walking on water and the Samaritan woman at the well.

At Water Newton, west of Peterborough in the English county of Cambridgeshire, what is now known as the "Newton Treasure" was found by a farm worker who was ploughing a field in February, 1975. Among the items which included twenty-seven silver spoons there were silver plates and bowls engraved with the "Chi Rho" symbol.[6] Of particular significance was a wine-mixing bowl inscribed with the words "Lord, I, Publius, relying on you, honour your holy sanctuary." There were also some pieces of pewter, a jug and beaker, and a silver bottle with a prayer inscribed on it. These finds have led archaeologists to posit the existence of a late–second-century house church.

Luff, *The Christian's Guide to Rome*, 108–9.

4. O'Grady, *The Victory of the Cross*, 24.

5. Scotland, *Rome City of Empire*, 9 and 75–81.

6. Chi and Rho are the first two letters of "Christ" in the Greek alphabet.

At Hinton St. Mary in Dorset a Roman Villa was excavated in 1964. It yielded among other things a mosaic pavement that depicts a clean-shaven man with a chi rho monogram behind his head. This is an obvious representation of Jesus which has been dated on the basis of coins found on the site as being not later that AD 340–350. The mosaics also include two pomegranates, the Christian symbol of immortality, one on either side of Christ's head. The pavement also has a large image of the Tree of Life. This was clearly the home belonging to wealthy Christians which was used as a church. At Lullingstone in Kent there is a house which was plainly being used as a place of Christian worship by AD 360. It had a number of brightly colored frescoes showing Christians with their arms fully outstretched in prayer. These are now preserved in the British museum. There was also a large decorated panel with a Chi Rho symbol in the center. These two houses are particularly significant since they appear to have remained as places of worship well after Constantine's Edict of Toleration.

A discovery in a house in the Roman town of Caerwent in Wales[7] brought to light a large flanged pewter bowl, a pewter plate, a knife, and some scraps of a woolen twill cloth. They had been buried level with the floor. On the bottom of the bowl there was a Chi-Rho monogram, devoting the vessel to Christian use. George Boon, who examined this collection, wrote: "It seems reasonable to claim that they were used in the Early Christian supper known as the agape, held after the Eucharist at the invitation of some well-to-do member of the community in his own house, for his poorer fellows."[8] Further archaeological study of the town revealed that house number 22 contained a very large room, number 7, some twenty-three feet long and thirteen feet wide with an apse at one end, and it seems likely that this was the place where the Christians of the town worshipped even after toleration had been granted by Constantine.

For most of the first and second centuries the Lord's Supper generally continued to be shared in the context of a fellowship meal with participants gathered in homes around the domestic table.[9] Writing to the Corinthian church about the Lord's Supper, the Apostle Paul referred to it as the

---

7. House VIIN.

8. Boon, "The Early Church in Gwent 1," 17.

9. There were occasions when the early believers broke bread in other contexts. For instance we know that there were times when the Eucharist was held in the catacombs of Rome.

sacrament of "the Lord's table,"[10] clearly indicating the domestic context of their gatherings. In a sermon John Chrysostom (c. 347–407) commented on the importance of this close link in earlier Christian times between the Eucharist and the fellowship meals. He wrote, "For when all the faithful met together, after hearing the instruction, and after the prayers, and the communion of mysteries, they did not immediately return home, upon the breaking up of the assembly, but the rich and wealthy brought meat from their houses; and called the poor and made common tables, common dinners, common banquets in the church itself."[11] These words must, at the very least, reflect something of the practice of Chrysostom's own time in and around the city of Constantinople where he served for a time as bishop.

It is possible in some places that the Eucharist was separated from the agape at a very early point. Indeed, as Jeremias pointed out in the *Didache*, the two separate prayers spoken over the bread and over the wine in the Last Supper have been joined together in one single prayer, possibly suggesting that no longer was there a shared meal between them. It is clearer in the writings of Justin about the year AD 160 that the Eucharist in his native area had been separated from the agape meal. In some cases it preceded the meal so that the congregation could participate having fasted and in others it came afterwards. Regardless of whether or not the Lord's Supper was celebrated in the context of a meal, the fact is that it would have been celebrated in a *home* and in the manner that resonated with the Jewish Passover with its blessings, remembrances, and ethos. Andrew McGowan has shown that in Tertullian's time, probably early in the third century, believers who had been present at the Sunday Eucharist took *home* some of the consecrated elements and were able to have a subsequent communion in their own *homes* by extension. Indeed even those who had been prevented from being present at the main service were able to share in these smaller home-based occasions.[12] In support of this Eusebius recorded that Irenaeus, in discussion with Pope Victor in Rome at the end of the second century, affirmed that "presbyters used to send the Eucharist to Christians who were not able to have it."[13]

10. 1 Cor 10:21.

11. Chrysostom, *Homily XXII.*

12. See Bradshaw, *Eucharistic Origins*, 100–101 citing McGowan, "Rethinking Agape," 165–76.

13. Eusebius, *History of the Christian Church*, 5:24.15

Throughout the third century when in many places the Eucharist began to be taken apart from the meal, it still continued to be located in houses on account of the persecuting Roman authorities. That said, the separation of the Lord's Supper from the meal context was very probably a slow process. This is suggested by the fact that in AD 367 the Council of Laodicea actually sought to forbid agapes in private homes. They ruled, "It is not permitted to hold love feasts, as they are called, in the Lord's houses, or churches nor to eat and to spread couches in the house of God."[14] The emphasis was still on eating and drinking to remember not a deliverance from slavery in Egypt but a greater deliverance from the consequences of sin and selfishness.

CHANGES AFTER CONSTANTINE

Following the Emperor Constantine's conversion to Christ in AD 312 and the end of suffering and persecution for the Christians, the celebration of Communion gradually moved out of peoples' homes and into the now newly legal official church buildings which began to be erected everywhere in the Roman Empire.[15] Thus, instead of the owner of the home or one of the prophets[16] or a deacon (priests only after Nicaea 325) leading the fellowship in simple prayers of thanksgiving to the Lord for the bread and wine at a domestic table (1 Cor 10:21), priests, though not at this point in time clad in special ecclesiastical dress, now stood before stone altars and uttered lengthy consecration prayers, some of which were designed and believed to change the bread and wine into the body and blood of Christ. Thus about the year AD 325 Cyril of Jerusalem wrote, "we beseech the loving God to send forth His holy Spirit upon the gifts lying before us, that He may *make* the bread the body of Christ, and the wine the blood of Christ."[17] That said, there still appear to have been occasions in the immediate post-Constantine years when Christians kept the Eucharist in their own homes. Basil the Great (c. 330–379) wrote:

> But as to a person's being compelled in times of persecution, in the absence of a priest or minister, to receive communion from

14. Council of Laodicea, "Canon XXVIII."

15. Eusebius, *History of the Christian Church*, 10:2:2–3.

16. *Didache*, 10.

17. Cyril of Jerusalem, *Catechetical Lectures*, 23.7.

his own hand—it is a waste of time to prove that this is no offence at all, since events themselves attest the long-standing, traditional character of the practice. For those living the solitary life in the wilderness, where there is no priest, reserve communion at home, and receive it from themselves.[18]

Basil went on in this letter to refer to the same practice of receiving "reserve communion" at homes in Alexandria and in other parts of Egypt. There, Basil remarked, "each one, even of the laity, very commonly keeps communion in his house and receives it from himself when he wishes." Basil's concern here was for isolated Christians who were cut off from priests and priestly ministry, but his comments show that homes and houses were still the venue for communion services in a number of areas of the Roman Empire.[19]

It has been argued that it was necessary for the Eucharist to be celebrated in larger groups, since the bigger and sometimes flamboyant buildings that began to be erected after Constantine's conversion demanded it. In fact, once the Emperor Theodosius made Christianity the established religion of the Roman Empire in AD 381 an ever-growing number of people wanted to become Christians and attend public worship in order to improve their status and employment opportunities. This increased the need for structured liturgy and more formal church leadership. That said, note has to be taken of the fact that the Passover feast was kept not in the Tabernacle or in the Jerusalem temple or in the synagogues but in *houses* (Exod 12:3). Indeed, there are clear indications in the Mishnah tractate Pesaḥim 5:5–7 that early first-century Jews collected their Passover lambs from the temple and then took them for the feast to their homes, or tents in the case of those who lived outside the city. There are early glimpses of this same practice at the time of Hezekiah and Josiah when lambs were given to their families or small groups (2 Chr 35:12) By calling the Last Supper "the Passover" and instituting it in a house rather than in the temple or a

18. Basil the Great, "To the Lady Caesaria concerning Communion, Letter 93."

19. Ibid. Interestingly, Basil went on to point out that the person who receives the bread directly from the hand of the priest in the church still "has it at his own disposal, and thus moves it to his mouth with his own hand. And so it is the same situation whether one receives a single portion or many portions at the same time from the priest." It was evidently the practice of some priests to give several portions of consecrated bread (he doesn't mention wine) to those who lived in isolated places. They could then serve themselves and when they did so it was in essence no different from to the communicant in church taking the bread and wine from the priest and then serving themselves.

synagogue, Jesus made it clear that he intended Communion to be part of a domestic spirituality rather than an aspect of public, temple, or synagogue worship. Paul clearly understood this when he referred to the Eucharist as the New Passover. "Let us keep the Feast," he wrote, "for Christ our Passover has been sacrificed for us."[20] The point therefore is that the home and the small group are the most appropriate and the best suited locations for the Lord's Supper.

During the Middle Ages the established Catholic churches in the West and the Orthodox churches in the East ensured that Christian worship took place in their official public buildings, many of which were large and impressive and designed to bespeak the power and influence of the Holy Roman Empire. The insistence on keeping all worship in public buildings of course also helped to secure political loyalty and solidarity. In this process the importance of the home and household spirituality was almost totally lost, apart from small groups such as the Waldensians and the Lollards. However, with the coming of the Reformation in sixteenth-century Europe there was a growing dissatisfaction over corruption in the established churches and a desire to recover the simplicity of the home-based spirituality of the New Testament Church. Puritans in particular began to focus on the importance of the home as the primary expression of Christian life and worship.

THE PURITAN HOUSEHOLD A CHURCH MINIATURE

The seventeenth-century American and English Puritans were concerned to make Christianity the religion of their home. J. I. Packer wrote, "It is hardly too much to suggest that the Puritans created the Christian family in the English-speaking world."[21] When a new home was occupied for the first time Puritans dedicated it to God and pledged all the members of the household to his service. Ties of mutual obligation bound the members of the household to one another. P. McGrath emphasized that "it was Puritanism which stressed an individual pietism, with the household as its essential unit rather than the parish."[22] Within a Puritan household the notion of making a family into a church was of great importance. It was seen as the husband's responsibility to ensure that his family attended Sunday

20. 1 Cor 5:7.

21. Packer, *Among God's Giants*, 28.

22. McGrath, *Papists and Puritans*.

worship. It was his constant endeavor to set a godly example at all times and he taught his household the essentials of the Christian faith and led them in Christian worship at least once a day. J. I. Packer, quoting a tract written by the Puritan John Geree (1601–1649), observed, "His family he endeavoured to make a church, both in regard of persons and exercises, admitting none into it but such as feared God; and labouring that those that were born into it, might be born again."[23] J. Stoughton relayed an account of a simple service held in the home of a Mr. Fox in 1592. The gathering shared a communion supper which was described as "a much stronger resemblance to the Passover scene in the Upper Room at Jerusalem than . . . the administration of the sacrament in St Pauls' Cathedral of that day."[24] In 1592 Arthur Billett and Thomas Settell, both of whom were members of the church which had been led by Henry Barrow, stated that they had received the Lord's Supper in the home John Barnes, a local tailor.[25]

Religious books were read to the Puritan family to promote piety. Puritan philanthropists were always eager to increase their number and donate them to poorer Puritan homes. It was a frequent custom in Puritan homes to read sermons as a method of religious education. Members were exhorted to listen carefully to the preacher so that they could write down parts of the sermon when they got home or repeat parts of it and other members would contribute by filling in the forgotten parts. Among the many Puritan devotional writers Richard Baxter was one of the most significant. In 1650 he published *Saints Everlasting Rest,* a book that was written for devotional reading in the home.

The singing of Psalms in the home was another prominent feature in many puritan homes. Family prayers, however, occupied the largest place in the discipline of the Puritan residence and it was generally accepted that in a well-ordered household family prayers should be held twice a day. The discipline of the individual soul was also felt to be the key to character and private devotions were therefore a very important part of Puritan homelife.

METHODISM AND THE HOME

One of the reasons why Wesleyan Methodism, and more particularly English Primitive Methodism, was so successful in reaching the poor was their

23. Packer, *A Quest for Godliness,* 270.

24. Stoughton, *Spiritual Heroes,* 54.

25. Burrage, *Early English Dissenters,* 42.

return to the New Testament emphasis on the home. Hugh Bourne, one of the movement's co-founders, described in his *Memoirs* how a revival broke out in the area of Harriseahead in 1801. It was, he recorded, a revival that was characterized by conversational style "preachings" that frequently took place in mine workers' cottages. These often humble dwelling places were frequently the scene of very fervent gatherings for prayer. Bourne described these gathering as being of "no ordinary kind." Liveliness was the key and "the people got to be in a great measures, Israelitish" a term which he went on to explain, meant "noisyish."[26] He quoted the Old Testament book of Ezra 3:12–13, "And the people shouted with a great shout . . . and the noise of it was heard afar off." Such proved to be the case at the prayer meeting which Bourne held at Jane Hall's Cottage, which was on the side of Mow Cop, a village in the English County of Staffordshire. H. B. Kendall, the first official historian of Primitive Methodism, related that the door was open and Elizabeth Baddeley, a miner's wife who was given to profane language, distinctively heard the sound of prayer and praise echoing across the hillside from Harriseahead which was a mile and a half away. In consequence she was convicted of her sinful ways and became a born again believer.

A similar story was carried in an 1850 issue of *The Primitive Methodist Magazine*. Hannah Wright, a servant girl, had come under the influence of the Spirit of God after a local preacher who had declared "Jesus is at home." Following this she was invited by friends to a Primitive Methodist prayer meeting but could not go because she had to mind the house for her master and mistress. According to the article, "The house of prayer being not far distant, she heard the exercises; and while a friend was besieging the throne of grace, the power of God smote her to the ground; and there she was laying when the family returned home. When she got up she explained that God for Christ's sake had pardoned all her sins."[27] Julia Werner in her study of the denomination commented, "The Cottage prayer meetings of Primitive Methodism were a 'form of revivalism' and that they were popular because they were held in rural areas where people were isolated and devoid of other forms of entertainment. They also appealed to women who were excluded from pub-based diversions."[28] Significantly, many of the first official church buildings erected by the Primitive Methodist church in Great Britain were designed in the shape and appearance of larger houses,

---

26. Kendall, *History*, vol. 1, 31.

27. *The Primitive Methodist Magazine*, 1850, 124.

28. Werner, *The Primitive Methodist Connexion*, 180.

which enabled ordinary people to feel more at ease and their worship more related to family and everyday life.

THE CHURCH IN THE HOME

One thing is clear and that is that the Christian church has often been most effective when it was based in houses. Probably at no time did the Christian church expand as rapidly as during the first three centuries. Paul and the early Christian missionaries often began their evangelistic endeavors by going initially to the Jewish community. For the Jew the home was of first importance. The Lord had set them apart in households and often dealt with them by households. Equally, in Roman society the house and the family were no less valued. The father was the undisputed head over a close-knit family unit that included slaves. The Romans worshipped domestic deities in their homes, a fact that has been borne out by the excavations at Pompeii where literally hundreds of small statues of household gods have been found.

BISHOP JOHN ROBINSON AND HOME-BASED EUCHARISTS

One of the great twentieth-century scholars who recognized the importance of the home for Christian spirituality and evangelism was Bishop John Robinson of *Honest to God* fame. Before the publication of that controversial book he had earlier written another challenging book entitled *On Being the Church in the World*.[29] In a chapter entitled "The House Church and the Parish Church," he reminded his readers it is always "the great Church" but nevertheless it can "and must be embodied in units which can be described as 'the church' as it finds expression 'at Corinth' and 'in your house.'" These units, Robinson pointed out, "are not simply bits of the church; they are the Church; they are the body of Christ in its totality, as it exists in this or that of its cells. Each cell is a microcosm, on its own scale perfectly reproducing the whole."[30] This is not an ecclesiological model which endears itself to most people in episcopal orders and many in priestly orders but it was one in which Robinson was wholly confident. "We should not," he wrote,

29. Robinson, *On Being the Church in the World*.
30. Ibid., 102.

"think of the house Church as a purely temporary expedient: a makeshift arrangement characteristic of the earliest Church in Jerusalem or in any other mission area" and nor are we to think of the house Church "simply as an evangelical weapon for the Church in the house is not an *ad hoc* experiment: it is a theologically necessary part of the life of the body."[31]

Robinson went on to reinforce this point by citing the Apostle Paul's reference to "Aquilla and Priscilla and the church in their house," and "Nympha and the church in her house" at Laodicea. These people were not working in "fringe areas of the parish (paroikia) where the church had not yet been established," rather "these were Churches within the 'parish' church, in much the same way as to-day the parish Church is a Church within the diocese."[32] "This conception of the cellular structure of each [large] or parish church," Robinson contended, "is something that has been grievously lost in the modern church."[33] Paul does distinguish between "the Church of the Laodicaeans" and "the church that met in Nympha's house," and this same distinction was seen in the Church at Rome and other major cities within the empire. Indeed, we know from the pen of Eusebius that in the middle of the third century the Church in Rome must have been composed of at least forty Christian households and probably considerably more. He records that the church was composed of "forty-six presbyters, seven deacons, forty-two acolytes, fifty-two exorcists, readers and door-keepers, and more than fifteen hundred widows and distressed persons." This "vast community . . . both rich and growing with laymen too numerous to count," Eusebius recorded, "was supported by the Master's grace and love for men."[34] On the strength of this figure the number of Christians in Rome has been reckoned as between 30,000 and 50,000.[35] Clearly on the Lord's Day the majority of these Roman Christians must have been "breaking bread" in their homes without one of the forty-six Presbyters being present. In other words, the majority were lay-led occasions. To return to Robinson we can now see the strength of his conviction on this matter. He wrote, "What is of theological significance is the application of the term 'the Church,' with all the high doctrine that goes with it, to the smallest unit of

31. Ibid., 103.
32. Ibid., 103–4.
33. Ibid., 104.
34. Eusebius, *History of the Christian Church*, 6:43.
35. Ibid., 282.

Christian existence within the larger whole."[36] In a later paragraph he was even more resolute and wrote:

> I believe that the theological recovery of this idea of "the church in the house" is one of the most important tasks of our generation. Whereas the organisation is an optional extra, of the bene esse of the parish, I believe that the cellular structure of the Church will be rediscovered as a necessity of life. . . . Here is something of theological necessity for the very essence of the Church and for the life of every member within it. We have a defective idea of the house church if we define it as something which is a half-way stage to the parish Church [or any major denominational church]. Rather it is a vital cell within the body itself, which should be reflecting in microcosm the *whole* life and activity of the community of the Holy Spirit—all that Paul meant by describing it as 'the Church', the great Church, in the house.[37]

If the logic of Robinson's ecclesiology has been followed thus far, it is hard to escape his conclusion that the house church is a right, if not the right and proper location in which to celebrate the Lord's Supper or Eucharist. Indeed he went further and wrote, "I should be very surprised, however, if we do not see its reintegration with the agape meal, so that once more the Eucharistic elements become something taken off the table 'as they were eating.' The special vestments, the special vessels, will either disappear at this level or be radically modified."[38]

If we can run with Robinson's contention thus far then we have reached the point that each house church can, and indeed should have, their own lay-led Communion services, as was the case in mid–third-century Rome! At once of course this suggestion will bring forceful objections particularly from those denominations such as the Roman Catholics, Orthodox, and Anglicans who hold to the view that only ordained ministers and clergy can preside at the Supper. In answer to such an objection, Robinson countered that "the Eucharist is always at every level, the Christian Community celebrating through the priest, and not the priest celebrating for a congregation." The Reformation indeed made marked changes to the theology of the Eucharist but, as Robinson so poignantly put it, "All that has changed is that instead of offering the sacrifice for the laity the function of the clergy is

36. Robinson, *On Being the Church*, 104.

37. Ibid., 106.

38. Ibid., 110.

now 'to provide communion' for the laity."[39] Even in those churches and denominations where lay men and women are allowed to preside at the Lord's Supper the focus is frequently on their performance for the congregation rather than on the whole community celebrating together. "It is perhaps," Robinson concluded, "an essential element of the Christian Passover that it should be eaten . . . among the tables and chairs of the home by men and women who like the Israelites of old must go on their way in the morning."[40]

RECOVERING HOUSEHOLD WORSHIP TODAY

The logic of what has so far been considered is that the church needs to recall the Apostle Paul's model of the church as "God's household."[41] The church in the house is indeed church at the basement level. It cannot be without significance that Christianity spread very rapidly in the first three centuries when it was almost totally home based and Eucharists must often have been lay led.

A survey of the subsequent centuries of Christian history reveals that churches were often at their most effective when the center and heart of their activities was the home. Such was certainly true of seventeenth-century Puritans, the Moravians and Wesleyans and nineteenth-century Primitive Methodists. Whilst it is not known to what extent the Lord's Supper was a significant part of the spiritual life and worship in these later religious movements, the fact is that the home was the locus of the church.

In summation it needs to be emphasized that is that Jesus chose the home rather than the synagogue or public sphere as the location for the central act of Christian worship. It is also abundantly clear that the early Christians in Jerusalem and other places mentioned in the book of Acts regularly and frequently shared the Eucharist in their homes.[42] The present-day churches need to seriously reconsider following this example. Contem-

---

39. Ibid., 108.

40. Ibid., 112.

41. Eph 2:19.

42. See Acts 2:42 and 46. The reason for this assertion is simply that Acts 2:42 records that the early Christians "devoted themselves to the apostles' teaching, and to the fellowship, to the breaking of bread and to prayer." Since it is impossible to imagine that as the Lord's Supper was the only instruction that Jesus gave regarding worship, the early Christians would have neglected it. The "breaking of bread" must therefore refer to the Lord's Supper or Eucharist. Indeed "breaking of bread" was a frequent designation of the Lord's Supper in the early days of the Christian church.

porary Christianity needs to strengthen, reclaim, and reprioritize home and family life. Prayer and shared listening to God through his Word, and the singing of worshipful songs can both unify and cement family ties and relationships. It can also be an important means of imparting wisdom and providing a moral framework.

In the present liberal and growing secular climate of North America and Western Europe homes are increasingly going to be the sphere where Christian friendships are forged and the Christian message shared. Above all, the homes and houses can and should be the places where Christian families and small groups of believers can share the Lord's Supper with each other. Whilst clergy and ministers of major denominations may not favor home-based Lord's Suppers, every encouragement can and should be given to Christians to hold them in their own homes as families or in small groups.

6

A Meal for Believers

ONLY FOR THE PEOPLE OF GOD

As has been already been noted, scholars such as Joachim Jeremias have sought to demonstrate that the Lord's Supper is the continuation of the Passover feast and although it was, and is still, intended to be an interactive informal joyous occasion in the home, it was nevertheless restricted to those who were God's people. The regulation in Exodus 12:43–49 clearly excludes those without faith in the Lord (foreigners) from sharing in the meal, although it does allow any slave who has been circumcised (presumably believers) to take part. Temporary residents and hired workers were to be excluded.[1] Clearly, therefore, the Passover was a meal intended for those who were committed worshippers of Jehovah.

NEW PASSOVER FOR BELIEVERS

From the very beginning this same restriction was clearly carried forward by the early Christian communities in their celebration of the Lord's Supper or New Passover. The *Didache,* which can perhaps be considered the first service book of the early church, lays down the following instruction, "Let

1. Exod 12:43–49.

no one eat or drink of your Eucharist except those baptised into the name of the Lord; for, as regards this, the Lord has said, 'Give not that which is holy unto dogs.'"[2] In a similar way, Justin Martyr in his *First Apology* which was written in Rome about the year AD 150 made it abundantly clear that only baptized believers were allowed to partake of the Eucharist.

> And this food is called by us "thanksgiving," of which it is permitted for no one to partake unless he believes our teaching to be true, and has been washed with the washing of forgiveness of sins and regeneration, and so lives as Christ handed down.[3]

The *Apostolic Tradition of Hippolytus* proffered the plain instruction that "A catechumen shall not sit at table for the Lord's Supper."[4] The *Apostolic Constitutions*, a fourth-century collection of church laws, laid it down that at the beginning of the Lord's Supper the deacon shall say, "Let none of the catechumens (those still under instruction), let none of the hearers (that is those who had come to the service because they were interested in Christianity), let none of the unbelievers, let none of the heretics, stay here."[5]

Serapion (d. after 360), Bishop of Thmuis and a close friend of Athanasius, gave similar instructions in his *Sacramentary* (c. AD 340). Before the time came for receiving the sacraments the catechumens were asked to leave with the deacons apparently proclaiming in a loud voice.

> "Bow down your heads for a blessing, O you catechumens" following which the bishop raised his hand in the sign of the cross and blessed them in the following words.
> "We raise our hand, O Lord, and pray that the divine and life-giving Hand be raised for a blessing unto this people; for unto You Eternal Father, have they bowed their heads through Your only-begotten Son Jesus Christ, by Whom glory and might be unto You in the Holy Ghost now and throughout all ages. Amen."[6]

In the North Syrian rite of the *Apostolic Constitutions* which dates to about 370 the dismissal of the catechumens follows a very similar pattern. After being commanded by the deacon to kneel he then recited a series of short petitions for them. After each one they were invited to answer *Kyrie eleison*

2. *Didache*, 9.
3. Justin, *First Apology*, 66:1.
4. Hippolytus, *Apostolic Tradition*, 82.
5. Hippolytus, *Apostolic Constitutions*, 8.
6. Serapion, *Sacramentary*, 42.

in the following way: "That He who is good and loves mankind will piti-fully receive their prayers (Kyrie eleison); that He will reveal unto them the gospel of his Christ (Kyrie eleison); that He will enlighten them and establish them with us (Kyrie eleison)." Altogether there are eighteen such petitions for the catechumens, after which they are invited to stand and pray for themselves and entreat the Lord for the peace of Christ all the days of their lives. When this is completed they are bidden to bow for the bishop to bless them and the deacon then dismisses them.[7] This having been done the deacons then announced, "Let the catechumens go forth; and when these had gone, cried again: 'The doors! The doors!' as a signal to those of their number, or their assistants, who guarded the doors, to close and lock them against all intrusion."[8] Once this had been done the congregation continued with prayers and the Eucharist.

Theodoret (c. 393–c.457), the church historian and Bishop of Cyrrhus in Syria, quoted what he said was an unwritten saying of Jesus, "My mys-teries are for myself and for my people." The *Egyptian Church Ordinances* made it clear that the Lord's Supper was solely for baptized Christian be-lievers. Ordinance 49 is very clear on the matter: "Let not (one) allow the catechumens to go into the Lord's Supper with one of the faithful."[9] In the Middle Ages as the Lord's Supper was gradually transformed into the Mass and it became the custom in many places for Christian men and women simply to receive the presence of Christ by gazing on and reverencing the consecrated host. As a result of this, the issue of unbelievers or nominal Christians partaking of the bread and wine became a diminishing issue.

THE PROTESTANT REFORMERS

However, the Protestant Reformers who had come to a rediscovery of the Pauline doctrine of justification by faith alone were very aware that the Lord's Supper was for those who had actively put their faith and trust in Christ who had died that they might be forgiven and had risen again to bring them new life. In England, Archbishop Cranmer made this fact ex-plicitly clear in his second *Book of Common Prayer*. To receive the bread and wine it was necessary "to earnestly repent" and "be heartily sorry for

7. Dix, *The Shape of the Liturgy*, 478.
8. Ibid., 42.
9. Keating, *The Agape*, 119.

these our misdoings."[10] At the Confirmation service Cranmer added a rubric which made it abundantly clear that the Lord's Supper was only for Christian believers. It required that there shall be none vadmitted to Holy Communion "until such time as he be confirmed or ready and desirous to be confirmed."[11]

THE PURITANS

The sixteenth- and seventeenth-century Puritans shared Cranmer's convictions. For example, the separatist Puritan, Henry Barrow (c. 1550–1593), was incensed that the Church of England admitted "a promiscuous multitude into the most sacred worship of the church." He was particularly "angered at the suggestion of some Puritans that while it was necessary for oneself to be 'a true believer of worthy life' no pollution ensued from taking Communion with the wicked." The Anglicans, in Barrow's view, were absurd to imagine "that it is lawful to receive all into the bozom of the bodie of the church, to delyver the most holly and pretious things of God to all, evene the sacraments."[12] Thomas Goodwin (1600–1680), the leader of the Independents at the Westminster Assembly in 1643, was also adamant that the Lord's Supper must be restricted to the church members. "The sacraments," he argued, "are never administered to begin or work grace."[13]

The Puritans in both America and England were concerned to pattern church life and practice on strict biblical principles and it is therefore no surprise that they were concerned to ensure that unbelievers were kept from the Lord's table. For this reason Stephen Mayor wrote, "They did not consider making the Eucharist the normal Sunday service, despite their indebtedness to Calvin, who did."[14] In England however, the regular week-by-week worship of the established church was non-sacramental and therefore did not arouse Puritan hostilities in the way that other issues did. That said, when there were Communion services the Puritans were insistent that only the worthy should be allowed to come to the Lord's table. They believed it to be the pastor's duty to judge who was or was not fit to be a partaker. Robert Browne (c. 1550–1633), who became known as "the father

10. Cranmer, "Confession," *Book of Common Prayer* 1552.

11. Ibid., "Rubric at the End of the Confirmation Service."

12. Barrow, *Writings*, 157.

13. Goodwin, *Works*, vol. 2, 389.

14. Mayor, *The Lord's Supper*, 27.

of English Congregationalism," stressed that it was essential to make proper spiritual preparation before going to a Communion service. This consisted of ensuring a person's life was separated from bad company, redressing ill or lax behavior, and the private examination by each individual of his or her conscience. John Smyth (c. 1570–1613), who founded the first English Baptist Church, albeit in Holland, was adamant that "in the outward supper only baptised persons must partake, for there is presented and figured before the eyes, of the penitent and faithful, that spiritual supper, which Christ maketh of his flesh and blood."[15]

In American colonies the Puritans adopted the same strictness in protecting the Lord's Table from unbelievers and those Christians who failed to live up to their profession. Those who had been baptized as infants were kept from receiving the sacrament until such time as they were able to make their own profession of faith. Francis Higginson (1588–1630), the Puritan minister of Salem, preached a sermon on Jesus' words, "Give not that which is holy to dogs" to those who had gathered to receive Communion. His intention was to be certain that only those who were true adult believers would receive the bread and wine.[16] John Cotton (1585–1652) wrote specifically on the matter in *The Way of the Churches of Christ in New England* (1645) as follows:

> But now for as much as wee all who are borne in Christian Churches, are baptised in our infancy, and such as are baptised infants, are not admitted to the Lord's Table in well-ordered Churches, till they have approved, and in their own persons publickly confirmed their profession of repentance and faith, which their parents, or others in their stead professed, and promised for them at their Baptisme.[17]

Cotton went on to relate that the members of other churches and their children were welcomed to the Lord's Table provided that they bring a letter of testimonial.[18] The practice of allowing the children of believers to share in the bread and wine resonates with children being allowed to share in the Passover meal.

The Reverend Jonathan Mitchel (1624–1688), Pastor of Cambridge, Massachusetts, was particularly careful to allow only those who were truly

---

15. Smyth, "Confession of Faith," in *Works*, vol. 2, 745.

16. Davies, *Worship of American Puritans*, 197.

17. Cotton, *The Way of the Churches of Christ*, 88.

18. Ibid.

converted to come to the Lord's Table. According to Cotton Mather he wrote a series of "propositions," the sixth of which was sharply focused on the matter. It stated, "Hence, either a relation of the work of conversion, such as hath been ordinarily used in most of our churches, or somewhat equivalent thereto, is necessary in order to full communion, or to admission to the Lord's Table."[19]

Richard Baxter (1650–1691) of Kidderminster was clear that the Lord's Supper was not a "converting ordinance" and stated that God gave no command to give the Lord's Supper to infidels to convert them. Faith, repentance, and consent to the covenant are all to be professed before reception.[20] As Baxter saw the matter it was essential that those coming to Communion should first be received into church membership. But even then they needed further instruction and teaching about the Supper.[21]

THE STRICT AND PARTICULAR BAPTISTS

In the later years of the eighteenth century England Abraham Booth (1734–1806) and William Gadsby (1773–1844) were prominent Particular Baptist pastors in London and Manchester respectively. They both adopted the practice of restricting Communion only to those who had been baptized as adults. Gadsby published a periodical, *The Gospel Standard*, in order to spread his views. During the Victorian years, however, most Baptists gradually abandoned the practice, though not quite all. Indeed, the Gospel Standard Baptists remain to the present time in England. Surprisingly perhaps, both Booth and Gadsby were active in itinerant ministry and in planting new congregations. In Scotland, Archibald McLean (1733–1812) adopted Strict Baptist principles in his Edinburgh congregation. They observed the Lord's Supper which they called "The Breaking of Bread" every Lord's Day, making it the central focus of their worship. They often held a Love Feast or agape between the morning and the evening service. They held to strict Communion practice, and retained the kiss of charity (1 Thess 5:26) and feet washing as an act of hospitality.[22]

19. Davies, *Worship of American Puritans*, 199–200.

20. Ibid., 133.

21. Mayor, *The Lord's Supper*, 133.

22. Underwood, *A History*, 189–90.

THE CHURCH OF ENGLAND

It is significant that Archbishop Cranmer inserted a rubric at the end of his 1552 Prayer Book Communion service which was retained in the later 1662 Prayer Book and stated "that every Parishioner shall communicate at least three times in the year, of which Easter shall be one." Clearly he did not anticipate that Communion would be the main regular central act of Sunday worship service. This may well have been because he recognized that the sacrament was intended only for those who had "truly repented and intended to lead a new life."[23] Cranmer's prescript held in the majority of English parishes right up to the early Victorian years with most English parishes holding only three or four communion services a year.[24]

Most contemporary universal mainline denominational churches, together with the vast swathes of indigenous Pentecostal fellowships and more recent apostolic network churches,[25] have followed Cranmer in trying to keep unbelievers from receiving the bread and the wine. Some do it by having the Eucharist as a kind of add-on short Communion at the end of their main Sunday preaching service. In many churches a blessing is pronounced and the people are invited to leave with those who want to break bread asked to remain seated. All this is done with laudable intent, but if such churches were following the ways of the early Christians of the first three centuries and encouraging believers to have the Eucharist in their own homes or in small groups, such provisions would be unnecessary.

CONCLUSION

Richard Baxter, the great pastor of Kidderminster, was concerned that clergy should not think to use the Eucharist as a means to convert the wicked or ignorant. The fact that such a practice might have produced this result—just as a stolen book might convert a thief—did not justify it. For the unbelieving to receive the bread and wine was "to tell God a lie."[26] It is of course easy enough to try and justify the practice of many present-day churches

23. Gibson, *First and Second Prayer Books*, 392.

24. See, for example, Scotland, *Good and Proper Men*, 151.

25. The Apostolic network churches are those which have emerged in the wake of the Charismatic movement of the later twentieth century. They included Covenant Ministries International, New Frontiers International, Salt and Light, Cornerstone, Icthus, Pioneer, Vineyard, and Partners in Harvest. See Kay, *Apostolic Networks*, 343–49.

26. Baxter, "Christian Directory," *Practical Works*, vol. 4, 313.

making Communion as their central or main act of Sunday worship but, as Baxter intimated, it is manifestly not the best idea. Most obviously for the reason that the Lord's Supper was never instituted or intended by Jesus to be or become a public ceremony, and certainly not one to which the uncommitted were invited to participate. In the secularizing of the Western world it makes little sense to think that large numbers of unchurched people are going to be won to Christ by watching a formal ceremony presided over by a minister clad in a black gown and sitting on the dais at the front of the auditorium in a big chair behind a large table set with a silver tray full of tiny pieces of bread and stacks of thimble-sized cups of black currant juice. Possibly even less attracting would be the sight of a small group of priests and Eucharistic ministers clad in white hooded garments standing round an altar laden with silver goblets of wine and plates of wafers with candles burning and incense rising up around it.

It is obvious from this survey of Christian history that through the ages most congregations have at the very least felt the need to confine the Lord's Supper to the Lord's people. In particular, at the time of the sixteenth-century Reformation Cranmer was seeking to bring the Anglican Eucharistic practice much more into line with that of the early church. Even though the England of his day was part of a nominal European Christendom in which all citizens were assumed to be Christians, he clearly did not envisage that the Eucharist would be the central weekly Sunday service. Fast-forwarding to the present time, it is hard to imagine that he would ever have countenanced the practice in the secularizing culture of the contemporary world. There are always those, as has been noted, who argue that the Eucharist is "a converting ordinance" but Cranmer was all too aware of the New Testament teaching and the custom of the early Christian churches of the first and second centuries to buy into such practice. In that early period of the church's history it was never anticipated that those who were not committed baptized Christians would be present at the Lord's Supper.

If the contemporary churches can recognize the Lord's Supper as the "New Passover," as the earliest Christians clearly did, they will return to their practice of keeping it as a home-based sacrament for the believing community. It would then be unnecessary to make it the main public central act of Sunday worship. Instead, if the words of Archbishop William Temple were to be taken seriously that "the Church is the only society on earth that exists for the benefit of non-members," local churches would be offering something on Sundays such that those who are strangers to the

Christian faith were able to attend without encountering anything awkward, embarrassing, or excluding.

7

A Sacramental Meal

In his Gospel the Apostle John does not record the events of the Last Supper in the Upper Room in the same way that the other three Gospels do. Instead, he links the words which Jesus spoke when he broke the bread and poured out the wine with the miracle of the feeding of the five thousand.[1] Significantly, at the beginning of his narrative he mentions that the Jewish Passover feast was near.[2] After the people had been fed and their hunger thoroughly satisfied, Jesus announced himself to them as "the bread of life" and went on to assert that "he who comes to me will never go hungry, and he who believes in me will never be thirsty."[3] He also drew a contrast between the manna which the Israelites had eaten in the desert following the Passover and their escape from Egypt and the bread which he himself would provide. Whereas their forefathers who ate the manna in the wilderness eventually died, whoever would eat the bread that he would bring "will live forever."[4] In this teaching Jesus made it abundantly clear that there is physical hunger which can be satisfied with material bread but there is a deeper spiritual hunger which can only be satisfied by feeding on his very presence. "My flesh," he declared, "is real food and my blood is real

1. John 6:1–15 and 53–54.
2. John 6:4.
3. John 6:36.
4. John 6:51.

drink and whoever eats my flesh and drinks my blood has eternal life and I will raise him up on the last day."[5]

It's clear from this that there is a spiritual presence in the Lord's Supper but it is not *in* the bread but rather it is received as the communicants consciously and purposefully take the presence of the living Christ into their lives. The communicants eat and drink what is and what remains as ordinary bread and ordinary wine but crucially they feed spiritually on the presence of the living Christ. As he himself put it, "I am the living bread that came down from heaven. If anyone eats of this bread he will live for ever," and again "the one who feeds on me will live because of me."[6] This spiritual feeding can begin as people gather round the table before the bread and wine are received and it can continue well after the bread and wine have been consumed. Indeed, the ideal is that the Lord's people should be those who feed continually on his presence. In this context William Barclay wrote challengingly,

> There is no doubt what John is saying—he is saying that for the true Christian every meal has become a sacrament. It may well be that there were those who—if the phrase be allowed—were making a fetish and a magic of the Sacrament, who were implying that the Sacrament was the one place where we might find and meet and enjoy and rest in the nearer presence of the Risen Christ. It is true that the Sacrament is a special appointment with God; but John held with all his heart that every meal, in the humblest home, in the richest palace, beneath the canopy of the sky with only the grass for a carpet, is a sacrament.[7]

Barclay further commented that John "refused to limit the presence of Christ to an ecclesiastical environment and a correctly liturgical service." Rather he thought that the Communion table, the dinner table, and the picnic on the sea shore or the hillside were all places where the sustaining presence of risen Christ can be made known.[8]

---

5. John 6:54–55.
6. John 6:51 and 57.
7. Barclay, *The Gospel of John*, vol. 1, 232.
8. Ibid., 233.

THE LORD'S SUPPER AS SPIRITUAL FOOD IN THE EARLY CHRISTIANITY

As might be expected, John's understanding of the Eucharist appears to have carried over into the understanding and praxis of many of the early Christian congregations. In the catacombs in Rome, for example, there are a number of frescos dating from the second and third centuries which depict the Eucharist with the disciples and Jesus gathered together with bread and wine, and with extra loaves and fishes either on the table or in baskets standing alongside.

As has been noted in Chapter 3, a belief sprang up at a relatively early point that the presence of Christ was in the bread and wine, as opposed to a spiritual presence in the Christian believer. Nevertheless, some of the early Christian writings and liturgies witness to a belief that the communicants received a spiritual presence rather than one that was contained in the elements. The thanksgiving prayer in the *Didache* gives thanks that "You did grant spiritual food and drink and life eternal, through your servant."[9] In Part 1 of his *Apostolic Tradition* which dates from around AD 217 Hippolytus gives a quotation from the consecration prayer with which he is familiar. It includes the following lines: "And we pray that You would send your Holy Spirit upon the oblation of your Holy Church and You would grant to all [Your saints] who partake to be united [to You] that they may be fulfilled with Your Holy Spirit for the confirmation of [their] faith in truth."[10] It is clear from these lines that Hippolytus believed that the strength and resources of the Holy Spirit were imparted to the recipients of the bread and wine. Athanasius wrote similarly in a letter to Serapion, "We receive the celestial food that comes from above."[11]

Origen stressed that Christ's body "is not both present here with us, and also gone hence and estranged from us."[12] Augustine wrote that "As concerning the presence of his Majesty, we have Christ ever with us; but as concerning the presence of his flesh, he said truly to his disciples, Ye shall not ever have me with you."[13] Similarly, Ambrose declared "that we must not seek Christ upon earth, nor in earth, but in heaven, where he sitteth

---

9. *Didache*, sec. 10.

10. Hippolytus, *Apostolic Tradition*, 1:4.

11. Athanasius, *Letter to Serapion*, 19.

12. Cited Cranmer, *Defence*, bk. 3, ch. 5, 129.

13. Ibid., bk. 3, ch. 5, 130.

at the right hand of his Father." Gregory followed suit and stressed that "Christ is not here by the presence of his flesh, and yet he is absent nowhere by the presence of his majesty."[14]

During the course of the Middle Ages the church came increasingly to the view that the sacramental grace of Christ's presence was contained *in* the sacrament. This development eventually reached its zenith in the pronouncement on transubstantiation at the Lateran Council of 1215 and the teachings of Thomas Aquinas (c. 1225–1274). That said, there were occasional voices who held a different view. Among their number were Ratramnus (d. 808), a monk from Corbie, and Bernard (1090–1153), Abbot of Clairvaux. In his book, *De Corpore et Sanguine Domini*, Ratramnus taught that the bread and wine of the Eucharist are not changed materially in any way but they remain exactly as they were before consecration. Communicants therefore eat only ordinary bread and ordinary wine. However, for the true believer there is an inward "spiritual feeding" in which the faithful feed on Christ by faith in their hearts.[15] Bernard held that grace was made available through the sacraments rather than in them.[16]

THE SUPPER, A MEAL OF SPIRITUAL FOOD, THE REFORMATION AND AFTER

John Calvin urged his followers "to believe that the sacrament is spiritual— a something whereby God will feed our soul, not our stomach." He continued, "Let us seek Christ not as he is seen and apprehended by the bodily senses, but as he is recognised by His presence in our soul."[17] Calvin reiterated the same point in the *Institutes*: "It is not the bread that brings Christ or contains Him. It is Christ Himself Who through His Holy Spirit gives himself to us."[18] Again in the *Institutes* Calvin underlined the point that the bread and wine are "signs" which "represent the spiritual food" which we receive by faith.[19] On that understanding Calvin posed the question, "Why should the Supper have been instituted if we had not had a faith needing to be strengthened? If we feel ourselves frail, let us approach the Table . . .

---

14. Ibid., bk. 3, ch. 5, 132.

15. Ratramnus, *De Corpore et Sangune*, in Cannon, *History of Christianity*, 100.

16. Courtenay, "Sacrament, Symbol," 111.

17. Barclay, *The Protestant Doctrine of the Lord's Supper*, 116.

18. Ibid., 133.

19. Calvin, *Institutes*, 41.

in order to be vivified by Him. The Supper is to strengthen believers and to restore sinners."[20]

Ulrich Zwingli (1484–1531), the Zurich Reformer, wrote in his final statement on the Eucharist in July 1530 that "when the Jews were arguing about the corporeal eating of Jesus' flesh his response was, 'The flesh is no avail.'" In contrast, however, Jesus emphasized that "eating spiritually" gives life.[21] In his major treatise *On the Lord's Supper* Zwingli again stressed that communicants "do eat spiritually." "To eat the body of Christ spiritually is equivalent to trusting with the heart and soul upon the mercy and goodness of God through Christ." Again in the same section he emphasized, "If I may put it more precisely, to eat the body of Christ sacramentally is to eat the body of Christ with the heart and mind in conjunction with the sacrament."[22]

Almost all the Protestant Reformers would have shared the views of the John Lambert, the Protestant martyr who died in 1538, that "our soul . . . into whom nothing corporal can corporally enter, doth not carnally receive the body and blood of our saviour."[23] During the sixteenth-century Reformation there was controversy among the Reformers as to precisely in what ways Christ was present in the Eucharist. Martin Luther defended the doctrine of consubstantiation which asserted that the presence of Jesus was in, on, and around the bread and wine. At the other end of the Protestant theological spectrum Ulrich Zwingli affirmed that there was no change in the elements and that the Lord's Supper was primarily a memorial. Zwingli did not believe that the sacrament could impart a specific grace as that was already in the elect on account of their faith.[24] He saw the Eucharist as a statement of faith[25] and maintained that Christ was present in "the apprehension of the believing communicant."[26] Somewhere between these two views were those of John Calvin (1509–1564) of Geneva and his followers. They denied any change in the nature or substance of the elements but maintained that the faithful received the power or virtue of the body and blood of Christ. This was a doctrine which in consequence became

---

20. Ibid., 41.

21. Zwingli, "Final Statement on the Eucharist," July 1530.

22. Zwingli, *On the Supper*, 259.

23. Lambert, *A Treatise*, fo. 30.

24. Reardon, *Religious Thought*, 107.

25. Gerrish, *Continuing the Reformation*, 64.

26. Berkhof, *Systematic Theology*, 653.

known as "virtualism." As Calvin put it in his own words, the Holy Supper "is a spiritual communion, by which, 'en vertu eten efficace,' He makes us partakers of all that we can receive of grace in His body and His blood."[27]

MARTIN BUCER, THOMAS CRANMER, AND DOUBLE-EATING

Among those whose views were close to those of Calvin were Martin Bucer and Thomas Cranmer. Cranmer emphasized that there is a spiritual presence of Christ in the sacrament but it is not found in or contained in the bread or the wine. Rather, it is found within those who rightly receive the bread and the wine. Having made it absolutely clear that there is no change in substance of the bread and wine, Cranmer then made it plain that as well as eating and drinking ordinary material bread and wine there is nevertheless "a spiritual feeding," in which those who receive the sacrament in faith feed on Christ spiritually. This doctrine, which was spoken of as "double eating," Cranmer had learned from Martin Bucer (1491–1551), the German Reformer, who came to England in 1549 and was made Regius Professor of Divinity in the University of Cambridge. Bucer taught that "we confess two things to be in the sacrament; an earthly, viz., bread and wine, which remain unchanged: and a heavenly, Christ our Lord himself who does not leave heaven . . . but gives himself in a heavenly manner for the food and sustenance of eternal life."[28] Charles Smythe commented, "For Bucer Christ is not merely signified, but . . . eaten by faith in the power of the Spirit."[29] The Church of England Article XXVIII—*Of the Lord's Supper*, underlined this fact that to receive the sacrament "rightly and worthily" means with faith. John Lambert shared the views of Bucer and Cranmer, asserting that "our souls cannot live except they be spiritually fed with the blessed body and blood of Him, spiritually eating and drinking them."[30]

Significantly, both the 1552 and 1662 English Prayer Book liturgies repeatedly refer to the Lord's Supper as "a feast of *spiritual* food." At the end of the first exhortation in the 1552 order, which is to be said when the curate sees people "negligent to come to the Holy Communion," the text speaks of it as "the banquet of the most heavenly food." At the beginning

27. Barclay, *The Protestant Doctrine of the Lord's Supper*, 123.
28. Smythe, *Cranmer and the Reformation under Edward VI*, 167.
29. Ibid., 168.
30. Lambert, *A Treatise*, fo. 30.

of the Second Exhortation in the 1552 book, the Communion is spoken of as "our *spiritual* food," though this phrase was removed by the compilers of the 1662 book. The third exhortation in both the 1552 and the 1662 books inform us that "the benefit is great when we *spiritually* eat the flesh of Christ, and drink his blood; then we dwell in Christ, and Christ in us."

REASONS WHY CHRIST'S PRESENCE IN THE SUPPER CAN ONLY BE SPIRITUAL FEEDING

In *On the Lord's Supper* Zwingli pointed out that the "lamb in Exodus 12 *is* called 'the Passover,'" even though the Passover had not yet taken place. Therefore, he continued, "the little word 'is' is necessarily figurative, that is it is used to 'signify' . . . the Passover." In the following paragraph Zwingli developed this thought, writing "The Paschal Lamb is the Passover, that is, the Paschal Lamb represents the passing over of the angel of God; and, 'This is my body,' that is, This represents my body, the eating of this bread being the sign and symbol that Christ, the soul's true consolation and nourishment, was crucified for us."[31]

In the third book of his *Defence*, Cranmer devoted a section to the Presence of Christ in the sacrament and set out a number of reasons why there could be no substantial or bodily presence of Christ in the consecrated bread and wine. Cranmer cited several passages from the Gospels in support of this, beginning with John 15 where Jesus says, "I leave the world and go to my Father." He then made reference to Jesus' words in Matthew 26 that "You shall not ever have me with you."[32] He pointed out from Mark 16 that "Jesus was taken up into heaven, and sitteth on the right hand of the throne of God's majesty." He also added a quotation from the Letter to the Hebrews that "we have a High Priest that sitteth in heaven at the right hand of the throne of God's majesty."[33]

Cranmer stressed this point that communicants feed only on material bread and wine but they receive a spiritual presence of Christ as they do so in faith. He cited Origen, Tertullian, and Chrysostom, and several other early church fathers who understood Jesus' words about eating and drinking his body and blood only in a spiritual sense. Cranmer summed the

31. Zwingli, *On the Lord's Supper*, 225–26.

32. Cranmer, *Defence*, bk. 3, ch. 4, 128 citing Matthew 26:11.

33. Ibid., bk. 3, ch. 4, 128. He also cites Colossians 3:2: "Set your hearts on things above where Christ is seated at the right hand of God."

matter by pointing out that Jesus himself frequently "spoke in similitudes, parables, and figures,"[34] obvious examples being his discourse on the vine, the bread of life, the good shepherd and the door. Cranmer was clear that "the bread and wine have no holiness in them."[35]

NOURISHMENT THROUGH FAITH

Calvin shared Cranmer's view and was clear that "the sacraments do not confer grace" and that "nothing is received except by faith."[36] Calvin wrote that "the only way to dispose our soules to receive nourishment, reliefe, and quickening of his substance, is to lift up our mindes by faith above all things worldlye and sensible, and therby to entre into heaven, that we find and receive Christ."[37] In 1523 Zwingli wrote in a letter to Thomas Waterbach, "I believe the Eucharist is eaten where there is faith . . . . [O]nly he who firmly believes that our Lord's death betokened salvation . . . knows that this food is given among other things to strengthen weak faith."[38] For Zwingli, "only for those with faith, however little and however imperfect was Christ present at the distribution."[39] Zwingli also quoted Christ's words, "He who believes on him feeds on him" and then asserted, "It follows then that to feed on Christ's body is to believe in him who was given up to death on our behalf. He who believes on him feeds on him."[40] John Frith (c. 1503–1533), the English Protestant martyr and one-time junior canon of Cardinal College, Oxford, asserted that "while a man eateth the bread of the sacrament with the mouth and teeth" yet "with his heart and faith inwardly he eateth the very thing which the sacrament outwardly dothe reperesent."[41]

In his *Defence* Cranmer laid great stress on this concept of *spiritual* eating. "Christ's body and blood," he wrote, "are not received in the mouth, and digested in the stomach, (as corporal meats and drinks commonly be) but is received with a pure heart and a sincere faith."[42] At the start of the

34. Ibid., bk. 3, ch. 11, 164.

35. Ibid., bk. 3, ch. 15, 181.

36. Calvin, "Article XVII—The Sacraments do not confer grace."

37. Calvin, *Order for Communion*, 8.

38. Zwingli, "Letter to Thomas Watterbach," 96.

39. Potter, *Ulrich Zwingli*, 35.

40. Zwingli, *On the Lord's Supper*, 198.

41. Frith, *A Boke Made by John Frith*.

42. Cranmer, *Defence*, bk. 1, ch. 16, 74.

third book of his *Defence*, in the section entitled, "the manner how Christ is present in his Supper," he draws the contrast between the Papists who "teach that Christ is in the bread and wine" and his fellow Protestants who say that "he is in them that worthily eat and drink the bread and wine."[43] Later, in another paragraph in the fourth book, Cranmer repeats the point. He begins by referring to the words of Chrysostom that in speaking of "very flesh and blood" Jesus was using "figurative speech," and that the bread and wine be "signs, figures, and tokens instituted by him to represent unto us his very flesh and blood." Then he continued, "And yet as with our corporal eyes, corporal hands, and mouths, we do corporally see, feel, taste and eat the bread and drink the wine, being signs and sacraments of Christ's body, even so with our spiritual eyes, hands, and mouths, we do spiritually see, feel, taste, and eat his very flesh and drink his very blood."[44]

CONSECRATION BY EATING AND DRINKING IN FAITH

Cranmer held the view that what facilitated spiritual feeding at the Lord's Supper had nothing to do with the priest or president but everything to do with the believer eating and drinking in faith. Spiritual feeding therefore did not come as a result of the priest reciting Jesus' words of institution over bread and wine, or by his manual acts of placing his hands over the paten and chalice, or even by his calling down the Holy Spirit (epiclesis) on to the elements to change them into the body and blood of Christ. Cranmer was clear that consecration was simply "the separation of any thing from a profane and worldly use unto a spiritual use."[45] Indeed, to make his point explicit Cranmer removed the words "consecrate," "bless," and "sanctify" from the 1552 liturgy. He pointed out that in baptism ordinary water is taken from other ordinary uses, and put to use for baptism. In the same way "ordinary bread and wine is taken and severed from other bread and wine, to the use of Holy Communion," although it remains the same substance as that from which it was severed.[46] In Article XXV, which drew on the Augsburg Confession, Cranmer stated that "in such only as worthily receive the same they have a wholesome effect or operation."[47] For Cranmer,

43. Ibid., bk. 3, ch. 2, 124.
44. Ibid., bk. 4, ch. 8, 209.
45. Ibid., bk. 3, ch. 15, 181.
46. Ibid., bk. 3, ch. 15, 181.
47. Neil and Willoughby, *Tutorial Prayer Book*, 561–62.

worthily receiving the bread and wine meant eating and drinking, trusting in Christ's forgiveness and in remembrance of his death and passion.

The Roman Church's view was that good Christian men and women only ate the body and blood "at that time when they receive the sacrament." In contrast, John Calvin was clear that the spiritual feeding doesn't always take place at the precise moment when we receive the bread and wine.[48] More broadly, Cranmer held strongly to the view that people can eat, drink, and feed on Christ "continually, so long as they are members of his body."[49] Cranmer did not believe there was a single moment when the bread and wine were consecrated and so became the body and blood of Christ. It was for this reason that in the 1552 consecration prayer there was no epiclesis or calling down the Holy Spirit on the bread and wine. Nor was the priest required to engage in any manual act by laying his hands on the cup or the paten, as later became the case in the 1662 Communion liturgy.

The English Puritan and first English Baptist, John Smyth (c. 1554–1612), was clear that the bread and wine of the Sacrament are "the nourishers and comforters of our life whereby the Lord doth seale up unto us the spiritual nourishment and comfort of our soules."[50] Likewise, the American Puritan Samuel Willard (1640–1707) wrote in his *Sacramental Meditations* that "the Lord's Supper is a sacramental sign of the sustenance and nourishment of the Christian Community." It is, he wrote, "mutual conjugal love between Christ and his spouse the Church."[51]

CONTINUAL FEEDING

In the sixteenth century the Reformers were clear that Jesus' body and blood were only received in a heavenly and spiritual manner as the communicants ate and drank in faith. Cranmer made this plain in his teaching by the words that he requires to be spoken as the bread was given to each communicant, "take and eat this . . . and *feed on him* [not in the mouth but] *in thy heart* with thanksgiving."[52] Cranmer was also clear, as were other Reformers, that this "spiritual feeding" need not and should not end in the Communion service. Rather, Christians can and should feed continually

48. Calvin, "Article XX."

49. Cranmer, *Defence*, bk. 3, ch. 2, 125.

50. Smyth, "The Bright Morning Star," in *Works*, vol. 1, 190.

51. Willard, *Some Brief Sacramental Meditations*, 205.

52. Gibson, *First and Second Prayer Books*, 389.

on the presence of Christ. Holy Communion should both encourage and assist Christian believers to grow in this practice. John Calvin in *Article* XX of his *Berne Articles* shared the same point, asserting that, "The advantage which we receive from the Sacraments ought by no means to be restricted to the time at which they are administered to us, just as if the visible sign, at the moment when it brought forward, brought the grace of God along with it."[53] John Bradford, the London-based Reformer and parish minister, also stressed the value of continual spiritual feeding on the presence of Christ, stating on one occasion that "though in the field a man may receive Christ's body by faith, in the meditation of his word."[54]

Continuous feeding can perhaps be likened to the way in which cattle feed. Cows have four chambers within their stomachs, the largest of which is known as the rumen. They can in some instances hold up to fifty gallons of partially digested food. Good bacteria in the rumen breaks the food down and provides protein for the cow. This is where the cud comes from and is eventually passed into the abomasum that is similar in function to the human stomach. Here it is finally digested and essential nutrients are passed into the blood stream. Although the illustration is not perfect it can be suggested that in a similar way Christian people may from time to time receive large deposits of spiritual food through the Word, Spirit, and sacrament. These spiritual recourses can be stored, processed, meditated on, and finally digested. In a parallel spiritual way the Lord's Supper can assist believers to develop the habit of "continuous feeding" as the Protestant Reformers suggested. It was for this reason that Calvin dealt in a section of the *Institutes* with the "Right Use of the Supper" and stressed the importance of taking time when receiving the bread and wine. "To rush forward to receive the Lord's Supper," he wrote, "is a failure to discern the Lord's Body."[55]

NOURISHMENT FROM THE WORD OF GOD, TEACHING, AND PREACHING

The Protestant Reformers were clear that preaching and teaching from the Bible went hand in hand with the sacrament of the Lord's Supper. They held that the expounding of Scripture was indeed both a preparation for the feast and also added to the spiritual food which the congregation could

53. Calvin, "Article XX," 175.

54. Bradford, "Sermon on the Lord's Supper," 96.

55. Calvin, *Institutes*, sec. 40, 219.

receive. In other words, the worshippers would feed by faith on the spiritual presence of Christ the Bread of Life through both bread and wine and through the truths of God's word. The fact that Cranmer saw the expounding of Scripture as a key part of this spiritual feeding is born out in the Collect for the Second Sunday in Advent, which he originally wrote for the 1549 Prayer Book. "Blessed Lord, who has caused all holy scriptures to be written for our learning; Grant that we may in such wise hear them, read, mark, learn and inwardly digest them, that by patience and comfort of thy holy word, we may embrace and ever hold fast the blessed hope of everlasting life, which thou hast given us in our Saviour Jesus Christ."[56] The key words of Cranmer's prayer in this context are "inwardly digest," reminding worshippers that they can be fed, nourished and sustained by God's word.

SERMONS PROVIDE ADDITIONAL SPIRITUAL FOOD

Luther, Calvin, Cranmer, and other Reformers all made provision for a sermon and a reading from an epistle and Gospel at each Communion service. They had no place for priests "as pretend to be Christ's successors in making a sacrifice to him . . . for no person made a sacrifice of Christ, but he himself only."[57] Cranmer did not believe Christian ministers had any priestly or sacrificial role. Their function was to be a preacher and teacher of Scripture, to pastor the people, and to minister the bread and wine of Communion. This fact was made abundantly clear in the ordination services of both the 1552 and the 1662 Prayer Books. Those who were made deacon received a New Testament from the bishop with the words, "Take thou authority to read the Gospel in the Church of God, and to preach the same." Similarly, priests received a copy of the Bible with the words, "Take authority to preach the word of God, and to minister the holy sacraments in this congregation where thou shalt be appointed." In his 1552 Prayer Book Communion service Cranmer made provision for a sermon immediately following the creed. If a minister was not licensed by the bishop to preach a sermon, he was required to read one from the *Book of Homilies* which had been published in 1547. Significantly, the first sermon in the book was written by Cranmer and entitled, "A Fruitful Reading of Holy Scripture." Other homilies included, "On the Salvation of all Mankind," "Of the true

56. Gibson, *First and Second Prayer Books*, 34.
57. Cranmer, *Defence*, bk. 5, ch. 5, 220.

and lively faith," "Of Good Works," and "An exhortation against the Fear of Death."

Cranmer did not believe the priest or minister to be in any way ontologically different from the laity. He certainly did not subscribe to any notion of the spirit of the apostles being passed down to or residing in the clergy by virtue of their ordination. He was adamant that the bishop's hands made no such change. "The difference between the priest and the layman in this matter," he wrote, "is only in the ministration; that the priest as the common minister of the Church, doth minister and distribute the Lord's Supper unto other, and the other receive it at his hands."[58] In the Lord's Supper, therefore, the Protestant Reformers held the minister's core roles and duties were to ensure that the Scriptures (a passage from a New Testament letter and a passage from a Gospel) were read, a sermon given, and the bread and wine administered to the people.

ALL OTHER BENEFITS OF HIS PASSION

When a person dies there are benefits accruing from their will. Jesus brought lasting forgiveness through his death on the cross which was "a full, perfect, and sufficient sacrifice, oblation and satisfaction, for the sins of the whole world."[59] But this was by no means the only spiritual benefit which flowed from his passion. The New Testament is clear that Jesus brought "peace through the blood of his cross." So as Christians drink the wine they can at the same time be imbibing "the peace of Christ which passes all understanding." The Apostle Peter's first letter includes the reminder that it is by Jesus' wounds believers have been healed (1 Pet 2:24). The author of the Letter to the Hebrews states that through his death Jesus is able to cleanse people's consciences from guilt (Heb 9:14). In addition to this, the prophet Isaiah foresaw that in his death Jesus would bear his followers' griefs and carry their sorrows (Isa 53:4). It is these, the healing and wholeness, the cleansing of guilt and other spiritual benefits that the congregation should be receiving by faith as they eat the bread and drink the wine. This in part is what the Catechism refers to when it states that "on such days [at the Lord's Table] chiefly we ought in faith and spirit fervently to pray to God, to give us all good things that we lack and have need of, and to defend and deliver

---

58. Ibid., bk. 5, ch. 11, 224.
59. Cranmer, *Book of Common Prayer*, 305.

us from all evil things."[60] It was these same benefits that the participants at the Puritan Assembly had in mind when they compiled and published the *Westminster Confession* in 1648:

> Worthy receivers, outwardly partaking of the visible elements in this sacrament, do then also inwardly by faith, really and indeed, yet not carnally and corporally, but spiritually, receive and feed upon Christ crucified, and all benefits of his death: the body and blood of Christ being then not corporally or carnally in, with or under the bread and wine.[61]

Recent approaches to the Lord's Supper still regard it as the vital means of experiencing the presence of Christ. Just as the participants at the Jewish Passover found a deep sense of God's presence through the eating and drinking at the Seder meal, so the majority of the world's Protestant Evangelical and Charismatic Christians still stress the importance of the intimate experience of the divine presence as they share in the bread and the wine of the Lord's Supper. It's an emphasis that is still seen, for example, in part of the consecration Prayer A in the Church of England's *Common Worship*, which prays that "as we eat and drink these holy gifts in the presence of your divine majesty renew us by your Spirit, inspire us with your love and unite us in the body of your son, Jesus Christ our Lord."[62]

CONCLUSION

The Lord's Supper is clearly a vital source of spiritual nourishment and strength and should be a regular part of every Christian's spirituality. As Calvin put it, "The celebration of the Lord's Supper should therefore be frequent. One has need of often reminding oneself of the death of Christ."[63] For this reason Calvin began his *Articles* with the statement as follows, "It is certain that a Church cannot be said to be well regulated, unless the Supper of our Lord is frequently celebrated."[64] He continued that "in view of the great comfort believers receive in every way," it should be held every week

---

60. Cranmer, "Catechism," *Writings of Thomas Cranmer*, 129.
61. *Westminster Confession*, Article VII.
62. *Common Worship*, 187.
63. Barclay, *The Protestant Doctrine*, 219.
64. Calvin, Introduction to the *Articles*.

as "was the practice of the ancient church."[65] In *Article* LIII of his *Ecclesiastical Ordinances* he wrote similarly, "our Lord instituted the Supper for frequent celebration, and it was thus observed until the devil overturned everything."[66]

One of the great advantages of locating the Lord's Supper in homes and houses is that there is more time available to sit quietly and eat the bread and drink the wine in an unhurried manner. Freedom from rush and hurry is vital if people are going to be able to meditate and feed on Christ's presence. The difficulty with a large congregation in a church building on a Sunday is that there is always the pressure of having to get up from the Communion rail or leave the bread and wine queues to make room for the next person in the line. To feed sacramentally requires time and space.

65. Barclay, *The Protestant Doctrine*, 219.
66. Calvin, "Ecclesiastical Ordinances," Article LIII.

8

A Meal for Remembrance

The Communion service was deliberately designed, not by Paul but by Christ himself, to give people an unmistakeable *reminder* why he died: his body given and his blood shed for our sins.

JOHN C. LENNOX, PROFESSOR OF MATHEMATICS
AT THE UNIVERSITY OF OXFORD

As is the case with all religious doctrines, the Passover ritual changed and developed over time. It seems to have been the case that at some point during the Roman rule over Israel the rabbis instituted the idea of having four cups of wine. It was customary for a Roman feast to be preceded by drinking wine. Then, after this initial celebration drink was over the banquet began, during which more wine was drunk. The rabbis, not to be outdone, quite possibly decided that the Passover should be celebrated with four cups of red wine and wrote the instructions concerning them in the Pesaḥim tractate of the Talmud. It was a requirement that everyone, even the very poorest, was to be given four cups of wine. The four cups of wine enable those at the Passover meal to *remember* four great redemption promises made by God and contained in Exodus 6:6–7: "I will bring you out from under the Egyptians," "I will free you from being slaves to them,"

"I will redeem you with an outstretched arm," and "I will take you as my own people."

THE PASSOVER AND REMEMBRANCE

The central aspect of the Jewish Passover was the commemoration of the Lord's deliverance of his people from slavery in Egypt. This is obvious from the food and the wine that are shared in the Seder. The unleavened poor person's bread caused them to remember the hardships in Egypt and the fact that they had to leave the land in a hurry with no time to make bread with yeast; the bitter herbs recalled the brutality of the persecution they endured in Egypt.

During the meal it is traditional for a child, often the youngest present, to question the one who presides over the meal as to the reasons for the ritual and the food. If no child is present another person is chosen. The most famous question is, "Why is this night different from all other nights"? Other questions include, "Why is it on all other nights during the year we eat either leavened bread or unleavened bread, but on this night we eat only unleavened bread"? Again, "Why is it that on all other nights we do not dip [our food] even once, but on this night we dip them twice"? and "Why is it that on all other nights we dine either sitting upright or reclining, but on this night we all recline"? After the questions the story of the change from slavery to freedom is told.

At the Passover meal three loaves of unleavened bread are placed on the table. The head of the family takes and breaks the middle one into two parts. Holding the broken pieces he says, "This is the bread of affliction which our forefathers ate in the land of Egypt: whosoever is hungry, let him come and eat; whosoever is in need, let him come and keep the Passover." As K. E. Keith well stated, it so clearly pointed to the greater deliverance of Christian people from bondage to sin.

> When Jesus took the bread at the Last Supper He was saying in effect, "Up to this time whenever you broke the bread, it reminded you of the 'Bread of Affliction' which your fathers ate in Egypt; but henceforth when you break the bread, let it remind you of the breaking of my Body. Heretofore, whenever you broke this bread, you thanked God for your redemption from the Egyptian bondage; henceforth, when you perform this action, thank God for your

redemption from a greater bondage, the bondage of sin. 'This do,' no more in remembrance of Egypt, but 'in remembrance of Me.'[1]

MEMORY IN JUDAISM

To commemorate is to preserve the memory of something by means of a public act or ritual. The Lord's Supper was designed to commemorate the death of Jesus. This emphasis on remembrance that we see in the Passover was a very important aspect of all Jewish life and worship. The Jews were people who constantly looked back to draw strength from the Lord's blessings, guidance, provision, and protection over their lives. They learned to take encouragement and to feed their spirits with these blessings that God had bestowed on them in the past. Indeed, the Old Testament relates that the Lord frequently appointed memorials of his past acts on behalf of his people. Thus, for example, circumcision was instituted as a memorial of the covenant with Abraham. Stones taken out of the Jordan were appointed as a memorial of Israel's passing through the Jordan on dry land. The Passover was of course appointed as a perpetually repeated memorial of Israel's deliverance from Egypt. The Korean scholar Seong Hye Lee has demonstrated that "the purpose and the arrangement of the Psalter and its integration and unity was to help people *memorize* the Psalms for their religious life."[2] The Jewish people constantly wrote things down in order to remember them. The rabbis also taught using memory techniques.

Gerhardsson has rightly reminded us that the chief content of Jewish culture and education was tradition and the memories of the past.[3] Memory was a vital part of Jewish spirituality. Indeed, the social and cultural identity of Israel was rooted in their corporate memory of their past experiences and dealings with Yahweh. One of the ways by which they sought to remember these great blessings of former times was by means of rituals. The simple act of having seen a symbolic ceremony such as the Passover and, more importantly, shared in it, intensified its impact on their memory as a people. Visual imagery of this kind not only illuminates the soul, it confirms great truths in the memory in a more intensive way. Clearly any performance, be it ritual activity, music, or art, greatly aids the process of

1. Keith, *The Passover in the Time of Christ*, 31–32.
2. Lee, "The Psalter as an Anthology," 223.
3. Gehardsson, *Memory and Manuscript*, 73.

remembrance. Throughout life from birth to death, therefore, Jews were constantly reminded by signs, symbols, and ceremonial rituals of the vital need to remember.

Just as the Jewish Passover called the participants to remember their deliverance from slavery, so in the New Passover Jesus laid stress on remembering his great act of redemption through his sacrificial death and resurrection. In the Lord's Supper we are reminded that "in him" every Christian has been freed from bondage to slavery, sin, and death. Importantly, both the Passover and the Lord's Supper were intended to be vivid remembrances or representations (re-presentations) of their divine deliverance, so that it was alive in their thoughts and hearts, indeed in their very beings. They were of course greatly helped in this by partaking of food and drink that so vividly symbolized and represented the divine act of redemption that they were recalling.

ANAMNESIS

In 1 Corinthians 11:25 Paul records Jesus' words, "This do in remembrance of me." Significantly, these words do not occur in either Matthew or Mark's account of the Supper, although they are found in Luke 22:19, suggesting that Paul and Luke are based on a different tradition. The Greek word *anamnesis*, which is translated "remember," means more than a mere commemoration of a past act: it emphasizes its present relevance. Very often "remembrance" includes both "memory and activity." In the Old Testament God "remembers" and "visits" or "forgives." The Eucharist is not in any sense a reenactment but it is a recalling of the sacrificial death of Jesus in such a way as to be able to receive its present benefits. John Calvin asserted that "bare" remembrance is not possible for the true Christian man or woman. He contended that "no spiritually-minded believer can remember the Lord without at the same time being in conscious fellowship with him through the Spirit, so that 'bare' remembrance is impossible, while genuine remembrance is fellowship with Christ, than which no higher blessing is possible."[4] Interestingly, G. D. Kirkpatrick suggested that "anamnesis" (remembrance) for Paul can also include the idea of proclamation. He examined the use of the word in the Septuagint and found that "anamnesis" is used to denote proclamation.[5] This is something that is readily recognized in day-to-day

4. Quoted in Knox, *The Lord's Supper*, 65.
5. Kirkpatrick, "Anamnesis," 41.

experience. A married woman looking at her ring remembers her husband away on a business trip but at the same time it is also a present declaration of her commitment to him.

REMEMBRANCE IN EARLY CHRISTIAN EUCHARISTS

The early church father Justin Martyr emphasized Christ's command to "do this in remembrance," both in his *First Apology* and in his *Dialogue with Trypho*. In the *Dialogue* he was explicit that the Eucharist is celebrated "in *remembrance* of the suffering which he underwent for the sake of those whose souls are cleansed from all wickedness."[6] In a later passage Justin commented "the bread which Christ commanded us to offer in *remembrance* of his being made flesh for the sake of those believing in him, for whom also he suffered; and the cup which he commanded us to offer, giving thanks in *remembrance* of his blood."[7] Justin clearly saw this as a vitally important aspect of the Supper since he returned to this same theme at a further point in the *Dialogue*, where he stated that "remembrance is effected by believers' participation in their solid and liquid food, in which the suffering which the Son of God endured for us is remembered."[8]

REMEMBRANCE AND THE REFORMERS

John Calvin regarded the Eucharist as an "appointed *memorial*" to "help our weakness for if we were sufficiently mindful of the death of Christ, this help would be unnecessary."[9] Later in the same paragraph Calvin made the important point "that Christ is not present in the Supper, because a *remembrance* applies to something that is absent." Although he is not therefore "visibly present and is not beheld with our eyes . . . the symbols excite our remembrance by representing him."[10] That said, although Calvin rejected any notion of Jesus being locally present in the bread and wine, "in order that he may be present with us, he does not change his place, but

---

6. Justin, *Dialogue with Trypho*, 41:1.

7. Ibid., 70:4.

8. Ibid., 117:3.

9. Calvin, *Commentary on the First Epistle to the Corinthians*, 381–82.

10. Ibid., 381–82.

communicates to us from heaven the virtue of his flesh, as though it were present."[11] In the *Institutes* Calvin stressed that Christians need "frequently to return" to the memory of Christ's Passion in the Supper "to sustain and strengthen their faith."[12]

In his "Admonition Concerning the Sacrament of the Body and Blood of our Lord," published in 1530, Martin Luther emphasized the Supper's importance as "a sacrament rich in grace," and "full of innumerable and unspeakable blessings." For this reason therefore we must, he urged, consider first of all that he has instituted this sacrament to be done in his remembrance. This remembrance is not only for our benefit but also for Christ's. Luther stated it as follows:

> "Do this in remembrance of me" [1 Corinthians 11:24]. Carefully ponder and consider this word "remembrance"; it will say much to you and will appeal to you greatly. But I am not now speaking of any benefit or necessity which we may look for in the sacrament but of the benefit which accrues to Christ and God himself and how necessary it is to his divine glory and service that we use and honor it diligently.[13]

Luther's focus is something we often lose sight of. If we do take time to remember the Lord and his sacrificial death, as indeed we should, we tend to do so with the intention of receiving the blessings of his divine presence, help, and strength. However, Luther reminds us that just as human beings are affirmed by being remembered so it is with Christ. "We will, then," he wrote, "partake of it [the Supper] frequently, in order that we remember him and exercise ourselves in this fellowship according to his example."[14]

Nicholas Ridley (1500–1555), Bishop of London, asserted in a conference with Hugh Latimer (c. 1485–1555) that "the commandment and institution of our Saviour Christ" was "for the oft frequenting of the remembrance of his death."[15] Latimer similarly declared, "The Supper of the Lord was instituted to provoke us to *remember* His death until He cometh again."[16] Ridley emphasized the supreme importance of remembrance of

11. Ibid., 382.

12. Calvin, *Institutes*, 3:44.

13. Luther, "Admonition Concerning the Sacrament," vol. 38, 105.

14. Luther, "The Blessed Sacrament," vol. 35.

15. Ridley and Latimer, "Conferences between Nicholas Ridley and Hugh Latimer," vol. 2, 120.

16. Ibid., vol. 2, 255.

Jesus. He was vehement that "This remembrance . . . as the author thereof is Christ (both God and man) so by the almighty power of God it far passeth all kinds of remembrance that any other man is able to make . . . for whosoever receiveth therewith this holy sacrament thus ordained in remembrance of Christ, he receiveth either death or life."[17] Ridley's one-time chaplain John Bradford (1510–1555) declared in a sermon on the Lord's Supper that "the end wherefore this sacrament was instituted was and is . . . that we should never forget that whereof we should be most certain." Bradford went on to explain that "the memory of Christ's death" is so important because of "what commodity it bringeth with it." The chief of those commodities is that "he which worthily receiveth should be certain of the remission and pardon of his sins and iniquities, how many and great soever they be. How great a benefit this is, only they know which have felt the burden of sin, which of all heavy things is the most heavy."[18]

The *Augsburg Confession* of 1530 also underlined the benefits which believers derive from remembrance:

> The institution of the sacrament . . . is enjoined that the body and blood of the Lord should be received: and that should be done for the *remembrance* of the benefit by Christ. For a remembrance signifies not only some representation of an historical fact, as if it were seen as a spectacle, as they dream who defend merit from the mere doing of a thing, but it signifies by faith to remember the promise and the benefit, to comfort the conscience and to give thanks for so great a benefit.[19]

In the sixteenth-century Communion liturgy of the Frankfurt Exiles the words spoken by the minister at the reception of the bread and wine emphasized the importance of remembrance. The rubric states "And when he delivereth the breade, he shall saye. 'Take, and eate this, in *remembrance* that Christe dyed for the, and fede on him in thyne hert by fyth with thenkesgeuinge.'" And in the giving of the cup the emphasis is the same, "Drynke this in *remembrance* that Christes bloude was shedde for the, and be thankful."[20]

In the third exhortation in Thomas Cranmer's 1552 Communion liturgy and in the later 1662 liturgy the priest charged the congregation that

17. Ridley, *Brief Declaration*, 8.
18. Bradford, "Sermon on the Lord's Supper," 106.
19. *Augsburg Confession*.
20. Leaver, ed., *The Liturgy of the Frankfurt Exiles*, 32.

they "should always *remember* the exceeding great love of our Master, and only Saviour Jesus Christ, thus dying for us." The consecration prayer calls the people not in any way to offer up the bread and wine but to receive the bread and wine "in *remembrance* of his (Christ's) death and passion." The words which were then spoken at the administration of the bread and wine in the 1552 rite were words of thanksgiving in remembrance of Jesus' death and passion.

The words spoken during the administration in Cranmer's 1549 Prayer Book were, "The body of our Lord Jesus Christ preserve thy body and soul unto everlasting life," and "The blood of our Lord Jesus Christ preserve thy body and soul unto everlasting life." When the 1549 book came into use a number clergy were of the view that these words made it still possible to retain a belief in the doctrine of transubstantiation. Following advice from Martin Bucer (1491–1551) and others, Cranmer changed the wording in his 1552 Prayer Book to, "Take and eat this, *in remembrance* that Christ died for thee, and feed on him in thy heart with thanksgiving," and "Drink this in *remembrance* that Christ's blood was shed for thee, and be thankful." When Queen Elizabeth I came to the throne and reintroduced worship in English she combined the 1549 words of administration with those of the 1552. In consequence, her 1559 Book of Common Prayer Book, which was almost entirely based on the 1552 Prayer Book, hinted at a compromise over the presence of Christ in the elements but nevertheless still invited the participants to *remember* his sacrificial death. It is the means, as Thomas Cranmer put it in the post Communion prayer in his 1552 liturgy, by which "we receive all other benefits of his passion."

Philip Hughes, in his *Theology of the English Reformers*, summed up the importance which they attached to remembrance as follows:

> The sacrament of holy communion, moreover, is commemorative in accordance with Christ's command: 'Do this in remembrance of Me.' As the third of the longer exhortations in the communion service explains, this sacrament was ordained by Christ 'to the end that we always remember the exceeding great love of our Master and only Saviour, Jesus Christ, thus dying for us, and the innumerable benefits which by His precious blood-shedding He obtained for us.'[21]

---

21. Hughes, *Theology of the English Reformers*, 214.

THE PURITANS AND REMEMBRANCE

Both the *Westminster Confession* and the *Savoy Declaration* stressed the importance of remembrance in the Lord's Supper. The Westminster statement declared that the Our Lord Jesus instituted the Supper "to be observed in his church for the *perpetual remembrance* of the sacrifice of himself in his death."[22] The *Savoy Declaration* was very similar, asserting that the Lord's Supper is to be observed "for the perpetual *remembrance* and shewing forth of the Sacrifice of himself in his death."[23]

The English Puritan, Richard Baxter (1615–1691) of Kidderminster, asserted that a crucial part of the Lord's Supper is "the Commemoration." This, he wrote, is "the visible representation of the sacrificing of Christ on the cross to the Father for the sins of man; to keep up the *remembrance* of it, and lively affect the church thereby, and to profess our confidence in Christ, for the acceptance of our persons and performances with God, as well as the pardon for our sins."[24] The Puritan Thomas Doolittle (1630–1707), who as a grammar school boy heard Baxter preach, wrote *A Treatise Concerning the Lord's Supper*. Published in 1665, it ran into twenty-six editions from that year until 1727. Doolittle asserted that "sacraments are glasses for our understanding, and monuments for our *memories*, that by mean and visible signs, we might perceive and *call to mind* sublime and invisible things. Here is bread, even bread of life to fill the hungry soul, and wine to satisfy the thirsty, and to cheer the drooping soul."[25]

It is of course easy enough to remember the sacrificial death of Christ in the quiet of a church with the bread and wine displayed on the Communion table, but by the same token it is all too easy to forget as soon as we leave the building. Against this background Baxter urged that we carry our remembrance with us. On returning home, each individual must "improve" the Lord's Supper by "serious remembering" of the mercies of God.[26]

The American theologian and New Testament scholar Charles Hodge (1797–1878) of Princeton put it in the following way:

> This do, 'Do what I have done; take bread, consecrate it, break it, distribute and eat it. In *remembrance of me*, that I may be

22. *Westminster Confession*, 31.
23. *Savoy Declaration*, 30.
24. Baxter, "The Poor Man's Family Book," vol. 19, 517.
25. Doolittle, *A Treatise on the Lord's Supper*, 9.
26. Baxter, "The Catechising of Families," vol. 4, 245.

remembered as he who died for your sins.' This is the specific, defi-
nite object of the Lord's Supper, to which all other ends are sub-
ordinate, because this alone is stated in the words of institution.[27]

Hodge went on to make the point that by this means "we are brought into
a real communion with Christ."[28] The great poet and Dean of St. Paul's Cathedral, John Donne (c. 1573–1631), was making the same point when he
wrote that "the art of salvation is the art of memory."[29]

TWO ASPECTS OF REMEMBRANCE

The Leading Victorian Anglican Evangelical clergyman, Edward Bickersteth (1786–1850), published *A Treatise on the Lord's Supper* in 1841 in
which he devoted a section on the importance to remembrance. In it he exhorted the reader of the supreme importance of constantly being reminded
that their sins had been forgiven.

> We may at all times with advantage remember Jesus Christ as a
> MARTYR, witnessing a good confession before Pontius Pilate, (1
> Timothy vi. 13) and sealing it with his blood—as an EXAMPLE of
> suffering obedience even to death triumphing over all his enemies;
> but particularly as A SACRIFICE FOR SIN, that we should regard
> his death when we surround his table.
>   Let not you minds be turned from this one point but remem-
> ber that Jesus Christ died for your sins, and keep in view the ben-
> efits thereby procured . . . . [M]any sincere worshippers deprive
> themselves of much comfort and strength which they might have
> received at the Lord's table . . . . Instead of keeping their minds
> steadily fixed on Jesus Christ, as the Lamb that was slain, and
> dwelling on his sacrifice, and the efficacy of his blood, they have
> by turns meditated on a variety of other religious truths.[30]

In his section on remembrance Bickersteth made the important point
that there are two parts or aspects to remembering Jesus. Most communicants, when they eat and drink in remembrance of Jesus, simply focus
their thoughts on what Jesus has done for them. They remember his sacrificial love in suffering and dying on the cross to bring them forgiveness of

27. Hodge, *Exposition of the First Epistle to the Corinthians*, 226.

28. Ibid., 226.

29. Davies, *Bread of Life*, 2.

30. Bickersteth, *A Treatise on the Lord's Supper*, 68.

their sins, a fresh start and newness of life through his Spirit. All of this is perfectly fine but, as Bickersteth, following Martin Luther, so importantly pointed out, we should also be remembering Jesus for who he is.

Everyone likes to be remembered. Indeed, they need to be remembered. People feel affirmed and encouraged when friends and family remember their birthday, anniversary, or perhaps some other significant milestone in their lives. Jesus is still at this very moment in time and indeed throughout all eternity, fully human as well as fully divine. In his humanity he must and does take joy and encouragement when his followers take time to remember who he is and thank and praise him for his love and goodness. Indeed, Jesus the man needs affirmation just as he did when Mary Magdalene anointed him with her jar of costly perfume shortly before his going to the cross. Bickersteth therefore included a section in which he invited his readers to remember who Jesus is. Significantly, he prefaces this section by stating, "This remembrance is so primary a part of our due receiving of the Lord's Supper, that it may be advantageous here to consider . . . how can we best remember our Divine Redeemer when we come to his table"?[31]

In answer to his question he exhorted Christian people "to remember him first as IMMANUEL, God with us" and "the joy of having God with me." He then urged that Jesus be remembered as "God our SAVIOUR." He is "the name above every other name, at which every knee shall bow,"[32] and He is the one "who purifies his people to be zealous for good works." "This is our God, we have waited for him, we will be glad and rejoice in his salvation." He should be remembered "as the MESSIAH" who bestows the gift of his Spirit to guide and equip his people. He should be remembered "as the PROPHET who teaches not only outwardly to the ear, and intellectually to the understanding, but also effectually to the heart."[33] He should be remembered as "THE HIGH PRIEST who reconciles us to himself and brings unspeakable comfort to the burdened sinner."[34] He should also be remembered as KING, the one "who is glorious in power and will ultimately overthrow the rulers of darkness." Lastly, Bickersteth invited his readers to "remember him as the REDEEMER" who "assumed our nature and at the costly price of his own blood, recovered our souls and obtained

31. Ibid., 246.
32. Ibid., 247.
33. Ibid., 249.
34. Ibid., 250–51.

eternal redemption for us."[35] Bickersteth concluded this section by reminding his readers "how sweet it is to fulfil Jesus dying charge—This do in remembrance of me."[36]

CONCLUSION

In Britain, America, and other countries of the world we take time to remember our dead, particularly those who have fallen in battle, and rightly so. In the UK Remembrance Sunday is kept on the nearest Sunday to November 11, which is Armistice Day and marks the ending of the war between the Allied nations and Germany. The sacrificial deaths of so many are remembered by the symbol of poppies. In America, Veterans' Day, which also takes place on November 11, brings to our remembrance the ending of the two great wars. Perhaps Christian believers need to allow these events to remind them of the need to be more serious about *remembering* the sacrificial death of Jesus which is the very core of the Christian faith. There is a need perhaps to take on board the words of Richard Baxter and take time to do "some serious remembering" of the mercies of God.

Few contemporary, and indeed the past liturgies, do much more than make a passing reference to remembrance. Almost none make it the central point or purpose of the Eucharist. Christian believers need therefore to take seriously the Passover context and the teachings of Calvin, Baxter, Bickersteth, and others and give time to seriously *remember* both who Jesus is and the wonderful benefits of his passion which he bestows on his people.[37]

Psychological studies have demonstrated the vital importance of feeding on positive memories for emotional health. A psychological study by faculty members at Stanford University underlined the importance of "remembering the good and forgetting the bad" as a major factor in emotional well-being.[38] Simply thinking back to times of happiness can change a person's emotional state to one of positivity. In particular, it has been shown that remembering by visualization can have a significant impact on present well-being. The same principle applies in terms of Christian experience. As Christian people mindfully think back to those times in their lives when the Lord markedly blessed or significantly guided or abundantly provided for

35. Ibid., 253.

36. Ibid., 254.

37. Ibid.

38. Joorman et al., "Remembering the good, forgetting the bad," 640.

them, the sense of his presence and his hand on their lives will be markedly strengthened. Along with the psalmist they will find themselves declaring, "Lord you have your hand on me." There is indeed power and emotional strength in positive remembering. As Solomon put it in the book of Proverbs, "As a man thinketh in his heart so is he."

Very few Communion services invite worshippers to take time and seriously spend some minutes *remembering* the gift and cost of their salvation and the wonder of having the slate of sin and wrongdoing wiped clean. At the distribution (giving of the bread and wine), communicants are frequently greeted in Catholic and Episcopal churches with a perfunctory-sounding "the body of Christ" as a wafer is pressed into their hands, or with "the blood of Christ" as some well-meaning Eucharistic minister tips the cup into open mouths. How much better it would be for communicants at least to hear the words "eat this in remembrance that Jesus died for you" and "drink this in remembrance that Jesus died for you," while they eat the bread and drink the wine. The reception of the elements and the moments immediately following is the time when worshippers could be invited to recall Christ's love, his provision and the blessing of life. In this context some of the verses at the beginning of Psalm 103 seem particularly suitable.

> Praise the Lord, O my soul;
> all my inmost being, praise his holy name
> Praise the Lord, O my soul,
> and *forget not* all his benefits—
> Who forgives all your sins
> and heals all your diseases,
> Who redeems your life from the pit
> and crowns you with love and good things
> so that your youth is renewed like the eagle's.[39]

In the early Christian centuries the groups of Christians who gathered in homes around the domestic table, as they ate portions of bread and drank wine from their own cups, must surely have taken time to *remember* the death and resurrection of Jesus which had brought them forgiveness and new life. They would have done this by meditating, by imagining, sharing, and uttering aloud short prayers of praise and gratitude.

39. Ps 103: 1–5.

9

A Celebration Meal

One of the marked characteristics of the Jewish Passover was a strong note of joy and celebration. Moses was told to instruct the people that all subsequent Passovers after the first one were to be extended for seven days, of which the first and the last were to be "a sacred assembly."[1] Children were to be a part of the meal and the rejoicing,[2] and those living nearby who were not Israelites were to be invited to join in the celebrations. The month of Nisan, when the Passover took place, was in spring and this was a season of special sacrifices and festivities. By the time of Jesus' earthly ministry several new features had been added to the Egyptian Passover, one of which was the drinking of four cups of wine. It was a requirement that every Jew on this night was required to drink *four cups of wine*, and it was asserted by some Rabbis that the four cups were the joyful reminders of the four Hebrew words used by God when he promised to bring the Israelites out of Egypt. This in itself speaks of celebration. One of Solomon's proverbs spoke of "wine which makes glad the heart of man" and the Jewish rabbis often declared that "without wine there can be no celebration."

Many careful preparations were put in place to ensure the Passover celebrations went really well. As K. E. Keith wrote,

1. Exod 12:15 and 13:7.
2. Exod 13:14.

> Housewives would be busily occupied in something approaching
> spring-cleaning, and in "washings," "baptizings," of cups, and pots,
> and brazen vessels (Mk. vii. 4); in carefully cleaning and storing
> cereals, and in making garments for themselves and their house-
> holds, in honour of the coming feast.[3]

Keith noted that special sets of kitchen and other household utensils were
generally used during the Passover. If it was necessary to use an everyday
set they were well scrubbed and then "literally immersed or baptized" in
boiling water. New vessels that had been purchased from Gentiles would
have to undergo the same process.[4]

At the time of the Passover the Sanhedrin sent out working men to
examine and repair the bridges and to keep the roads in good condition,
for the convenience of pilgrims. About a month before the feast, all the
graves were freshly whitewashed so that their dazzling brightness might
make them unmistakable, thus warning pilgrims from coming near and
inadvertently making themselves ritually unclean.[5]

On the evening of 15th Nisan the Israelites got together in companies
of not less than ten and not more than twenty to eat the Passover meal at
home. As Keith put it, "They would sit at table and in the same jovial spirit
that Christians sit at the Christmas table. The Jew regards the Passover as a
joyous, religious feast."[6]

CELEBRATION IN JEWISH WORSHIP

Joy and celebration were a recurring characteristic of Jewish worship. When
the Israelites returned from exile under Ezra and Nehemiah they celebrated
the Passover[7] and they "celebrated it with joy . . . because the Lord had
filled them with joy."[8] This same mark of joy continued after Ezra had
read the book of the Law to the assembled people. Both Ezra the priest and
scribe and Nehemiah the governor instructed the people "not to mourn
or weep" but "to go and enjoy choice food and sweet drinks," and to "send
some to those who have nothing prepared." They were further exhorted

3. Keith, *The Passover*, 12.
4. Ibid.
5. Ibid., 13.
6. Ibid., 23.
7. Ezra 6:19.
8. Ezra 6:22.

"not to grieve for this is a sacred day and the joy of the Lord will be your strength." All the people "then went away to eat and drink, to send portions of food and to celebrate with great joy, because they now understood the words that had been made known to them."[9] In short, Nehemiah was telling his people to indulge in celebration in order to recover their spiritual strength.

The Psalms are full of expression of joyous worship as those who come are exhorted to offer praise with a variety of joyful sounding instruments. It's perhaps small wonder that C. S. Lewis, the author of the Narnia books, wrote that "Joy is the serious business of heaven."[10] Dietrich Bonhoeffer, a German Lutheran pastor who died in 1945 in one of Hitler's concentration camps, wrote in his *The Cost of Discipleship*, "The Christian life is not one of gloom, but of ever increasing joy in the Lord."[11]

THE NATURE OF JOY

Joy is generally defined as "a feeling of great delight or happiness caused by something exceptionally good or satisfying. It is keen pleasure, elation and feelings of gladness, fun, happiness or excitement." The New Testament word translated "joy" is "chara" and it can also mean "to enjoy" and "to have fun." In both the Old and New Testaments it is about celebration, merry-making, pleasure, delight, and happiness. Horton Davies noted that for the Jews of ancient Israel joy "was the simultaneous expression of physical, psychological, and spiritual well-being. Consequently, joy was unembarrassingly associated with the body in "the pleasure of a good meal" and a "drink of good wine."[12] Joy, Davies also pointed out, "was also a characteristic of the sacrificial banquets of the Hebrew when they made pilgrimages to the temple and gave the tithe offering" (Deut 12:7; 14:23).[13]

Joy obviously exists at two levels. There is "common joy" which everyone in the world at large experiences when external circumstances are favorable and the course of their lives is seemingly positive. Within the Judaeo-Christian tradition, however, there is deeper divine joy which is

9. Neh 8:9–12.

10. Lewis, *Letters to Malcolm*, 93.

11. Bonhoeffer, *The Cost of Discipleship*, 335.

12. Davies, *An Experimental Liturgy*, 93; quoted in Davies, *Bread of Life and Cup of Joy*, 97.

13. Ibid.

implanted in the hearts of believers. Such joy comes from the Lord whose very nature is joy. Indeed, Jesus promised his followers, "My joy will be in you that your joy may be complete."[14] Again in John 16, Jesus said with emphasis, "You will rejoice and no one will take away your joy."[15] Paul, in his First Letter to Timothy, wrote of Jesus as "God the blessed and only ruler, the King of kings and Lord of lords."[16] The Greek word that is translated "blessed" is "makarios," which actually means "happiness" and is the same word which is used in the beatitudes in the Sermon on the Mount. Jesus is therefore the Lord of joy and happiness who imparts this same disposition to his followers.

Quentin Hogg, Lord Hailsham and a former Lord Chancellor of England, wrote of Jesus in his autobiography that the world "needs to recapture the vision of this glorious and happy man whose mere presence filled his companions with delight. No pale Galilean he, but a veritable Pied Piper of Hamelin who would have the children laughing all around him and squealing with pleasure and joy as he picked them up."[17] Again, in another paragraph, Hailsham "came to the conclusion that we should have been absolutely enhanced by his company. Jesus was irresistibly attractive . . . intensely fond of life, and intensely vital and vivacious."[18]

Jesus evidently enjoyed good worship and attended the great Jewish festivals and unsurprisingly he was critical of the somber and legalistic nature of the worship of his day. He warned his followers that they should not be sitting in the big chairs at the front of the synagogues or using titles such as "rabbi" or "father." He also spoke against wearing long religious robes and said that those who did so "would be severely punished."[19] Jesus poured out joy wherever he went and there can be no question but that he intended that worshipping him should be both a joyful and convivial experience. He described the gift of salvation as "a great feast or a wedding banquet given by a monarch to celebrate the marriage of his son (Matt 22:4), or as a great supper prepared by a wealthy landowner (Luke 14:26f)."[20]

14. John 15:11.

15. John 16:22.

16. 1Tim 6:15.

17. Hogg, *The Door Wherein I Entered*, 55.

18. Ibid., 55.

19. Luke 20:46.

20. Davies, *Bread of Life*, 95.

CELEBRATING AND THE EUCHARIST

One of the sad things is that on very many occasions the Lord's Supper or New Passover is often a far cry from anything which could be construed as "celebratory." Horton Davies wrote that is difficult for us "to imagine a meal either at the Lord's Supper or at Mass or Holy Communion, even more difficult is perceiving the service as a celebration. For us its character is solemn, sacred, and staid, not joyful, jubilant, and celebratory."[21] Church newspapers frequently carry announcements about Eucharistic "celebrations" and even give the names of the celebrants but how much celebration is there? And what is it that is actually being celebrated? For most Christians who belong to a mainline church the Sunday Eucharist is more often than not a somber affair. Few are able to come away from them saying they had just experienced "royal joy" or "overwhelming happiness." Anglican, Episcopal, and Roman Catholic Eucharists are usually lengthy liturgical affairs with wordy introductions, confession, absolution, collects, readings, sermon, creed, intercessions, the peace, and offertory all coming after one another in fairly quick succession. This is then often followed by a small procession of lay people up the center aisle carrying flagons, silver goblets, and other ecclesiastical tableware. After another hymn, there is a lengthy consecration prayer, the Lord's Prayer and finally the distribution of the elements for which people of Roman Catholic, Anglican, and Episcopal traditions queue in somber lines, first to receive the bread and then to receive the wine. All this often has to be got through at speed in order to be completed it in the prescribed time. So as soon as the final hymn has been sung people are rushing to get out and collect their children from Sunday school or the kids' clubs. The result of all of this is there is often little or no time left in which to engage in any form of joy or celebration.

And yet Paul and the apostles urged the early churches to pursue joy. Paul exhorted the Christians at Philippi to "Rejoice in the Lord always" and he repeated himself in order to stress the point, "I will say it again, rejoice."[22] Here the Greek is in the imperative tense, *chairete*, meaning that this is not an option, it is a must. In writing to the congregation in Thessalonica Paul again urged them to "Rejoice always . . . for this is God's will for you in Christ Jesus."[23] It was against this background that the Victorian English

21. Ibid., 91.
22. Phil 4:4.
23. 1 Thess 5:16–18.

Baptist preacher, Charles Spurgeon, wrote in his *Lectures to My Students*, "Sepulchral tones may fit a man to be an undertaker.... An individual who has no geniality about him had better be an undertaker, and bury the dead, for he will never influence the living"![24]

Things may be a little different in some of the more Protestant mainline and free churches where there is less ritual and the congregation remains seated while the bread and wine are served to them in their seats or pews. But here Communion or the Lord's Supper can often be a short, fifteen-minute "add on" at the end of a main preaching service. Such "breaking of bread" occasions can be helpfully quiet and reflective but they too often lack the convivial atmosphere of joy and fellowship which is characterized by the Passover meal and that Jesus undoubtedly intended should be there at his Supper.

THE IMPORTANCE OF JOY IN CHRISTIAN WORSHIP

If there is one thing that stands out in the worship of the people of God in both the Old and New Testament times it is the mark of joy. It needs always to be remembered that it is not the Last Supper which is now celebrated but the Lord's Supper! It was this that the early Christians shared in their homes "with glad and sincere hearts" and "praising God."[25] Davies suggested that "the dominating sense of overwhelming joy so characteristic of those early Eucharists" was due in part to the recollection of the post-resurrection meals that the disciples had shared with Jesus. They were an anticipation of the messianic banquet which he had promised at the Last Supper.[26] Whilst it is the argument of this book that Jesus' ideal and intended location for the Lord's Supper should be in peoples' homes, it is vital that wherever it takes place it should be an occasion of joy and convivial table fellowship. It is of course true that when Christians gather round the table they remember and give thanks for the sacrificial love and death of Jesus for the forgiveness of sins. But they should come not solely for the reason that it is Good Friday but because they are, or certainly should be, living as Easter people. Christians don't only celebrate Jesus' death, they rejoice in his resurrection and conquest of death. They gather not so much because Jesus died but because he lives! The Lord's table is a celebration of the resurrection, a joyous feast

24. Spurgeon, *Lectures*, 1.

25. Acts 2:46–47.

26. Davies, *Bread of Life*, 97.

and a foretaste of the heavenly banquet.[27] Horton Davies suggested that the atmosphere should be something akin to a birthday party or wedding anniversary.[28] The Puritan Thomas Brooks (1608–1680) wrote that "it is the duty and the glory of a Christian to rejoice in the Lord every day, but especially on the Lord's Day."[29]

There is always a danger of over seriousness. Robert Louis Stevenson once wrote in his diary as though it was something strange, "I have been to church to-day and am not depressed."[30] As Charles Hodge of Princeton put it in earlier times, the Lord's table should not be a place of gloom.[31] In too many churches the atmosphere at the Lord's Supper is more akin to a funeral than a festival. Congregations should not be like the two sorrowful disciples on the Emmaus road. They should come alive with joy as they did when Jesus made himself known in "the breaking of bread."[32]

Celebration joy should be one of the chief characteristics of biblical and Christian worship. In October 1891 John Trevor (1855–1930) left the pulpit of his Upper Brook Street Unitarian Church in Manchester to found the first Labour Church and what became known as the Labour Church Movement that eventually numbered 121 churches in the British Isles.[33] He did so because he came to the realization that the historic denominational churches had nothing to offer the working poor of the city. In his new denomination Trevor and the early leaders sought to ensure that "there was an atmosphere of royal joy in the worship."[34] The secretary of the Bolton Labour Church wrote in 1893 of "the heartiness and vigour with which labour hymns are sung in contrast to the conventional style of most churches and chapels."

THE NEED TO RECOVER JOY AND CELEBRATION

Throughout the history of the Christian church there has been a constant pull to formalize and ritualize the simplicity and joy of the Supper which

27. Matt 13:43; 26:29 and Rev 2:7 and 21:6, 22:1–2, 14 and 17.

28. Davies, *Bread of Life*, 91.

29. Grosart, ed., *The Complete Works of Thomas Brooks*, 299.

30. Barclay, *The Gospel of Matthew*, 116–17.

31. Hodge, *Exposition of the First Epistle to the Corinthians*, 233.

32. Luke 24:17, 21.

33. Inglis, "The Labour Church Movement," 451.

34. *Labour Prophet*, August, 1893, 80.

Jesus instituted in the Upper Room. Indeed, sociologists of religion understand this to be recurring phenomenon of church life in general, which they have designated "routinization." It works in the following way. Because informal and celebratory worship occasions require considerably more energy and care to manage, it eventually becomes easier and less demanding to put them into a set fixed pattern or ritual. In this way a sacrament such as the Lord's Supper then happens by rote with a minimum of planning or preparation required. Sadly, in the process there is the constant danger of it becoming dull and perfunctory.

Among the many who in their generations tried to restore joy and celebration to the Lord's Supper were the Moravians, some of the early Puritans, and John Wesley's Methodists. The American Puritan Samuel Willard (1640–1707) of Boston, whose *Sacramental Meditations* were published posthumously in 1711, stressed the importance of joy in Communion. Wine, he pointed out, symbolizes "the refreshing and cheering of life." As wine makes the body happy so in a similar way "Christ cheers the heart and soul of his people." He went on to labor the point in the following paragraph.

> Wine is used in some countries for their drink; and it was more especially liberally made use of at their feasts, weddings, and more free entertainments, being accounted the more noble sort of drink . . . . Wine is good to drive away sorrow, and make cheerful. . . . Wine is a cordial, it comforts the heart, recruits the fainting spirits, and greatly refreshes them that drink it, when labouring of infirmities. Wine puts boldness and courage into persons, and drives away fear. . . . Wine is used in surgery, to cleanse and purge the wounds men have gotten.[35]

This same note of joy was sounded by Benjamin Colman (1673–1747) in *A Discourse of the Pleasure of Religious Worship in Our Public Assemblies*, which was also published in Boston in 1717. He made this same point in a sermon preached in the city.

> Here is a Banquet of Wine and the Sceptre of Grace held forth. . . . As some happy People keep the day with Joy the day of their Espousals, so is or should be the frequent Communion of Saints to them at the Table of Christ, and in remembrance of his love.[36]

---

35. Davies, *The Worship of American Puritans*, 205–6.
36. Colman, *A Discourse of the Pleasure of Religious Worship*, 157.

When John Wesley's Methodist followers were rebuffed from some of the Anglican Communion services they turned to their own buildings. In their own premises there were regular celebrations with large congregations. In 1784 Wesley produced his own *Order for The Administration of the Holy Communion or Lord's Supper* for the Methodists in North America.[37] From the very early beginnings of the movement the Methodist Communion services were, as Wesley said, "enlivened by hymns suitable to the occasion."[38] In 1745 Wesley published his *Hymns on the Lord's Supper*, which was a collection of some of his own compositions and some that were by his brother. They were particularly intended for singing at the Lord's Supper. Many of these hymns, according to Trevor Dearing, "express the joy of the Eucharist."[39] Dearing continued, "The singing of hymns and the use of extempore prayer brought people together in the joy of what can well be called a 'Gospel Feast.'"[40] Again Dearing commented, "The sense of joy and peace, of acceptance and sonship, were inevitably and naturally expressed in his 'Gospel Feast' Eucharist."[41]

Dietrich Bonhoeffer captured something of the joy that should be in evidence as Christian people gather around the table and invite Jesus to be the guest of honor. In a piece entitled "The Fellowship of the Table," based on the supper at Emmaus in Luke 24:30–33, he focused on the note of joy which he asserted should be a marked characteristic of such occasions.

> The fellowship of the table has a festive quality. It is a constantly recurring reminder [that] our life is not only travail and labor, it is also refreshment and joy in the goodness of God. We labor, but God nourished and sustains us. And this is the reason for celebrating. Man should not eat the bread of sorrows (Psalm 127:2); rather 'eat the bread with joy' (Ecclesiastes 9:7); 'I commend mirth, because a man hath no better thing under the sun, than to eat, and to drink and to be merry' (8:15); but of course, 'who can eat, or who can have enjoyment apart from Him?' (2:25, A.R.V.) It is said of the seventy elders of Israel who went up to Mount Sinai with Moses and Aaron that 'they beheld God, and did eat and drink' (Exodus 24:11 A.R.V.) God cannot endure that unfestive, mirthless attitude

37. Tucker, *American Methodist Worship*, 119.

38. Wesley, "Letter to a Friend on Public Worship."

39. Dearing, *Wesleyan and Tractarian Worship*, 12.

40. Ibid., 13, 99–100.

41. Ibid., 100.

of ours in which we eat our bread in sorrow, with pretentious, busy haste, or even with shame.[42]

Bonhoeffer concluded by reminding his readers that the fellowship of the table teaches Christians that while they are on their earthly pilgrimage they still need to be sustained with "perishable bread." But if they share this bread with one another, they will ultimately receive the imperishable bread together in the Father's house. "Blessed is he that shall eat bread in the kingdom of God" (Luke 14:15).

In earlier times I served as a chaplain in a college of higher education that later became the University of Gloucestershire and once or twice a term we made an attempt to capture something of the celebratory atmosphere which the undergraduate students felt was lacking in our Sunday Communion services. On these occasions we asked the college kitchens to provide us with a fork supper including drinks and dessert. About sixty or seventy students would gather in an informal circle with the Communion table in the center on which was placed the bread and wine. We began with grace and the breaking of bread in remembrance of Jesus' death and passion. Then with background music we ate and enjoyed a two-course meal during which time there was a good deal of joy, informal sharing of things spiritual and the affairs of the day. At the end of the meal, "after supper," we shared the wine, thanking the Lord for his blood so generously poured out in love and forgiveness. We ended with informal prayers and time of singing. For many including myself these occasions proved a wonderful combination of joy, serious remembrance, and thankful celebration.

It's now a good many years since I left the chaplaincy and my wife and I are members of a Church of England church where, until very recently, we have been active members of a small midweek fellowship group which met in members' homes. One of the meetings each month was always a bring and share meal at which there was often a very simple Communion. We were usually about twelve in number and ate around the leaders' dining room table. We most often began with a grace and then each member broke decent-sized pieces of bread and we ate together slowly and in thankful remembrance. A full cooked meal then followed with wine, background music, and plenty of joy and good conversation. When we had finished the dessert and coffee we each poured some more red wine into our glasses and drank taking several sips in remembrance of Christ's blood so freely shed for us. We usually ended with prayers of thanksgiving and prayers for one

42. Bonhoeffer, *Life Together*, 66–69.

another. This to me really captured a glimpse of what Jesus intended the New Passover to be like—a time of joy, thanksgiving, and serious remembering of the Lord for who he is and his redeeming love for us his people. My wife and I still belong to the same church and will be moving on to become part of a similar group nearer to our own home.

CONCLUSION

As Davies and others[43] have pointed out, there is no doubt that the Eucharist has become a largely somber and serious affair, dominated by the cross rather than the resurrection. It seems to be largely the Pentecostals and Charismatic Christians who have attempted to express something of real joy in their worship in the way that the early Christians did so fully. In order for the Lord's Supper to be a joyous celebration it is not necessary for it to become a festive party with special décor, communion balloons, and party poppers which can be purchased from online Communion party stores such as "Ceremonial Celebrations" that can be found on the internet. Rather, it is simply a matter of creating meals that have an atmosphere of normal, natural happiness and enjoyment. Sharing the Lord's Supper in smaller more intimate gatherings in a house or home makes this more readily possible.

43. Davies, *Bread of Life*, 121. See also Hardy and Ford, *Jubilate*, 68.

10

A Sit-Down Meal

SITTING AT THE TABLE

At the very first Passover the people of Israel clearly would not have reclined while they ate their roasted lambs and unleavened bread. It was a meal that had to be eaten in haste so that the people could escape from the clutches of the Egyptians. However, the custom of sitting in a more relaxed manner came to be adopted in the subsequent memorial Passover meals. At some point it became a requirement to recline at the Passover meal, rather than just sit as people did for other meals. The actual point in time when the rabbis proscribed reclining as a requirement is not known, though it has been thought that it was likely to have been during the Roman rule over Israel. The reason for this conjecture is simply that it is known that reclining was the rule for celebration meals in Roman society.

Strictly speaking, therefore, Jesus and his disciples reclined at the table during the Last Supper. Indeed, as has already been noted,[1] it was required that the guests at the Passover always reclined. At other meal times Jesus is frequently stated to have *sat* although on some occasions he did also recline. For example, Luke recorded an occasion when he was a guest at the home of Simon the Pharisee and reclined (*kateklithe*) at the table.

---

1. See chapter 1.

In the early period before Constantine's conversion the Eucharist was shared in the context of a home-based meal. Clearly the invited guests would have been seated for these occasions. Certainly when Paul broke bread at Troas the guests appear to have been sitting.[2] Tertullian wrote, probably at the beginning of the third century, and gave a description of the Lord's Supper as he knew and experienced it. He mentioned that those who attend "recline" at the table but "not before prayer to God has been offered."[3]

The *Egyptian Canons* state, "Let not the catechumen *sit* down at the Lord's Supper,"[4] making it clear that sitting for the sacrament was the norm. In Hippolytus' time it is clear that the people *sat* to receive the sacrament. Canon 172 of his *Constitutions* reads, "Let no catechumen *sit* with them at the Lord's Agape." In *De Virginitati*, which is thought to be an early fifth-century document, details are given concerning the Eucharist. The opening instruction is as follows: "When you sit down at table and come to break bread, having signed yourself three times, say thus, giving thanks . . . ."[5]

THE INTRODUCTION OF STANDING

The early frescos of the Eucharist on the walls in the catacombs of Rome depict the participants sitting. During the fourth and fifth centuries, however, the Eucharist gradually ceased to be in a domestic setting and began to be held in officially legalized public church buildings. In consequence, the role of the person who presided at the Eucharist grew in importance. Instead of overseeing of a small informal group in a home, the leader of the Eucharist now became a significant public official, often responsible for leading a sizeable congregation. This in turn resulted in the development of ritual, liturgical structures and the growth of the clerical office which came to be regarded as imbued with sacramental grace. Thus, when a priest invoked the Holy Spirit on the bread and wine, their substance was held to have been changed. They were now believed to have become the body and blood of Christ. The practice of standing to receive the bread and wine

---

2. Acts 20:9.

3. Athanasius, *De Cult. Fem.*, 2/11. Scholars believe that the writer is possibly referring to the Eucharist here on the grounds that the Supper includes only moderate eating characteristic of earlier Eucharistic meals and religious songs and other prayers.

4. *Egyptian Canons*, LXXV.

5. Some scholars have attributed this document to the pen of Athanasius.

thus emerged more widely in the post-Constantinian church partly out of reverence for the consecrated elements but also out of convenience. Clearly, it was easier for large numbers to receive the Eucharistic elements from the hands of the priest while standing. The practice of standing to receive the bread and wine is therefore an ancient one, though not as early as sitting. It is a practice that has remained throughout the centuries and indeed at the present time in the Eastern churches where clergy and laity alike stand to communicate.

KNEELING

The practice of kneeling for Communion appears to have come into the Latin Western church at some point in the early Middle Ages. The reasons for this change from standing to kneeling are not altogether clear, although it seems likely that it was associated with the supposition that the bread and wine had changed in status and subsequently in substance. Later, when it was believed that the elements were the very body and blood, it was felt appropriate to kneel in reverence and adoration before the real presence of Christ in the sacred host.[6]

Roman Catholics still do stand or kneel to receive the bread and wine as do many Anglicans including both Evangelicals and Anglo-Catholics. However, during the Protestant Reformation of the sixteenth century many churches began to return to the early Christian practice of sitting to receive the bread and wine rather than kneeling. Not only was this in keeping with the biblical traditions, it was also normal to sit for a meal, particularly in the early period when the Eucharist included a shared agape meal.

PROTESTANT OPPOSITION TO KNEELING

In England the move in favor of sitting at Communion was sparked off by John Knox (1505–1572), who had been made one of the royal chaplains in 1551. At the time when Cranmer's Second English Prayer was being discussed he was summoned to preach before the king. Knox had earlier been sent by the Archbishop first to Berwick and later to Newcastle, where he had given both the bread and wine to communicants while they were

---

6. This supposition is borne out by the fact that Cranmer's Black Rubric was specifically designed to impress upon worshippers that there should be no adoration of the bread and wine.

seated, arguing that it better corresponded to the method used by the Jews at the Passover. He used his sermon and the discussions that followed to have the instruction to receive the bread and wine kneeling removed from the Prayer Book service. Initially the king and some of the bishops were persuaded, but Cranmer overcame Knox's opposition in a letter dated October 7th, 1552 to the king's council. His principal argument was that Christians are not bound in religious services to adhere to the exact words of the original institution, nor to the exact form of the original service. Cranmer set out these points in a rubric that was only just in time to enable its inclusion in the first edition of the second Prayer Book. Because it was inserted at the last moment it had to be printed in black as opposed to red, the color of all the other rubrics. Hence it became known as the Black Rubric. That said, Cranmer was obviously not totally convinced in his own mind over the matter and in his *Reformatio Legum Ecclesiasticum,* which was published in 1553, he did experiment with sitting.[7] There were still differences of opinion over the matter in the English Church in the reign of Elizabeth I. Matthew Parker, her Archbishop of Canterbury, found on coming to office that there were considerable variations of practice at communion services with some kneeling, some standing and others sitting.[8] In the end, his celebrated *Advertisements* of 1566 required that all were to receive the bread and wine "kneeling."[9] Edmund Grindal, who was Bishop of London and later succeeded Parker at Canterbury, found "the administration of Communion is done by some with a surplice and cap, some with a surplice alone, others with none ... some with leavened bread, some with unleavened; some receive kneeling, others standing, others sitting."[10]

THE BATTLE OVER KNEELING

One of the problems with Elizabeth's 1559 Prayer Book was the removal of the Black Rubric, which explicitly stated that kneeling to receive the bread and wine did not imply the communicant was engaging in adoration of the host. This meant that many clergy, and not just those who were Puritans, were themselves apprehensive about receiving the bread and wine kneeling. There were of course much larger numbers of laymen and laywomen who

7. Cited in Buchanan, *What Did Cranmer Think He was Doing?*, 29.

8. Brook, *A Life of Archbishop Matthew Parker*, 167.

9. Ibid., 189.

10. Grindal, British Museum, Lansdowne MS. 8, F.16.

were also concerned over the matter. At Beeston in Nottinghamshire in 1584 a man was taken to court for not receiving the bread and wine kneeling. At the Primary Visitation of Nottinghamshire by Archbishop of York Toby Matthew (1595–1628) in 1607, a leading layman was brought before him. The charge was made that "he doth refuse the taking the communion at Easter until he be resolved whether he may take it kneeling, sitting or standing lawfully."[11]

Two years later at Sutton-in-Ashfield, also in the county of Nottinghamshire, a man and a woman were cited for receiving communion standing and admitted the offense. At Worksop the practice was more general under the ministry of Richard Bernard, a clergyman of noted Separatist tendencies. His successor, James Collie, was charged with the same offence in 1614 but countered that this was the usual custom in the parish. Other subsequent references to this practice of receiving without kneeling in Worksop were noted in the registers but none of the offenders were taken to court. At Attenborough in 1616, German Ireton, the father of Henry Ireton who later became one of Cromwell's generals, was charged with five others for refusing to kneel and leaving the church without receiving Communion. At Woodkirk in Yorkshire, which was a noted Puritan center, five parishioners were summoned in 1619 before the authorities for refusing to kneel for the sacrament. The books of the church courts show that under Toby Matthew's episcopate his policy became more lenient with the passing of time and that any clergyman who was unable to conscientiously keep the rubrics of the Prayer Book was allowed to follow the dictates of his conscience.[12] The problem for many clergy was that the omission of the Black Rubric in the publication of the 1559 Prayer Book meant that kneeling could be interpreted once again as adoration of the sacrament.

Richard Neile (1562–1640), who became Archbishop of York in 1632, developed a more vigorous policy against the Puritans. In 1632 John Okell, Vicar of Bradford, was ordered only to give Communion to those who knelt to receive. In 1635 Ezekiel Rogers of Rowley near Hull was charged and admitted to seven or eight offenses of administering Communion to worshippers who refused to kneel.[13] However these harsh prescripts were reversed during Cromwell's Protectorate when the Westminster Assembly produced

11. Biggs, "The Controversy," 51–62.

12. Mayor, *The Lord's Supper*, 50n1.

13. This information has been taken from Biggs, "The Controversy," cited by Mayor, *The Lord's Supper*, 50–51.

A Directory for the Public Worship of God that was approved by Parliament on March 16th, 1645. It encouraged people to sit or stand.[14]

SITTING AT THE LORD'S TABLE

When the Catholic Queen Mary Tudor succeeded Edward to the English throne in 1553 John Knox fled to Geneva and for a short time he served as pastor to the English congregation there. His *Geneva Liturgy* prescribed that Communion was to be received *sitting*: "the minister *sitteth* . . . at the Table, every man and woman likewise taking their place as occasion best serveth."[15] Robin Leaver also observed that *sitting* for Communion was the practice of the Dutch Stranger Congregation which met in the church of the Austin Friars in London during the reign of Edward VI.[16]

The English Puritans complained strongly against kneeling to receive Communion. One of their published tracts stated that among "the remnants of Antichrist" preserved in the *Book of Common Prayer* were "to knocke and kneele to the sacrament using the Rownde God which did deface Christ's Supper."[17] According to Horton Davies, the Puritans justified the receiving the bread and wine *seated* on the ground, saying that "it signified the rest which Christ promised to his people, as well as by the parallel of the Last Supper."[18]

At this very time, the American Puritan John Cotton published *The Way of the Churches of Christ in New England* in 1645. In it he dealt with the Lord's Supper and gave a description as to how it was administered. He wrote:

> The Lord's Supper we administer for the time, once a month at least, and for the gesture, to the people *sitting*; according as Christ administered it to the disciples sitting, (Mat 26:20,26.) who also made a Symbolicall use of it, to teach the Church their majoritie over their Ministers in some cases, and their judicial authoritie, as co-sessors with him at the last Judgement, (Luke 22.27 to 30) which maketh us to looke at the Lords Supper, not only as an adoration devised by man, but also as a violation by man of the

14. Davies, *The English Free Churches*, 77.

15. Leaver, ed., *Liturgy of the Frankfurt Exiles*, 32; Mayor, *The Lord's Supper*, 8.

16. Leaver, ed., *Liturgy of the Frankfurt Exiles*, 32.

17. *Seconde Parte of A Register*, 100; quoted in Mayor, *The Lord's Supper*, 18.

18. Davies, *The Worship of English Puritans*, 55.

institution of Christ, diminishing part of the counsel of God, and the honour and comfort of the Church held forth in it.[19]

The great Puritan John Owen (1616–1683) was appointed Dean of Christ Church by Oliver Cromwell in 1651 and vice-chancellor of the University of Oxford the succeeding year. However, following the restoration of the monarchy in 1660 the Church of England became intolerant of those who had been given free rein during the Protectorate and by the provisions of Cromwell's *Directory for Public Worship*. Owen spent much time defending the now persecuted Puritans.[20] In his *An Answer to Two Questions*, Owen considered the question as to whether Dissenters might still receive Communion in the Church of England. He gave a negative answer for several reasons, one of which was that to do so involved "the reception of the elements kneeling."[21]

The early New England Puritans were reported in the 1640s by Thomas Lechford to receive the sacrament with "the Ministers and Elders sitting at the table, the rest in their seats or upon their forms."[22] In his *The Lord's Supper in Early English Dissent* Stephen Mayor summarized the Nonconformist concern to sit for the sacrament in the following lines.

> Sitting came to be the normal posture: first perhaps simply because it was not kneeling, which was idolatrous; then because it followed (in principle) the practice at the Last Supper; then, with some, because it had symbolic value—perhaps signifying the rest promised by God to His people. What was important was that the communicants should not kneel.[23]

SITTING AT THE COMMUNION TABLE IN THE MODERN CHURCH

People sat at the great sacramental services at the time of the Second Great Awakening in America. In August 1801 a Presbyterian Sacramental meeting was organized at Cane Ridge which turned out to be the prelude to a revival which lasted for six or seven days and at which, according to

19. Cotton, *The Way of the Churches of Christ in New England*, 89.

20. Thomson, *John Owen Prince of Puritans*, 91–113.

21. Owen, ed., "An Answer to Two Questions," xxi, 527.

22. Lechford, *Plaine-Dealing*, 16–17.

23. Mayor, *The Lord's Supper*, 156.

estimates, as many as 10,000 people attended. About 2,500 gathered on the Sunday with around 1,500 taking Communion. Tables were set up in the aisles of the meeting place and the people sat down in sessions throughout the day.[24]

Fast forwarding to the present time, at Lochcarron Free Church of Scotland in Ross County the Communion table is open to all believers. During the singing of the psalm people come out and sit on benches which are placed along both sides of two long trestle tables. Approximately thirty are seated with the presiding minister sitting at one end. Other sittings of up to thirty people follow until all have shared the bread and wine. This custom of sitting is common among Free Church of Scotland congregations.

IMPLICATIONS FOR PRESENT CHURCH PRACTICE

Significantly, Luke records in his Gospel that following the Last Supper Jesus said to his disciples, "I confer on you a kingdom, just as my Father conferred one on me, so that you may eat and drink at my table in my kingdom and sit on thrones and, judging the twelve tribes."[25] Sitting therefore is the sign of acceptance. When a visitor comes to a person's home they demonstrate their acceptance of them by saying, "please come in and sit down." When people enter a church building there are others who welcome them by showing them to a seat. Jesus called his followers "friends" and friends sit together in mutual acceptance of one another. In his vision of the seven churches of Asia Minor the Apostle John saw the risen Jesus knocking on the door of the church at Laodicea. If anyone was willing to welcome him in, his one desire was to have supper with them, presumably sitting![26]

In churches, particularly Roman Catholic and Anglican, where people kneel at a rail or queue cafeteria style to receive the bread and wine from the hands of the priest or minister, everything tends in consequence to happen in a rush. It is sad that this most important of meals is often such a hurried affair. Indeed, it is a waste to spoil any meal by being in a hurry. How many are parents heard saying to their children "don't eat so quickly," and that is what so often happens when it comes to sharing the bread and wine of the Lord's Supper. It's often all over in a minute or two.

24. *Methodist Magazine*, 1802, vol. 25, 263.
25. Luke 22:29–30.
26. Rev 3:20.

The Bishops at the Savoy Conference in March 1661 stated: "The posture of kneeling best suits at the Communion, as the most convenient, and so most decent for us, when we receive, as it were from God's hand, the greatest of seals of the Kingdom of Heaven."[27] Many present-day Roman Catholics and Anglicans are of course still of this same view. That said, the fact is such a posture stems from a wrong understanding of the nature of Jesus' character and his relationship with his followers. Jesus called his disciples "friends" and at the Last Supper he sat together with them on equal terms around a domestic table and shared his food and friendship with them in an intimate, relaxed, informal, and friendly manner. To this must be added the fact that kneeling is not a normal posture in which to eat a meal. Such a practice militates sharply with the Jewish custom of fellowship eating which Jesus both endorsed and practiced.

A FINAL WORD ON SITTING

Whilst standing to receive Communion may have been an early practice on certain occasions in some places in the early Christian communities, that doesn't mean it needs to be replicated by the contemporary churches. Nor for the same reason is it necessary to kneel to eat and drink the bread and wine simply because that became the practice in medieval western churches. Some of course still argue that communicants should kneel at the altar rail to receive the bread and wine as a sign of reverence to the King of Kings. However, it needs to be remembered that at the Last Supper Jesus was the "servant king" who washed his disciples' feet. The fact was, Jesus and his disciples *sat* together to share the Last Supper, as was the custom at all Passover meals. As has already been noted,[28] in the first three centuries almost all Eucharists were held in houses in the context of a meal for which people would have *sat* around a domestic table. It is not normal to queue for a meal cafeteria style, least of all a celebration supper, and then to eat it while still standing. Jesus called his disciples "friends" and sat with them as a seal of acceptance, friendship, love, and equality. Sitting is the normal way to eat a meal and Christians need to be seen as people who do things normally and well.

As is well-known, since the Reformation almost all the Nonconformist churches have adopted the normal and ancient custom of the early

27. See text in Buchanan, *The Savoy Conference*.
28. See chapter 2.

church and sit to receive the bread and wine. If the churches now return to the practice of sharing the Lord's Supper in houses and homes the issue of sitting will become a nonissue. Indeed, Stephen Mayor wrote, "In later Nonconformity sitting for Communion became so normal that anything else is forbidden by immemorial custom."[29]

29. Mayor, *The Lord's Supper*, 90.

11

A Thanksgiving Meal

THANKSGIVING AT THE JEWISH PASSOVER

Significantly the Jewish Passover took place in the month of Abib, which later came to be called Nisan. This was the month of the ripening grain and thanksgiving for the harvest. Thus there is a strong note of thanksgiving in the Passover. It was seen supremely as the people praised and gave thanks to the Lord for their marvelous deliverance from slavery and the bitter and harsh conditions of the land of Egypt. At the point in the meal when the second cup is drunk in accordance with the instruction in Exodus 13:8, the Jewish father has to tell his son about the importance of this feast. By tradition the youngest child asks, "Why is this night distinguished from all other nights"? The father then explains how the Lord delivered Israel from the hands of the Egyptians, the significance of the Passover lamb, the unleavened bread, and the bitter herbs. In view of this freedom the Mishnah states, "Therefore, we are bound to give thanks."[1] The host of the meal then invites the whole gathering to join in thanksgivings and praise to God. This was done by the singing of the first part of the Hallel. As the priests prepared the Passover lambs in the outer Temple court they also sang the early part of the Hallel, which consists of Psalms 113–14. These have an

1. Mishnah, Pes. 10.

emphasis on joy and praise but also thanksgiving. In the latter part of the Hallel, Psalm 117, the psalmist declares, "I will sacrifice a thank-offering to you." At the beginning of Psalm 118 the congregation are exhorted to "give thanks to the Lord, for He is good: his love endures for ever." Later in the same psalm there is an exhortation to thanksgiving.

> Open the gates of righteousness,
> I will enter and give thanks to the Lord.
> This is the gate of the Lord
> Through which the righteous may enter.
> I will give thanks, for you answered me;
> You have become my salvation.[2]
> . . .
> You are my God, and I will give thanks;
> You are my God and I will exalt you.
> Give thanks to the Lord, for he is good;
> His love endures for ever.[3]

Significantly the first cup of the Passover meal is often referred to as the Cup of Thanksgiving. The meal itself is one of profound thanksgiving and gratitude for the deliverance of God's people from the land of Egypt. The last or seventh day of the Passover was a day of thanksgiving in which the Lord's people celebrated with feasting.

THANKSGIVING IN THE LORD'S SUPPER OF THE EARLY CHURCHES

In view of this it is no surprise that Jesus stressed the importance of thanksgiving when he introduced the New Passover to his disciples as an integral part of their worship. This is markedly clear in his words of institution. In the Lukan account he took first the cup and *gave thanks* and said, "Take it and divide it among yourselves." Then, a little later, "he took the bread, *gave thanks* and broke it and gave it to them."[4] Nolland commented that this emphasis on thanksgiving "has its own secure place in Palestinian Judaism and is notable in the language of the Qumran thanksgiving hymns."[5] He continued that "the use here in Luke of eucharistesas may reflect a Chris-

2. Ps 118:19–21.

3. Ps 118:28–29.

4. Luke 22:17 and 19. See also Matt 26:26–27; Mark 14:22–23:1 Cor 11:24–25.

5. *Didache*, 9.

tian emphasis on partaking the Eucharist with thanksgiving (cf. 1 Timothy 4:4–5)."[6]

First-century references to the Lord's Supper outside the New Testament continue the emphasis on thanksgiving. Significantly, the *Letter of Clement of Rome to the Corinthians*, which is generally agreed to have been written about AD 95, contains some passing allusions to the Eucharist. Clement wrote, "Let each of you in his own order, give thanks (eucharisteito) unto God, preserving a good conscience, and adhering to the appointed rule of his service (leitourgias) with all reverence."[7] Whilst this is in the nature of a passing reference, it is sufficient to indicate that the early Christians in Rome understood the Lord's Supper to be a Eucharist or thanksgiving, much in the way that the Jewish communities gave thanks to the Lord in their homes and particularly at their meal times.

In the second century this same emphasis on thanksgiving remained central in the keeping of the Lord's Supper. The *Didache*, which is generally dated early in the second century, gives directions regarding the sacraments. Chapter 9 is introduced by the words: "Concerning the thanksgiving (eucharistias) give thanks (eucharistesate) in this manner." Then follow two prayers, one for the cup, the other for the broken bread (*klasmatos*). The prayer to be said over the cup is as follows:

> We *thank* You, our Father for the holy vine of David Your servant,
> which You made known to us through Jesus Your servant.

The prayer to be said over the broken bread is parallel in form, but contains a supplementary petition for the gathering of the church from the ends of the earth.

> We *thank* You, our Father, for the life and knowledge which You
> did make known to us through Jesus Your servant . . . . [T]his
> bread that is broken was scattered on the mountains and gathered
> together from the ends of the earth into Your kingdom, for yours
> is the glory and the power through Jesus Christ for ever.

In section 10 of the *Didache*, "after the people have been satisfied," the liturgy includes a further lengthy thanksgiving prayer. It includes thanksgivings for "your holy name which you have enshrined in our hearts," and for "the knowledge and faith and immortality which you have made known to

---

6. Nolland, *Luke*, 1053.
7. Staniforth, *Early Christian Writings*, 44.

us through Jesus your Servant." It also gives thanks for the creation and for the gifts of "food and drink for the sons of men for enjoyment."[8]

Justin Martyr, who was beheaded in Rome in AD 165 for refusing to sacrifice to the gods of the Roman Empire, was one of the great defenders of early Christianity. In both his *Apology* and his *Dialogue with Trypho* he wrote at some length about the Eucharist in order to explain its practice and meaning to those outside the Christian community. In chapter 13 of his *First Apology* he wrote that Christians ought "to send up praises and hymns for our creation and all the means of health, the varieties of creatures and the changes of the seasons, and to send up petitions that we may live in incorruption through faith in him." Probably alluding to the Eucharist, Justin also urged that Christians "give thanks to God for having created the world with all the things in it for the sake of humanity, and for freeing us from the evil in which we were born, and utterly destroying the principalities and powers through him who suffered according to his will."[9] Then in chapter 65 of the *Apology* he commented that "the President sends up praise and glory to God the Father of all, through the Name of the Son and of the Holy Ghost; and *gives thanks at length* for our being counted worthy of these things."[10] In one passage of the *Dialogue with Trypho* Justin wrote:

> The *bread of thanksgiving,* which Jesus Christ our Lord command-ed to be offered for a memorial of the Passion that he suffered for those who are being cleansed from all evil, in order that we should at the same time *give thanks* to God for having created all that therein is for man's sake, and also for delivering us from the evil in which we had been, and for utterly overthrowing principalities and powers by him, who suffered according to his will.[11]

Justin then went on to quote Malachi 1:10–12, which he stated referred to those "who in every place offer sacrifice to Him, the bread of *thanksgiving* and also the cup of *thanksgiving,* affirming thus that we glorify His Name and you (Jews) profane it." Later, in chapter 70 of the same work, Justin wrote of "the bread which Christ commanded us to offer for a memorial of His being made flesh for the sake of those who believe in Him, and the cup which He commanded us to offer *thanking* over it for a memorial of His blood." These two passages both contain a strong note of thanksgiving. In

8. *Didache,* 10.

9. Justin, *First Apology,* 13:2.

10. Ibid., 65.

11. Justin, *Dialogue with Trypho,* 41.

fact at one point Justin even stated: "Prayers and thanksgivings are the only perfect and well-pleasing sacrifices to God."[12]

Hippolytus (c. 170–235) of Rome gave details in his *Apostolic Tradition* (c. 215) of the liturgy with which he was familiar in his part of the imperial city. It is clear that thanksgiving was an important aspect and that it was prominently focused on "Jesus Christ, whom you have sent to us in the last times as Saviour and Redeemer." The lengthy prayer gives thanks for his role in the creation of all things, his death which destroyed the works of the devil and for his resurrection presence which illumines the just.[13]

Cyril of Jerusalem (c. 315–386) spoke of the Eucharist in his fourth *Catechetical Lecture*, reminding his hearers of the point in the liturgy where the priest says, "Let us give thanks to the Lord." "Indeed," Cyril asserted, "we ought to give thanks to the Lord for calling us, when we were unworthy, to so great a grace, for reconciling us when we were enemies, and for granting us the spirit of adoption." Cyril continued, "In giving thanks we do, indeed, a fitting and right act; but He did, not a right act, but one which went beyond justice, by His kindness counting us worthy of such marvellous blessings."[14]

John Chrysostom (c.349–407), spoke much on the subject of thanksgiving in connexion with the Eucharist during the course of a Homily on various passages in Matthew. After commenting on the cure of the leper in Matthew 8:1–4, Chrysostom moved on to a discussion of the church's thanksgiving in the context of the Eucharist. He began by saying, "Pondering these matters . . . let us continually give thanks to God." He then continued,

> God does not need anything of ours, but we need all things that are His. And so thanksgiving adds nothing to Him, but causes us to be closer to Him. For if men's kindnesses, when we call them to mind, warm us with greater love for them, so, when we continually recall the Lord's undertakings for our sake, we will be more diligent in respect of His commandments. . . . For this reason also the mysteries [Eucharists], awesome and full of abundant salvation, which are celebrated at every assembly, are called a thanksgiving [eucharistia], because they are recollections of many benefactions

---

12. Ibid., 117.

13. Hippolytus, *The Apostolic Tradition*, 4.

14. Cyril of Jerusalem, *Catechetical Lectures*, 4:5.

and exhibit the totality of God's care for us and dispose us in everyway to be thankful.[15]

A little later in the same homily Chrysostom went on to be more specific as to the nature of the blessings for which thanksgiving needs to be expressed at the Lord's Supper.

> But let us give thanks not for our own blessings, but also for those of others, for in this way we shall be able to destroy envy and to intensify charity and make it more genuine, since it will be quite impossible for you to go on envying those on whose behalf you give thanks to the Lord. For this reason, when the sacrifice is offered, the priest also bids us to give thanks for the whole world, for those who have gone before, for those now living, for those now being born, and for those who will come after us . . . . For they too form a choir, and give thanks to God for His good things bestowed on us saying: 'Glory to God in the highest, and peace on earth, good will among men' (Luke 2:14).[16]

In the *Liturgy of John Chrysostom*, before the bread and wine are actually placed on the Holy Table there is an opportunity for extempore prayers. Holding the chalice and the paten the priest faces the congregation and invites prayers for people, needs and various situations.[17]

Georges Florovsky wrote that "Gratitude is the proper response of man to the benevolence or *philanthropia* of God. As a response to man to the saving Providence of God, especially to the mystery of our Redemption, by Jesus Christ and in Him, and to the unfathomable gift of New Life in the Spirit, Christian worship is primarily an expression of grateful acknowledgement, of praise and adoration. It culminates ultimately in doxology."[18] This note of thanksgiving of course runs right back to the Day of Pentecost and has been at the heart of Christian worship since the very birth of the church. Indeed, the early Christians were exhorted to give thanks in all circumstances and to make their requests with thanksgiving. In view of this when they gathered around the domestic table for their agape Lord's Suppers there must have been many joyous short expressions of thanksgiving.

15. Chrysostom, *Homily on Matthew 25*, in Sheerin, ed., *The Eucharist*, 287.

16. Ibid., 288.

17. Fenwick, *The Eastern Orthodox Liturgy*, 20.

18. Florovsky, *The Festal Menaion*, 31.

THE GRACE OF THANKSGIVING

It cannot be without significance that the Lord's Supper became spoken of as the Eucharist from a very early point in time, Ignatius of Antioch using the term in his letter to the Philadelphians about the year AD 107.[19] By the end of the second century the term enjoyed widespread usage. The actual word *Eucharist*, as Gregory Dix pointed out, is simply the direct translation into Greek of the ordinary rabbinic term, *berakah*. To "bless" something is simply to "give thanks for it." The two terms are synonymous in Jewish thinking because for the Jew to bless something meant to give thanks for it. There were thus two Greek words with which to translate the one Hebrew word *berakah*. *Eulogia* speaks of God blessing a thing while *eucharistia* puts the emphasis of thing for which God is being thanked. Paul uses both *eulogein* as in 1 Corinthians 10:16: "the cup of blessing which we bless"; and *eucharistein* as in 1 Corinthians 11:23–24: "He took bread and when he had given thanks."[20]

Down through the centuries there have been endless debates over the nature of sacramental grace, how it is generated and who receives it and when. One thing that can be said is that there is a very close connection between thanksgiving and grace. Indeed, the word *Eucharist* meaning thanksgiving is very close to the word *charis*, meaning "grace." In the Romance or Latin based languages the words *grace* and *thanks* are almost identical. At the very least there is a direct connetion between the two. In French, the word *grace* is "to be thankful." In Italian, the word for "thankful" is *grazie*, and in Spanish *gracias* means "thankful." In English, to say grace before a meal is to give thanks. So there is a direct connection between grace and thanksgiving. To be in the grace of God is to be thankful. Conversely, to be unthankful is to be outside of the grace of God. It seems that it's not possible to separate thankfulness and the grace of God. This means that by coming to the table at the Lord's Supper with thanksgiving we open up the possibility of receiving grace. Indeed, by coming in an attitude of thanksgiving we are by that token in a state of grace. It is for this reason that offering up of prayers of thanksgiving is a vitally important aspect of the sacrament.

19. Ignatius, *Letter to the Philadelphians*, 4.
20. For a full discussion of this see Dix, *The Shape of the Liturgy*, 79–83.

THE NEW TESTAMENT AND THANKSGIVING

It is clearly important that communicants be reminded of the necessity of coming to the Lord's table with thanksgiving in their hearts and on their lips. In Colossians 3:15–17 Paul wrote, "And let the peace of God rule in your hearts to which also you are called in one body and be *thankful*." Here it is plain that thanksgiving was not an option but a command! "Be thankful"! Paul then continued his discourse in verse 16, "Let the word of Christ dwell in you richly in all wisdom, teaching and admonishing one another in psalms and hymns and spiritual songs with gratitude ('charity') in your hearts to God (verse 17) and whatever you do in word or deed, do all in the name of the Lord Jesus giving thanks ('eucharistountes') to God the Father through him." In these two verses the intimate connection between thanksgiving and grace is also clear in "singing songs of grace and do all things with thanks." The implication of this is that Christians must always be living in an attitude of thanksgiving to Jesus and coming to the Lord's Supper with thanksgiving in their hearts.

Thanksgiving for the people of God is not an optional extra, it is essential. In his Letter to the Ephesians 5:18, the Apostle Paul wrote of what it means "to be filled with the Holy Spirit." "Do not be drunk with wine in which is dissipation but be filled with the Spirit." It is perhaps a reflection on the negativity of some sections of the church that they have been overly focused on "don't be drunk with wine" rather than "be filled with the Spirit." The apostle then underscored the key mark of being filled with Holy Spirit. It is "speaking to one another in psalms, hymns and spiritual songs and making melody to the Lord and (verse 20) *giving thanks* always for everything in the name of the Lord Jesus Christ." The mark of a life that is filled with the Spirit of God (sacramental grace) is continuous thanksgiving.

The New Testament makes it plain in a number of places why thanksgiving is a vital aspect of Christian living. Perhaps the most obvious reason is simply that it is the will of God. Writing to the Thessalonians, Paul urged his readers, "Be joyful always, pray continually, *give thanks* in all circumstances, for this is God's will for you in Christ Jesus."[21] The will of God, Paul stated, was that the people of God are "to give thanks in everything." The injunction is not to give thanks for everything but in everything (*en panti*). It may be there are things for which Christians cannot give thanks such

---

21. 1 Thess 5:16–18.

as abuse, pain, or injustice, but they can never the less be thankful for the Lord's sustaining presence as they come to his table.

It is apparent from Psalm 100 that thanksgiving is a designated way into God's presence. Verse 4 invites the people of God to "enter his gates [the place of worship] with *thanksgiving* and into his courts with praise; to give *thanks* to him and praise his name." Here entry into the presence of God is presented as a two-stage process. The gates open the way into the courts. Gaining access to the presence of God is only possible *with thanksgiving*. There may of course be moments when God's people feel they have little or nothing for which to be thankful. If that were ever to be the case, the psalm concludes by underlining the fact that there are three great truths for which thanksgiving can always be made, "For the Lord is good and his love endures for ever; and his faithfulness continues throughout all generations." Clearly, when life's circumstances turn individuals away from feelings of thankfulness it is a time to refocus on these eternal, unchanging aspects of God's nature.

Thanksgiving is also a major ingredient in wholeness and healing. In Luke 17:11–19 the Gospel writer recounted an occasion when ten lepers met with Jesus. As lepers they were unclean and not allowed to come near to the general public. They were required to continually warn people of their coming by shouting out "unclean, unclean." When they saw Jesus in the distance they shouted out, "Jesus, Master have mercy on us." Jesus gave a very simple reply, "Go show yourselves to the priests." This was necessary in order that they might attain a certificate that they were clean. By telling them to go to the priest Jesus was indicating that on the way they would be healed. By the time of their arrival the priests would be able to certify that they were indeed no longer leprous. On their way all of the small company were healed but one of them, a Samaritan, came back praising God in a loud voice. He threw himself at Jesus' feet and *thanked* him—and he was a Samaritan. Jesus said to him, "Rise and go; your faith has made you well." All ten were healed but this man's thanksgiving brought him into the saving (*sesoken*) presence of God.

Closely related to this incident is the fact that thanksgiving unlocks the power of God. One very obvious example of this is found in the feeding of the five thousand in the Gospel of John, chapter 6. Significantly John incorporated into his account of this miracle teaching on the meaning of Jesus' eucharistic words of institution in verses 47–59. Interestingly, in verse 4 John records that this miracle of feeding took place at Passover time. The hungry crowd numbered five thousand. The resources were a mere five small barley loaves and two small fish. According to verse 11 Jesus took the loaves and the fish and gave *thanks*. There was then more than enough for every one to have as much as they wanted. Indeed after they had all eaten they took up twelve baskets full of the barley bread. It was the act of *thanksgiving* that released God's extraordinary provision. John was evidently impressed by this fact, since in verse 23 he noted that "other boats came from Tiberias near the place where the people had eaten the bread after the Lord had given *thanks*." It is significant that a number of frescos in the catacombs in Rome depict the Eucharist with the miracle of loaves and fishes on or beside the table.

Thanksgiving clearly lay at the heart of early Christian prayer. In his Letter to the churches in Rome Paul wrote, "I thank my God through Jesus Christ for all of you" (Rom 1:8). Paul thanked God every time he remembered the Philippians (Phil 1:3). He went on to urge them in "everything by prayer and petition with *thanksgiving* to make their requests known to God" (Phil 4:6). The apostle urged the Colossian church to live lives "overflowing with *thankfulness*" (Col 2:7). In further instruction to the church Paul urged them, "Devote yourselves to prayer, being watchful and *thankful*." Writing to his young co-worker, Timothy, Paul stressed that food is to be "received with thanksgiving," and "everything that is good is to be received with thanksgiving" (1 Tim 4:3–4). Paul wrote to the Corinthian church that he "always *thanked* God for them" (1 Cor 1:4). In his First Letter to the church at Thessalonica, Paul and his co-workers Timothy and Silas thanked God continually for the way in which they had received God's word and allowed it to work in them (1Thess 2:13). Writing again to them in his Second Letter, Paul declared, "We ought always to thank God for you brothers, and rightly so, because your faith is growing more and more, and the love every one of you for each other is increasing." Again the writer of the Letter to the Hebrews urged that "since we are receiving a kingdom that cannot be shaken, let us be thankful, and so worship God acceptably with reverence and awe" (Heb 12:28).

This strong note of thanksgiving which is so emphatic in the pages of the New Testament was visible in the early Communion liturgies, but became obscured during the Middle Ages when the Supper was gradually transformed into the Mass. But in the sixteenth century when the church rediscovered the Greek texts of the New Testament there was a desire to recover the emphasis on thanksgiving.

THANKSGIVING AND THE LORD'S SUPPER IN THE
REFORMATION AND AFTER

Martin Luther, for instance, wrote in his "Admonition Concerning the Sacrament of the Body and Blood of Our Lord" (1530), "There are two reasons for receiving the sacrament. The first one is that you thereby thank and praise Christ." "By thanking him," he continued, "we honor him on account of the blessings and gifts of grace we have already received . . . is not the person who goes to the sacrament with this attitude in reality saying: 'Lord, I thank you for all your grace given to me.'"[22] John Calvin (1509–1564), writing in the *Institutes*, was clear that "The Lord's Supper exhorts us Thanksgiving and Praise." He went on to assert that "in His divine goodness the Lord assures us by this mystery of great benefits as if He made us touch them with the finger." Indeed, it is by the Lord's Supper that He exhorts us "to be grateful to Him for them . . . and to exalt His goodness by our praises."[23]

At about the same time in England Archbishop Thomas Cranmer recognized this importance of thanksgiving in worship and wanted to express it in his new service book. This gave him the opportunity to replace the unbiblical sacrificial offering of the consecrated bread and wine made by the priest in the Mass for the sins of the people. In its place he substituted "a sacrifice of praise and thanksgiving" made by the people. In support of this, he cited the Letter to the Hebrews that endorsed exactly this change, pointing out that the animal sacrifices made by the priests in the Temple were no longer in force but "there was another kind sacrifice which is very necessary, the sacrifice of praise and thanksgiving."[24]

Cranmer also made this emphasis on the need for praise and thanksgiving very clearly at the beginning of chapter 3 of his celebrated *Defence.*

> Another kind of sacrifice there is, which doth not reconcile us to God, but is made of them that be reconciled by Christ, to testify our duties unto God, and to show ourselves thankful unto him: and therefore they be called sacrifices of laud, praise and thanksgiving. The first kind of sacrifice Christ offered to God for us; the second kind we ourselves offer to God by Christ. And by the first

22. Luther, "Admonition Concerning the Sacrament," 133.
23. Calvin, *Institutes*, sec. 37 and 38.
24. Heb 13:15.

kind of sacrifice Christ offered also for us unto his Father; and the second we offer ourselves and all that we have, unto his Father.[25]

Cranmer included a number of passages in his *Defence* that underline the importance of thanksgiving as an integral part of the Lord's Supper. At the beginning of chapter 12 of the fifth book he noted that the prophet Malachi foresaw that everywhere all faithful people would bring to God not "any oblation propitiatory to be made by the priests," but rather "in what place soever [sic] they be with pure hearts and minds, sacrifices of laud and praise."[26] In another paragraph in the following chapter Cranmer wrote that the Supper was ordained "that every man eating and drinking thereof should remember that Christ died for him . . . and so give unto Christ *most hearty thanks*, and give himself also clearly unto him."[27] After briefly surveying the writers of the early Christian church he concluded that "when the old fathers called the Mass, or Supper of the Lord, a sacrifice, they meant that it was a sacrifice of lauds and thanksgiving."[28] The Protestant Reformer and Bible translator George Joye (1495–1553) shared Cranmer's conviction and wrote, "Christ said, 'This thing do ye into remembrance of me, that is to say, so oft as ye celebrate this supper, give *thanks* to me for your redemption.'" Joye, it should be said, wished to revive the name "the thanksgiving," for the service. It was "a thanksgiving for redemption as was the Passover."[29]

The Elizabethan Puritan Separatist, Henry Barrow (c. 1550–1593) wrote of "the Supper of the Lord" as "a livelie and most comfortable symbole of our communion with Christ . . . excellently shewing unto us the meanes and maner of our redemption, *to stir us up to thankfulness*, to rejoice in our God and praise his name, to the general strengthening of all our faiths, and to the mutual binding us together in all our holie duties."[30] The Baptist John Smythe wrote that the Lord's Supper has a sacrificial aspect, but this was a sacrifice of thanksgiving, not of the body and blood of Christ. "The sacrifice," he asserted, "is Eucharisticall [sic], and not propitiatorie."[31]

---

25. Cranmer, *Defence*, bk. 5, ch. 3, 217.

26. Ibid., ch. 12, 225.

27. Ibid., ch. 13, 227.

28. Ibid., ch. 16, 229.

29. Knox, *The Lord's Supper*, 36.

30. Barrow, *The Writings of Henry Barrow*, 169.

31. Ibid., 70.

THANKSGIVING FOR OUR REDEMPTION AND ALL THE BLESSINGS OF LIFE

These two aspects of thanksgiving were an important focus in Cranmer's Eucharist. When he produced his second Prayer Book in 1552 he therefore set both the Prayer of Thanksgiving and the Gloria after the consecration and reception of the bread and wine. In this way, communicants were reminded of the importance of giving praise and thanksgiving to the Lord, supremely for the gift of salvation but also for "all other benefits of his Passion." The Prayer of Thanksgiving begins, "O Lord and heavenly father, we thy humble servants entirely desire thy fatherly goodness, mercifully to accept this our sacrifice of praise and thanksgiving."[32] In the Gloria the worshippers declare, "We praise thee, we bless thee, we worship thee, we glorify thee, we give *thanks* to thee for thy great glory, O Lord God heavenly king, God the Father Almighty." Cranmer's pattern clearly resonates with the Gospels of Matthew and Mark, which both record that at the conclusion of the Last Supper the disciples sang a hymn, presumably one of the Hallel Psalms of thanks and praise to God.[33] Significantly, the Collect for Cleansing at the very beginning of Cranmer's service focuses the attention of the worshippers on the importance of praise and worship, as the congregation are invited to pray that "we may perfectly love thee, and worthily magnify thy holy name through Christ our Lord."

Cranmer would certainly have agreed with the great Victorian English preacher, Charles Spurgeon (1834–1892), who once wrote as follows on the importance of thanksgiving.

> It is all we can give him, and the least we can give; therefore let us diligently render to him our thanksgiving . . . let us be at all times thoroughly fervent in the praises of the Lord, both with our lips, by thanksgiving and thanksliving. Jehovah is . . . not to be worshipped with groans and cries, but with thanks, for he is good; and these thanks should be heartily rendered, for he is no common goodness, for he is good by nature, and essence, and proven to be good in all acts of his eternity.[34]

At a similar point in time in 1863 President Abraham Lincoln, himself a committed Christian, decreed that the fourth Thursday in November

---

32. Gibson, *The First and Second Prayer Books*, 390.

33. Matt 26:30 and Mark 14:26; Pss 113–18.

34. Spurgeon, *Treasury of David*; Ps 107:1.

should be set aside as a day of national thanksgiving to God for the establishment of the American nation. In a public proclamation he declared:

> It has seemed to me fit that the gracious gifts of the Most High God should be solemnly, reverently, and gratefully acknowledged . . . I do therefore invite my fellow citizens in every part of the United States . . . to set apart the last Thursday of November next as a day of thanksgiving and praise to our beneficent Father who dwelleth in the heavens.[35]

THANKSGIVING AND CONTEMPORARY EUCHARIST

This emphatic note of thanksgiving was clearly apparent in the worship and Eucharistic liturgies of the early Christian churches. The need for it was emphasized by Luther, Calvin, Zwingli, Cranmer, and a host of other Protestant Reformers, as well as great Christian men and women down through the ages. Yet this emphasis on thanksgiving is often lacking in the Eucharistic worship of the contemporary churches. It is hard not to imagine the early Christians eagerly coming together around the domestic table in their homes and houses to utter many short joyous prayers of thanksgiving and praise as they shared a common agape meal and the bread and wine of the Lord's Supper. Whatever else contemporary Christians do when they gather together to share the Eucharist, time must surely be set apart so that members of the congregation can earnestly and joyfully share and speak out their thanks and praises. After all, it is the Eucharist and we ought at least to do what the name says it is!

---

35. Lincoln, "Proclamation of Abraham Lincoln," in *Collected Works,* vol. 6, 339.

12

Healthy Eating and Drinking

_____

HEALTHY SPIRITUAL EATING AND DRINKING

In 1 Corinthians 11:27–30 the Apostle Paul expressed his concern that some members of the church at Corinth were seriously damaging their health and well-being because they were taking the bread and wine of the Lord's Supper in a careless and casual manner. In truth, in verse 30 he warned that "many among you are weak and sick and a number of you have fallen asleep [died]." The reason for this state of affairs was simply that "whoever eats the bread or drinks the cup of the Lord in an unworthy manner will be guilty of the body and blood of the Lord." Paul is clear that an "unworthy manner" is "to eat and drink without recognising the body." To what exactly the "body" refers to has been a source of debate among biblical scholars. Is it the Eucharistic bread which Jesus declared was his body which is for you? Or is it their Corinthian fellow believers, whom Paul referred to as "the body of Christ" in the sense of the whole church?

In verse 27 Paul wrote, "Whoever eats the bread or drinks the wine in an unworthy manner will be guilty of sinning against the body and blood of the Lord." Here it seems plain enough that "to eat and drink unworthily" is simply to come to the Communion table in a careless and casual spirit and not really concerned to commemorate the death of Jesus as the sacrifice for sins. In short, it appears the Corinthians were treating the Lord's Supper as if were like any other ordinary meal. They were coming together to have a good feed and satisfy their own hunger, but not to feed on the body and blood of Christ. Charles Hodge (1797–1878) of Princeton Theological Seminary illustrated the meaning of Paul's words in the following analogy: "The man who tramples on the flag of his country, insults his country and offends the sovereign himself. In like manner, he who treats the symbols of Christ's body and blood irreverently is guilt of irreverence to Christ."[1]

That said, there is also a sense in which "not recognising the body" in verse 29 refers to the failure of Christians to treat other members of "the body of Christ" in a loving and respectful manner. It is the case that to treat Christ's people in an unworthy manner is to treat Christ who died for them in an unworthy manner. As has been seen in chapter 2 of this study, it was the practice of the early Christian churches to share the Lord's Supper in the context of a bring and share agape meal or Love Feast. It was customary on such occasions for all the different dishes which the people brought to be shared out and everyone then sat down to a common meal. This was a way of bringing about deep Christian fellowship and friendship. It is fairly obvious that the church in Corinth was a broad social mix, ranging from those who were rich to others who were either slaves or poor people who were living close to the bread line. Somewhere along the way the vital importance of fellowship that meant sharing with one another had escaped some of the membership. The rich, it seems, were not sharing their food but sitting apart in small exclusive cliques. Some were apparently even hurrying through the food they had brought along to avoid having to share it with others. This meant that a number of the poorer folk had almost nothing to eat and drink. The result of all of this was that what should have been a very happy and convivial shared meal at which there was no emphasis on social class had degenerated into small separate friendship factions. It may well also have been that some of these small groups had differences of opinion as to what was sound and solid Christian teaching. There is certainly more than a hint of this in the opening paragraphs of this letter which Paul penned, most probably from Ephesus about the year AD 55. In chapter 1 verse 10 Paul regretted that he had learned from some of the members of the congregation in Chloe's house that there were divisions among them. Some were asserting that they followed him while others announced themselves as disciples of Apollos or Peter. Paul challenged them by posing the question, "Is Christ divided?" Then at the beginning of chapter 3:1–8 he

---

1. Hodge, *The First Epistle to the Corinthians*, 230.

underlined the fact that he and Apollos and the other apostles were merely "servants through whom you believed." In fact, they were dependent on each other. "I planted the seed," Paul wrote, "Apollos watered it, but God made it grow."

In the next section of his letter (chapter 12) Paul went on to explain to the Corinthian Christians that a church that is pulled apart by social distinctions can hardly be considered a church at all. A true church is a body of men and women each contributing to the needs of the others and each dependent on the others. A true church is one where there is generosity and real sharing. Indeed it has been said that a true church is where the greatest privilege is not in jealously guarding privileges but rather giving them away.[2] So Paul urged the Corinthians to "wait for one another when they come together for their shared supper and Communion."[3] It is very clear that in no way did Paul condemn having food at the Eucharist, what he condemned was the failure to share it and eat it in a Christlike manner.

In summary, to eat the bread and drink the wine "in an unworthy manner" is to fail to come to the Lord's table consciously aware of his presence and intent on remembering his love and sacrificial death. It is also to fail to be consciously aware and lovingly respectful of his people and their needs. According to Paul, those who fail in either of these two aspects are in danger of damaging their health. In short they are engaging in unhealthy eating!

HYGIENIC SPIRITUAL EATING AND DRINKING

At this point it is important to recognize that there is another kind of unhealthy eating the bread and drinking the wine of Communion. This is a medical issue which relates to the spread of germs, bacteria, and viruses resulting from unhygienic practices, particularly those connected to the way in which the bread is shared and, more particularly the wine, which is often from a common cup.

From the earliest times people have been concerned about the unpleasantness of sharing common drinking vessels. In the Church of England in early Victorian times the Eucharist was celebrated in most parish churches only four times a year at most. Yet even on those few occasions the poor of the village were often required to receive the wine after the rest

2. Barclay, *The Letters to the Corinthians*, 113.
3. 1 Cor 11:33–34.

of the congregation in case they polluted the cup either with bits or food or bread and passed on any germs.

In the nineteenth century the Canadian physician Howard S. Anders published widely, imploring Christians to use individual cups during Holy Communion in order to prevent the spread of disease. One of those who responded was Dr. Thomas Mays, who argued that no conclusion should be drawn about the dangers of the communion cup producing "any special havoc" without statistics to prove his assertions. Anders expressed his disappointment that he was unable to obtain any convincing statistics "showing whether or not communicants are more susceptible to diseases than non-communicants" but he nevertheless remained adamant in his resolve to convince the Christian population to use individual cups because "cleanliness is next to godliness."[4]

The Times of London newspaper in November 2014 printed an article entitled "A Kiss is not just a Kiss, say scientists." It pointed out that when a kiss takes place eighty million bacteria are transferred in a ten-second kiss. Couples who kiss nine times a day develop communities of bacteria. Not all of these, it should be said, would be pathogenic. It doesn't take much imagination, however, to recognize that when thirty to perhaps as many as a hundred people sip from the same communion cup they too are establishing a veritable community of oral bacteria. Research shows that where undiluted twelve per cent alcoholic wine is used the majority of germs are eliminated from a common cup, but by no means all.[5] A report published in April 1993 "showed that strains of bacteria, which could cause respiratory infections and other diseases, were found on Communion cups at an Episcopal Church in Kentucky."[6] There are a number of diseases which can result from droplet infection and which could be transferred by the wine in a shared Communion cup. Such diseases include the common cold and influenza.[7] Both droplets and bacteria can of course be attached to the outside of a Communion cup. Much apparently depends on the person who serves wiping the outside of cup as well as the inside and of making sure that the cup is rotated and the cloth constantly turned to fresh patches. In an article in the journal *Infection Control*, Gina Pugliese and Martin Favero pointed

4. Loving, "The Effects of Receiving Holy Communion on Health," 15–18.

5. Adams, "Drinking from the Same Cup."

6. Ibid.

7. It is known that measles, diarrhea, and Ebola can also be contracted by droplet infection.

out that "Experimental studies have shown that bacteria and viruses can contaminate a common communion cup and survive despite the alcohol content in the wine. Thus, any ill person or asymptomatic carrier drinking from the cup potentially could expose other members of the congregation to pathogens present in the saliva." The authors of the article state that generally speaking the risk is low but they do go on to conclude that "churches may wish to advise their congregations that sharing the communion cup is discouraged if a person has an active respiratory infection (i.e., cold or flu) or moist open sores on their lips (e.g., herpes)."[8]

Frank Baker, the distinguished Methodist historian, wrote in 1956 that "Modern views on hygiene have driven the common cup into almost total banishment from the Methodist Communion, and they would almost certainly engender qualms about its introduction at a love-feast, even with the doubtful precaution of a cloth with which stewards could wipe away from the rim the obnoxious germs left behind at each sip."[9]

The health issue of the Common Cup came to the fore in England during the summer of 2009 with the outbreak of Swine Flu. After receiving a circular from the Department of Health not to share "common vessels" for food or drink, the Archbishops of Canterbury and York issued a letter dated July 22nd, 2009. In it they stated that following advice from the Department of health on the flu pandemic: "It makes good sense to take precautions to limit the spread of disease by not sharing common vessels for food and drink." They went on "to recommend those presiding at Holy Communion to suspend the administration of the chalice during this wave of pandemic flu." For those presiding at Holy Communion who still wished to offer both bread and wine the Archbishops advocated "the practice whereby the presiding minister, whose hands should have been washed with the appropriate alcohol-based rub before handling the elements and the vessels, personally intincts[10] all wafers before placing them in the hands of the communicants."[11] Significantly, "intinction" is quite widely practiced in parts of Africa where the chances of spreading disease by droplet infection is much greater. The full text of the Archbishops' letter was as follows.

8. Pugliese and Favero, "Low Risk of Infection from the Communion Cup," 443.

9. Baker, *Methodism and the Love Feast*, 61.

10. Intinction is the practice of dipping communion wafers in the chalice before handing them out to communicants.

11. Williams and Sentamu, "Swine Flu."

The Feast of Mary Magdalene
22nd July, 2009

Dear Colleague,

It now seems right to offer guidance at a national level about how the Church of England's worship might best take into account the interests of public health during the current phase of the swine flu pandemic.

The Department of Health have recently advised us that "in a pandemic it makes good sense to take precautions to limit the spread of disease by not sharing common vessels for food and drink." In the light of this advice, we recommend the practice whereby the presiding minister, whose hands should be washed with appropriate alcohol based rub before handling the elements and the vessels, personally intincts all wafers before placing them in the hands of communicants. This is a practice widely observed in the Anglican churches throughout Africa. Communicants receiving in this way need to be confident that the clergy and all assistant ministers follow the relevant hygiene.

The Bishop of Ripon and Leeds circulated substantial guidance, including a summary of the government's advice, with his letter of 23 June. Many of you have already issued local guidance based upon its content. We regard it as important that those presiding at Holy Communion are aware of this advice and of that contained in this letter. They should offer guidance to the congregation about appropriate precautions in receiving communion and exchanging the peace.

We shall keep this advice under review and will ensure that the detailed guidance provided on the Church of England website is kept up-to-date. In the meantime, we wish to express our gratitude to you and those who share your ministry for the pastoral care and service offered at this time of national concern.

+ Rowan Cantuar
+ Sentamu Ebor

The practice of "intinction" referred to in the archbishops' letter above has become widespread in many churches, where it is considered to be more hygienic than drinking from a common cup. However, it is necessary for the whole congregation to take part otherwise those who "intinct" will be dipping their wafer into everyone else's germs and residue. Furthermore, research by David Gould for the Anglican Church of Canada demonstrated that intinction used in parishes does not diminish the threat of infection, and may actually increase it. Hands, children's and adults', were "at least as likely to be the source of infection (often more so) as lips." Retention of the wafer in the hand of the recipient then intincting meant that the wafer was now contaminated by the hand of the recipient, which was then placed in the wine, thus spreading the infection to it.[12]

However, the practice of intinction doesn't reflect the way in which Jesus gave the bread and wine separately at the Last Supper. Indeed, as has been seen, there was a meal between the breaking of the bread and the taking and giving of the cup *after* supper. Horton Davies opined that "one could of course take strong exception to the use of wafers in the Roman Catholic and Anglican Churches, which are detrimental to the corporate celebration in Holy Communion."[13] It should nevertheless be countered that to eat tiny morsels of bread Catholic and Anglican style still doesn't reflect corporateness since each communicant eats one after another rather than together at the same time.

Whilst still on the subject of hygiene, it has to said that there can be few more unhygienic rituals than that of an Anglican or Catholic priest at the end of a Communion service, drinking down the dregs in the bottom of a chalice to which some fifty or sixty people have already contributed droplets, germs, and bacteria. Research carried out by Forbes on wine remaining in the chalice at the end of the church service found that it "contained among other things, bacteria, mucus and epithelial cells."[14] There must surely be a more sensible way of disposing of any remaining wine. There is little logic in reverencing the wine in this way when most clergy then also wipe the inside of the chalice with a linen cloth, which means some at least of the consecrated wine is lost in the washing machine!

NOT ONE CUP BUT INDIVIDUAL CUPS

It is still something of a mystery why the Anglican, Catholic, and Orthodox churches have become so wedded to the idea of drinking out of a common cup of wine. In reality, of course, one cup is often insufficient for a whole Sunday congregation. If the need for more than one cup is then conceded, why not let each communicant have their own cup? This has the added advantage of everyone being able to drink together, whereas in the case of

12. Gould, "Eucharistic Practice and the Risk of Infection."

13. Davies, *Bread of Life*, 131.

14. Loving, "A Controlled Study on Intinction."

one shared cup each person drinks in turn one after the other. The notion of one common cup seems to have developed from a later misunderstanding of the New Testament narratives of the Last Supper. At a Passover meal each of the participants would have had their own individual wine cups. Indeed, such is still the case in the present day. So what is very likely is that Jesus simply passed his own personal cup to each of his disciples in turn, inviting them to pour a little of his wine into their own cups. It is by no means certain that he would have been inviting each of them to take a sip from his own cup.

The reason for this assertion is that it was common in Roman society for a host or the president of a feast to pass his cup around to his guests or favored friends for each of them to pour a little of his wine into their own drinking vessels as a sign of companionship. On the occasion of the Last Supper this was simply Jesus' way of binding himself in friendship with the disciples as he sought to inaugurate the new covenant and work of his kingdom. One thing that is clear is that those who shared the Passover meal together all drank at the same time together. As K. E. Keith well expressed it:

> The head of the family takes the cup, pronounces the usual Sabbath (our Saturday) blessing on it, and adds the following: 'Blessed art Thou O Lord, our God, King of the universe, *Who hast kept us alive, and sustained us, and permitted us to reach this season*'. Then all drink their cups at the same time. Sometimes, in the East, the celebrant alone fills his cup, blesses it, drinks of it, and passes it round. Then each one would pour a little into his own cup and drink. This seems to have been the usage followed by our Lord. The cup mentioned in Luke xxii.17, refers to this cup. The cup with which He instituted His own Supper was the third cup.[15]

It needs to be remembered that at Passover meals each guest drank the wine from their own cups, and in apostolic times and the second century, and in many places beyond that time, the Lord's Supper was shared in the context of a meal at which the participants would have had their own drinking vessels.

It should by now have become clear that the most likely earliest Christian practice was for everyone present to have their own cup and drink together at the same time. We see this custom, for instance, in Hippolytus' *Apostolic Tradition* which contains this instruction: "And before they drink

15. Keith, *The Passover*, 29.

let each of those who are present take a cup and give thanks (eucharistein) and drink; and so let the baptised take their meal."[16] The use of one common cup in the Lord's Supper does not appear to be in accord with early Christian practice and it excludes the possibility of communing by drinking together.

The question then arises, how was it that the idea of a common cup emerged in some places at a comparatively early point in the second century? The answer would appear to be connected to development of a belief in a change in the elements of bread and wine through a consecration prayer and manual acts of the one presiding over the Supper. Priests thus came to be seen as a Christ figure who could make bread and wine into his body and blood at the altar. The words "took the cup" were widely misunderstood to mean that there was only one cup at the Last Supper and at the early Christian Eucharists. This understanding became more deeply entrenched in later times when the priest came to be seen as representing Christ to his people at the altar. This notion has persisted strongly down through the ages, particularly in the Roman and Orthodox traditions, and to a lesser extent in the Anglican tradition.

THE SHARED CUP

Where grape juice or unfermented liquids are used in a common cup instead of alcoholic wine, the dangers of spreading bacterial germs and disease is inevitably much greater. Thomas Connelly, in an article entitled "Sharing Drinks with Others," asked the question "Can you catch diseases or other sicknesses from sharing drinks"? His answer to his own question was "a resounding yes." The most common, according to Connelly, are "strep throat, the common cold and mumps."[17]

To sum up, it is by no means certain that the disciples all drank out of Jesus' own cup at the Last Supper. It is more likely that they each poured a little wine from his cup into their own cups. In the early agape Lord's Suppers each person would have had their own drinking vessel. Drinking out of the same Communion cup is not therefore convincingly supported by the biblical evidences and early Christian practice. It is very likely unclean, certainly unhealthy, unnecessary, and unhelpful. It is unhelpful for the reason it prevents the worshippers from drinking together. In other words,

16. Hippolytus, *Apostolic Tradition*, in Dix, *The Shape of the Liturgy*, 82.
17. Connelly, "Sharing Drinks."

each person drinks individually on their own, followed by the next person queuing in the line or kneeling at the altar rail.

REGULAR EATING AND DRINKING

One obvious difference between the Passover and the Lord's Supper is in the frequency with which they were and are taken. The Passover was and is kept annually, whereas the Lord's Supper or New Passover was taken frequently, at least in the early centuries.[18] It is generally accepted that healthy eating and drinking is regular eating and drinking. In this way the body receives a steady supply of nourishment and energy on a regular basis. The same practice holds good when it comes to sharing the Lord's Supper. The New Testament suggests that the early Christians probably shared the sacrament regularly each Sunday.[19] Indeed, it may well be that some of their number in Jerusalem and elsewhere shared the bread and wine considerably more frequently.[20]

The *Didache* assumes that on every Lord's Day there would be "a gathering together to break bread."[21] Ignatius and many of the early church fathers followed suit.[22] Justin Martyr recorded that "on the day called Sunday . . . when our prayers are ended, bread and wine are brought."[23] During the later Middle Ages, however, when the bread and wine were increasingly regarded as holy and propitiatory, the Eucharist was celebrated less and less frequently. In 1215 the minimum requirement was reduced to Easter Sunday, at which time the cup was withdrawn from the laity.[24] Jacques de Vitry (c. 1160–1240), a French Canon who later became Bishop of Acre, was a theologian of the period. He noted that the reason for this change was that "sins have become so multiplied in the land, it is permitted that Communion be received by the laity only once per year, that is Easter."[25]

---

18. The Ebionites, a Jewish Christian sect held that the Lord's Supper should only be celebrated once a year as the Passover was on 14–15 Nisan. See Higgins, *The Lord's Supper*, 56.

19. 1 Cor 11:20–21 and 16:2.

20. Acts 2:42.

21. *Didache*, 14.

22. Ignatius, *Letter to the Ephesians*, 20.

23. Justin, *First Apology*, 67.

24. Maxwell, *A History of Christian Worship*, 65.

25. Rubin, *Corpus Christi*, 155.

The sixteenth-century Protestant Reformers recovered much of the theology of the New Testament Lord's Supper. However, some of them fell well short of early Christian practice when it came to the matter of frequency. Zwingli, for instance, suggested four times a year: Easter, Whitsun, Autumn, and Christmas.[26] Cranmer required members of the Church of England to communicate only three times a year, of which one was to be Easter.[27] If, however, the home or small group is considered to be the most appropriate context for the Lord's Supper, as this book has argued, once a week would seem to be both practicable and spiritually healthful.

CONCLUSION

The Lord's Supper, as has been made evident in this study, is spiritual food. Indeed, it is the means through which the very presence of Jesus is felt and known by believers as they eat and drink the bread and wine with faith and trust in him. As in the case of all meals there is an etiquette to be observed at the Lord's Supper. Those invited come thankfully and respectful of the one who has invited them to the meal, as well as mindful of the needs of the other guests who are present at the table. Just as the guests at a banquet should look to the needs of those sitting near them, so at the Lord's Supper there is a call to be in fellowship with others who share the feast. To derive the full benefits of the Lord's Supper Christian people therefore need to come regularly, expectantly, and eat and drink in a healthful manner.

26. Maxwell, *A History of Christian Worship*, 65.
27. Post-Communion Rubric, *Book of Common Prayer*, 1552.

13

Celebrating the New Passover

THE NEED FOR A NEW APPROACH TO THE LORD'S SUPPER

Anyone who has followed the argument of the preceding pages of this book thus far will be aware that there is a vital need for the mainline denominational churches to undertake a radical rethinking about the ways in which they celebrate the Lord's Supper, Holy Communion, or Eucharist, whichever is the preferred term.

In the first place it is manifestly obvious that from a very early point in time the churches transformed this central act of Christian worship from the domestic setting of a simple informal fellowship meal in homes and houses to a formalized public ritual in large ecclesiastical buildings. Within 400 years, almost every trace of the Last Supper that Jesus shared with his disciples and with which apostolic Christianity was familiar had been lost. In some liturgies, to be sure, there were still allusions to Jesus' words of institution, but in most cases they had become encrusted with notions of change, offering, and sacrifice, and so had lost the purpose and emphasis that Jesus had intended. The contemporary public versions of the Lord's Supper are of course varied in style and atmosphere. At one end of the ecclesiastical spectrum there is the theatre of the High Mass, an esoteric ceremony in which a cluster of priests and Eucharistic ministers clad in white hooded albs and ornate robes process to the central high altar. There, aided by thurifers and the sound of bells, they change circlet wafers and cups of wine into the body and blood of Christ. There are also grand Non-conformist versions of the same. Here sedate, formally dressed men and women glide efficiently and quietly around an auditorium in the manner of smartly dressed waiters and offer worshippers a nibble of bread and a thimbleful of grape juice.

Virtual communions are growing in popularity, particularly among the elderly where participants join in online from their own homes. Having prepared their own bread and wine the congregation all eat together after the TV "president" or minister has said the consecration prayer and given the invitation. There are also the drive-in churches in parts of America where worshippers drive into the church lot and park by one of the many stands where there is a microphone ready to be dropped in through the car window. On occasions when it is Communion the bread and wine are slipped in through the car window in a little plastic container by one of the parking attendants. There are also help-yourself Communions in a number of churches. Here the bread and wine are placed on a table at the front of the building and worshippers are invited as in a buffet-style meal to go and help themselves at any point when they feel ready during the service.

All these expressions of communion have one thing in common. They have moved away from the simple home-based family or small group meal that Jesus so obviously intended. Instead of each company of believers eating together in a natural way, as they would at any normal meal, a bizarre situation has been reached where people imagine the only valid Eucharist is a large public gathering where they receive the bread and wine from the hands of a specially or ordained or designated official clad in special dress.

It was against a background of such developments that Eleanor Kreider wrote:

> How far we have come from the meal table services of the early communities! Is our "Lord's table" a contradiction or at least a misnomer? The church's table might be a more exact name. Who has access to this table? Who serves as host, and what does that role symbolise? Wrestling with these questions, the early Christian's sharp focus on Jesus with his friends around a common table has gone fuzzy. Food has become minimal and its meaning spiritualised. Eyes are either spiritually turned inward or riveted on the stylised gestures of the one presiding. Specific words, particular

patterns of doing things, and the proper credentials of the ministers have become what makes the service valid.[1]

In the light of these words from Kreider and other comments of a similar
nature there is an obvious need to recover the home-based meal that Jesus
instituted. Not least because research has consistently demonstrated that
the majority of churches that have the Eucharist or Communion as their
regular main or central Sunday service are, generally speaking, not growing
churches. The main issue, however, is simply that Jesus intended the Last
Supper to be the New Passover and therefore to be kept in the manner and
character of the old Passover.

So how should the Lord's Supper be kept?

AS AN EVENING SUPPER MEAL

As has been noted, both the Apostle Paul and all four Gospel writers indicate that the Last Supper was, like the Passover Meal, a Supper. As has
been noted, Paul and all four evangelists clearly linked the Lord's Supper
with the Passover meal and spoke and wrote of it in Passover terms. The
bread which Jesus took and broke marked the beginning of the meal and
the cup of wine that Jesus took he took *after* supper corresponded to the
third Passover cup, the Cup of Blessing.

It is simply not possible to organize meals for large gatherings of
people in public buildings on a regular basis. Even if it were, the chances of
such occasions providing opportunities for convivial speech and intimate
sharing, thanksgiving and fellowship are very unlikely. This is why many
church Communion services end up being rushed affairs with token wafers
or pieces of bread that are hardly big enough to go on a fisherman's hook.
Whilst churches will feel they want to have Communion from time to time
for the whole of their congregation, there is clearly a vital need to return
to small groups sharing the bread and wine in homes and houses after the
fashion of the early Christian practice of agape meals. The Last Supper was
clearly intended by Jesus to be the central part of a domestic spirituality
rather than a public ceremony.

Churches therefore need to teach husbands, wives, and children or
small groups of Christian friends to share the bread and wine on their own
in a relaxed home context and, if possible, during an *evening* meal. It is clear

1. Kreider, *Given for You*, 23.

that in the main the early churches endeavored to share the Lord's Supper in the evenings. The meal is important because it is the eating together that forges the bond of intimacy with the Lord and with other Christians that is so often lacking in current church Eucharists.[2] Denominational churches will of course want to set their own guidelines as to who should preside over or lead their public church-based Holy Communion services, and rightly so. That said, all Christian believers have the democratic right to do as they think fit and right in their own homes. They should be encouraged by their church leaders and fellow Christians to set aside some bread and wine at one of their weekly evening meals in order to meet with the Lord as they eat and drink together in remembrance of his death and resurrection. If the meal is a family one, the Passover practice could be followed with children sharing in the bread and wine if that seems right and appropriate. These occasions could simply be an ordinary supper made special by beginning with a prayer of blessing and sharing bread. During the eating and drinking there could perhaps be opportunities to share the events of the day and offer some prayers of thanksgiving and praise. The meal could then simply end with the sharing of wine. Occasionally the meal could be a more special celebration with special food and a more festive atmosphere.

AS A MEAL WITH ORDINARY BREAD AND ORDINARY WINE

In the Jewish Passover each family group was instructed to take ordinary bread (in this case unleavened bread) and ordinary red wine. The Jewish Passover began with a preliminary meal or starter in which the host broke bread in thanksgiving. The first of four cups of wine was also drunk at this point. The Passover lamb, the bread, the wine, and the bitter herbs were symbols. Just as there was never any notion that the Passover lamb was in any sense the substance of Jehovah or the means of forgiveness, so there was never any suggestion in the mind of Jesus or the early Christians that the bread changed in any way or form into his body, or for that matter the wine into the blood of Christ, or that they could be the means of forgiveness. They were simply symbols or representations of his body and blood. The early Christians never confused these symbols with the reality they represented.

2. Rev 3:20.

It is therefore not appropriate to kneel down to receive the bread and wine at a Communion rail and it is clearly idolatrous to venerate or worship portions of consecrated bread and wine contained in a pix or in an aumbry on or near the church altar. The teaching of transubstantiation and the priest offering up Jesus' body and blood at the altar for people's sins is unbiblical and erroneous. It needs always to be remembered that Jesus said, "I tell you I will not drink of this fruit of the vine from now on until the day when I drink it new with you in my Father's kingdom," the point being Jesus still called it "the fruit of the vine," not "my blood."[3] All this means that it makes sense to recognize that the very heart of the Lord's Supper is sharing some ordinary bread and wine as symbols and signs of remembrance of Jesus' sacrificial death and resurrection in order to bring us forgiveness and new life.

AS A FELLOWSHIP MEAL

The word *fellowship* means "to share," or "to have things in common." For this reason the Lord's Supper is sometimes called "Communion." The focus is on worshippers coming together to share their common life in the presence of their Lord. This is an aspect which has been lost in the Communion services of many contemporary churches and needs to be recovered. It is directly derived from the Jewish Passover meal, where those present share in storytelling, convivial conversation, and informal prayer and praise. Children are also present and one of the most important traditions is that the oldest child, often the son of the host or head of the household, asking the question, "Why are we holding this feast?" The Father then replies and explains the symbolism of the bread and the wine and bitter herbs. The worship of the old covenant included the children and the new or better covenant should therefore and does include children, who should be encouraged to share in household family Communion services.

Breaking bread and drinking wine should be "a communing with one another," that is, talking and sharing as people do at a meal with friends and as the guests certainly do at the Jewish Passover. It is, however, difficult for people to have fellowship if the bread and wine are passed to them while they're sitting in long lines in a large auditorium. It is even more difficult when people are queuing up cafeteria style in a long lines in a large church building to get a tiny cube of bread and sip of the wine. Some

3. Matt 29:29.

Roman Catholic and Anglican churches come close to "McDonaldizing Communion" into a kind of Christian "brunch on the run"! The central act of the Lord's Supper should be eating a reasonable portion of bread slowly and thoughtfully, followed by a proper sip of wine taken slowly with space and time for the participants meditate and remember the Lord's wonderful love and gracious "passing over" their sins. Instead, in many instances, particularly in Catholic, Episcopal, and Anglican churches, it's often all over in thirty seconds. Indeed in reality in these churches people don't commune by eating and drinking together at the same time. Rather, each person receives the bread and wine in a long line on their own one after another! Furthermore it's often not possible for most worshippers "to fellowship" or share with those sitting nearest to them in a church building because they may well be strangers and as likely as not there would be time constraints.

AS A HOME-BASED MEAL

When the Israelites were given the instructions for the first Passover meal they were told to hold it in their houses. And for obvious reasons they were not to go out of the house, because it was the only safe place when the angel of death passed over the land of Egypt. But in the years following the first Passover the Israelites were still told to keep the meal in their houses. Exodus 12:46 is very clear, "It must be eaten inside one house; take none of the meat outside the house."

Jesus, who was after all a rabbi, could so very easily have initiated the Lord's Supper in a public building or more likely in a synagogue, but he didn't. Jesus plainly intended that, like the old Passover, the New Passover was to be home-based worship. It was never his plan or purpose that his Supper should become a largely attended grand public spectacle with altars, incense, bells, and special officials parading themselves up and down in brightly colored robes. In the first century the Jewish Passover was a thoroughly domestic occasion. It was usually for a maximum of fifteen or sixteen people, which was probably the largest number able to share one lamb and capable of sitting round a household table.

One of the problems of contemporary Christianity is that it has lost the emphasis on the home and the family unit. The great English Puritans of the sixteenth and seventeenth centuries who held the home to be "the church in miniature" were one of the few groups who understood this divine principle and sought to recover it. Indeed, the expression "Christianity begins at home" seems to have originated from among them. It is not without significance that the Christian church was so vibrant and outgoing in the first three centuries when it was rooted in the home. It is also abundantly clear from the New Testament that the early Christians broke bread from house to house with their fellow believers in the context of their common meals. For the Jews, liturgical praise and prayer and formal preaching took place in the synagogues under the supervision of elders and deacons while the Passover and Pentecost were home-based occasions.[4]

AS A MEAL FOR BELIEVERS

The instructions which Moses received from the Lord and which he passed on to the people made it absolutely clear that the Passover was only for the people of God. Exodus 12:43–44 states that, "No foreigner is to eat of it." Slaves could share in the meal if they had been circumcised but no temporary resident or hired worker could do so. It is clear that Jesus and the early church restricted the New Passover to those who had faith in him.

The *Didache* stated that only those who have been baptized were to attend the Lord's Supper. But even in the third century it was still expected that the Lord's Supper was only for believers. In fact, as late as the fourth and fifth centuries when Christianity had moved into the public sphere, the church still insisted that those who were not committed believers should leave the building before the bread and wine were consecrated and shared. Such a regulation still makes perfect sense for the contemporary church. After all, if someone drops into Sunday morning worship as a stranger or very occasional visitor they are not going to be comfortable and relaxed watching a strange mystical ceremony that by its very nature excludes the uncommitted. There needs to be a recognition that the Lord's Supper is by its nature exclusive and something that can only be appreciated and understood by Christian believers. For this reason it is best kept in the privacy of people's homes.

AS A MEAL OF SPIRITUAL FOOD

At the Lord's Supper Christian believers eat ordinary bread and drink ordinary wine, yet at the same time they also able to "eat and drink spiritually."

4. Acts 2:2.

They feed on the spiritual presence of Jesus who is "the living bread"[5] and whose Spirit is "living water."[6] Thomas Cranmer believed and taught, as has been noted, what is known as "double eating." Christian believers feed on bread at the Lord's table, but at the same time they can and should continue to feed on Jesus' unseen spiritual presence. In fact, in the Church of England *Book of Common Prayer* service of Holy Communion when the minister distributes the bread, he or she does so with the words, "Take and eat this bread in remembrance that Christ died for you *and feed on him* in your hearts by faith." Cranmer made a further and very important point that believers don't merely feed spiritually on the Lord's presence at the point when they are eating the bread and drinking the wine, but they will hopefully go on feeding on his presence continuously. This is an important truth that needs to be taught and brought to people's minds during the sacrament.

AS A MEAL FOR REMEMBRANCE

In his instructions to the people of Israel in Exodus 12:14 Moses emphasized that the Passover was "a day you are to *commemorate* for generations to come." This was one day on which the Lord's people were to *remember* his faithfulness to them in delivering them from the harshness and brutality of their slavery in the land of Egypt. And they were helped in this by the symbols of the Passover meal. The unleavened bread, sometimes called "the bread of affliction," reminded them of the pain and suffering of the land of Egypt from which they had been set free. The bitter herbs which they dipped in sauce *recalled* the blood which the Israelites put on the posts and lintels of the doors of their houses. In a similar way, the New Passover invites the participants to *remember* the Lord's amazing sacrificial love in coming as "the spotless lamb of God" and perfect sacrifice for sin. And in that coming to bring freedom to his people from slavery, not a slavery in Egypt but rather a slavery to their selfish desires and all that holds their lives in bondage.

Remembrance of the Lord's blessings and the good times of the past is vital for both spiritual and emotional health. There needs to be a store of good memories that believers can recall and feed on in the hard and difficult times. Remembrance in Communion is about believers recalling and

5. John 5:51.
6. John 4:10.

reliving the spiritual blessings that they have stored away in their memory banks. It was something that the Old Testament people of God tried to do as often as they were able. In Psalm 78:9–16, for example, the psalmist expressed his regret that his people "forgot what he had done, the wonders he had shown them." He then specifically mentioned the deliverance from Egypt, the Red Sea crossing, and God's guidance and provision during the wanderings in the desert. There needs to be space for worshippers to both remember the Lord for who he is, as well as his supreme act of love and sacrifice in dying for the sin of the world.

AS A SIT DOWN MEAL

At first thought this seems to be a small point and yet it is perhaps more important than people's first thoughts. As was made clear in the early part of this book, people always reclined for Passover because it was a relaxed and convivial meal. Luke 14:14 is explicit that Jesus and his disciples reclined at table. Why people stand or kneel to receive the bread and wine has to be something of a mystery. It seems that the practice of standing to receive the bread and wine first began at the time when the early Christians started to construct official church buildings and it was decided they needed a special president to put the bread and cup into their hands. The custom of kneeling appears to have developed a little later in the Western churches in the Middle Ages when people began to believe that the bread and wine were in some sense Jesus' body and blood. So they knelt down in worship.

It seems both obvious and normal that sitting should be the accepted posture when the Lord's Supper is administered. It has clear biblical precedent in the Last Supper and in the practice of the primitive Christian church. It also has theological significance in that sitting is a sign of affirmation and acceptance by Jesus who welcomes his people to his table. Sitting is also a place of authority and it looks forward to the time when Jesus will welcome his people to sit with him at the heavenly banquet in the kingdom of God.

AS A THANKSGIVING MEAL

For the Jews the Passover was a thanksgiving for their deliverance from the hand of the Egyptians and this came to be expressed as the Passover developed in the four cups of wine that were drunk during the course of the meal. The third cup in particular was called the Cup of Blessing or the "Cup of Thanksgiving." Before Jesus took the bread at the Last Supper he gave thanks and he did the same before he took the cup of wine. It is important that Christian believers remind themselves that *thanksgiving* is the way into God's presence and it's also the most obvious sign that someone is filled with the Holy Spirit. The Lord's Supper should therefore be characterized by thanksgiving with adequate time for participants to share and contribute prayers of thanksgiving.

A HEALTHFUL MEAL

The Lord's Supper is an occasion when believers should to be exhorted to come together fully focused to remember the sacrificial love and death of Jesus for the forgiveness of their sins. They need to be made aware that to come casually is to fail to discern the Christ's body on which their salvation depends. More than this, for the sacrament to be healthful; each guest needs to be reminded that it is vital to be in a loving, respectful, and right relationship with the others who gather with them around the Lord's table. If either of these two aspects are lacking the proceedings could indeed be detrimental to their health (1 Cor 11:30).

A FINAL WORD

So the last word of this study is a plea to churches and Christian people to rethink the ways in which they keep the Lord's Supper today. Even if the links between the Lord's Supper and the Passover and Jewish fellowship and agape meals are not altogether clear, it is plainly obvious that the way it is practiced in most churches has moved a long way from the meal which Jesus shared with his disciples shortly before his crucifixion. Ideally, the Lord's Supper should be a sit-down evening meal for small groups of Christian believers. It doesn't need a priest or a special minister to make it valid. It should be a joyous celebration time in homes or houses. It should be marked by thanksgiving and convivial, informal fellowship. It's a time for the Lord's people to recall and testify and share stories of their faith journeys. Above all it's the occasion to remember the Lord's gift of forgiveness, his covenant love, goodness, and provision to his people. It's also a time for feeding on his presence and receiving "all other benefits of his passion" as well as refreshing our lives with the life-giving Holy Spirit.

Bibliography

Achelis, Hans. "The Canons of Hippolytus." In John F. Keating, *The Agape and the Eucharist*. London; Methuen, 1901.

Adams, Damon. "Drinking from the Same Cup, the Episcopalians Shared More than the Blood of Christ." *Sun Sentinel*, April 19, 1993.

Ambrose. *On the Sacraments*. The Nicene and Post-Nicene Fathers, 2nd series, vol. 10, edited by Philip Schaff and Henry Wace. Grand Rapids: Eerdmans, 1955.

Anon. *Acts of Thomas*.

Anon. *The Covenant to be the Lord's People and Walk After the Lord*. London: n.p., 1700.

Athanasius. *Letter to Serapion*. The Nicene and Post-Nicene Fathers, 2nd series, vol. 5, edited by Philip Schaff and Henry Wace. Grand Rapids: Eerdmans, 1955.

———. *On Female Dress* [*De Cult. Fem.*]. The Nicene and Post-Nicene Fathers, 2nd series, vol. 5, edited by Philip Schaff and Henry Wace. Grand Rapids: Eerdmans, 1955.

———. *To the Newly Baptised*. The Nicene and Post-Nicene Fathers, 2nd series, vol. 5, edited by Philip Schaff and Henry Wace. Grand Rapids: Eerdmans, 1955.

Augsburg Confession. In *Martin Luther*, edited by E. Gordon Rupp and Benjamin Drewery. London: Edward Arnold, 1970.

Augustine. *Reply to Faustus the Manichean*. The Nicene and Post-Nicene Fathers, 1st series, vol. 8, edited by Philip Schaff and Henry Wace. Grand Rapids: Eerdmans, 1956.

———. *Tractate 50*. The Nicene and Post-Nicene Fathers, 1st series, vol. 8, edited by Philip Schaff and Henry Wace. Grand Rapids: Eerdmans, 1956.

Baker, Frank. *Methodism and the Love Feast*. London: Epworth, 1957.

Barclay, Alexander. *The Protestant Doctrine of the Lord's Supper*. Glasgow: Wylie & Co., 1927.

Barclay, William. *The Gospel of John*. Edinburgh: St. Andrew, 1964.

———. *The Gospel of Matthew*, vol. I. London: SCM, 1965.

———. *The Letters to the Corinthians*. Edinburgh: St. Andrew, 1962.

———. *A New Testament Word Book*. London: SCM, 1955.

Barrow, Henry. *The Writings of Henry Barrow*. London: Routledge, 2003.

Basil the Great. "To the Lady Caesarea concerning Communion, Letter 93." *The Nicene and Post-Nicene Fathers*, 2nd series, vol. 8, edited by Philip Schaff and Henry Wace. Grand Rapids: Eerdmans, 1955.

Baxter, Richard. "The Catechising of Families." In *Practical Works of Richard Baxter* [1830], vol. 4. Peabody, MA: Hendrickson, 2010.

———. "Christian Directory." In *Practical Works of Richard Baxter* [1830], vol. 4. Peabody, MA: Hendrickson, 2010.

———. "The Poor Man's Family Book." In *Practical Works of Richard Baxter* [1830], vol. 19. Peabody, MA: Hendrickson, 2010.

———. *The Saints' Everlasting Rest.* Marshalton: n.p., n.d.

Berkhof, Louis. *Systematic Theology.* Edinburgh: The Banner of Truth Trust, 1958.

Bettenson, Henry. *Documents of the Christian Church.* Oxford: Oxford University Press, 1967.

Bickersteth, Edward. *A Treatise on the Lord's Supper.* London: R. B. Seeley and W. Burnside, 1841.

Biggs, Charles. *The Christian Platonists of Alexandria.* Oxford: Bampton Lecture, 1886.

Biggs, William W. "The Controversy Concerning Kneeling in the Lord's Supper—after 1604." *Transactions of the Congregational Historical Society*, xvii (1953) 51–62.

Bock, Darrell. *Luke.* Downers Grove, IL: InterVarsity, 1994.

Bonhoeffer, Dietrich. *The Cost of Discipleship.* London: SCM, 2011.

———. *Life Together.* London: SCM, 1971.

Book of Common Prayer. Oxford: Oxford University Press, n.d.

Boon, George C. "The Early Church in Gwent 1: The Romano British Church." *The Monmouthshire Antiquary* VIII (1992) 11–24.

Bouyer, Louis. *Eucharist.* London: University of Notre Dame Press, 1968.

Bradford, John. "Sermon on the Lord's Supper." In *The Writings of John Bradford.* Cambridge: Parker Society, 1848.

———. *The Writings of John Bradford.* Cambridge: Parker Society, 1848.

Bradshaw, Paul F. *Eucharistic Origins.* London: SPCK, 2004.

Bromiley, Geoffrey. *Zwingli and Bullinger.* London: SCM, 1953.

Brook, Victor J. K. *A Life of Archbishop Parker.* Oxford: Clarendon, 1962.

Bruce, Frederick F. *The Spreading Flame.* Carlisle: Paternoster, 1992.

Buchanan, Colin O. *The Savoy Conference Revisited.* Bramcote: Grove, 1976.

———. *What Did Cranmer Think He was Doing?* Bramcote: Grove, 1976.

Burrage, Champlin. *Early English Dissenters* [1912], vol. ii, 42 and 44. In *The Lord's Supper in Early English Dissent*, Stephen Mayor, 43. London: Epworth, 1972.

Cairns, David. *In Remembrance of Me.* London: Geoffrey Bles, 1967.

Calvin, John. "Article XVII." In *The Protestant Doctrine of the Lord's Supper*, Alexander Barclay. Glasgow: Jackson Wylie & Co, 1927.

———. "Article XX." In *The Protestant Doctrine of the Lord's Supper*, Alexander Barclay, 160. Glasgow: Jackson Wylie & Co, 1927.

———. *Commentary on the First Epistle to the Corinthians.* Edinburgh: The Calvin Translation Society, 1848.

———. "Ecclesiastical Ordinances, Article LIII." In *The Protestant Doctrine of the Lord's Supper*, Alexander Barclay, 160. Glasgow: Jackson Wylie & Co, 1927.

———. *Institutes of the Christian Religion.* Grand Rapids: Associated, n.d.

———. "Introduction to the Articles." In *The Protestant Doctrine of the Lord's Supper*, Alexander Barclay, 125. Glasgow: Jackson Wylie & Co, 1927.

———. *Order for Communion* [1545]. In *The Lord's Supper in Early English Dissent*, Stephen Mayor, 8. London: Epworth, 1972.

———. "Short Treatise on the Holy Supper of our Lord Jesus Christ." *Calvin Translation Society* 2 (1849), vol. 2, sec. 15.

Cannon, William R. *History of Christianity in the Middle Ages.* New York: Abingdon, 1960.

Canons of Hippolytus. Bramcote: Grove, 1987.

Chilton, Bruce. *A Feast of Meanings: Eucharistic Theologies from Jesus Through Johannine Circles.* Leiden: E. J. Brill, 1994.

Chrysostom, John. "Homily on Matthew." In *The Eucharist,* edited by Daniel J. Sheerin, 355. Wilmington: Michael Glazier, 1986.

————. *Homily III, Homily XX, Homily XXII, Homily XXV, Homily XXVII. The Nicene and Post-Nicene Fathers,* 1st series, vol. 11, edited by Philip Schaff. Grand Rapids: Eerdmans, 1968.

————. *The Liturgy of Chrysostom.* In *The Eastern Orthodox Liturgy,* edited by John Fenwick. Bramcote: Grove, 1978.

Clement of Alexandria. *Miscellanies [Stromateis]. The Ante-Nicene Christian Library,* vol. 4, edited by Alexander Roberts and James Donaldson. Edinburgh: T & T Clark, 1909.

————. *Paedagogus. The Ante-Nicene Christian Library,* vol. 4, edited by Alexander Roberts and James Donaldson. Edinburgh: T & T Clark, 1909.

Clement of Rome. "Letter of Clement of Rome to the Corinthians." In *Early Christian Writings, Andrew Louth.* London: Penguin, 1987.

Cole, Richard L. *Love-Feasts: A History of the Christian Agape.* London: Charles Kelly, 1916.

Colman, Benjamin. *A Discourse of the Pleasure of Religious Worship in our Public Assemblies* [1717]. In *The Worship of the American Puritans,* Horton Davies. Princeton, NJ: Peter Lang, n.d.

Common Worship. London: Church House, 2000.

Connelly, Thomas P. "Sharing Drinks with Others: Can I Actually Catch a Disease"? *Huffington Post,* July 21, 2013.

Cotton, John. *The Way of the Churches of Christ in New England* [1645]. In *The Worship of the American Puritans,* Horton Davies. Princeton, NJ: Center of Theological Inquiry, n.d.

Council of Laodicea. "Cannon XXVIII." *The Nicene and Post-Nicene Fathers,* 2nd series, vol. 14, edited by Philip Schaff and Henry Wace. Buffalo: Christian Literature, 1900.

Courtenay, William J. "Sacrament, Symbol and Causality in Bernard of Clairvaux and Scholasticism." In *Bernard of Clairvaux: Studies Presented to Jean Leclerq.* Kalamazoo, MI: Cistercian, 1973.

Cranmer, Thomas. *Book of Common Prayer.* Oxford: Oxford University Press, n.d.

————. "Catechism." In *Writings of the Rev. Dr Thomas Cranmer,* 129. London: The Religious Tract Society, undated.

————. "Confession," *Book of Common Prayer* [1552]. In *The First and Second Prayer Books of Edward VI,* edited by Edgar C.S. Gibson. London: J. M. Dent & Sons, 1932.

————. *A Defence of The True and Catholic Doctrine of the Sacrament of the Body and Blood of Our Saviour Christ.* Appleford: Sutton Courtenay, 1962.

————. "Post-Communion Rubric." In *The First and Second Prayer Books of Edward VI,* edited by Edgar C.S. Gibson. London: J. M. Dent & Sons, 1932.

————. "Rubric at the End of the Confirmation Service." In *Book of Common Prayer* [1552]. In *The First and Second Prayer Books of Edward VI,* edited by Edgar C.S. Gibson. London: J. M. Dent & Sons, 1932.

————. "Rubric Following the Sermon." In *The First and Second Prayer Books of Edward VI,* edited by Edgar C.S. Gibson. London: J. M. Dent & Sons, 1932.

————. *Writings of the Rev. Dr. Thomas Cranmer.* London: The Religious Tract Society, undated.

Cross, Frank L. and Elizabeth Livingstone, eds. "Mithraism." In *The Oxford Dictionary of the Christian Church*. London: Oxford University Press, 1974.

———. *The Oxford Dictionary of the Christian Church*. London: Oxford University Press, 1974.

Cullman, Oscar. *Early Christian Worship*. Philadelphia: Westminster, 1953.

Cyprian. *Concerning The Unity of the Church, Epistle 53*. In *Early Latin Theology*, vol. 5, edited by Stanley L. Greenslade. London: SCM.

———. *Epistle 53. The Ante-Nicene Fathers*, vol. 5, edited by Philip Schaff and Henry Wace. Grand Rapids: Eerdmans, 1957.

———. *On Works and Alms. The Ante-Nicene Fathers*, vol. 5, edited by Philip Schaff and Henry Wace. Grand Rapids: Eerdmans, 1957.

Cyril of Jerusalem. *Catechetical Lectures*. In *Library of Christian Classics*, vol. 4. London: SCM, 1950.

———. *Mystagogical Catechesis*. In Library of Christian Classics, vol. 4. London: SCM, 1950.

Davids, Peter H. *The Letters of 2 Peter and Jude*. Nottingham: Apollos, 2006.

Davies, Horton. *Bread of Life and Cup of Joy*. Leominster: Gracewing, 1993.

———. *The English Free Churches*. Oxford: Oxford University Press, 1952.

———. *The Worship of the American Puritans*. Princeton, NJ: Peter Lang, n.d.

———. *The Worship of the English Puritans*. Princeton, NJ: Soli Deo Gloria, 1997.

Dearing, Trevor. *Wesleyan and Tractarian Worship*. London: Epworth, 1966.

Didache. The Ante-Nicene Fathers, vol. 7, edited by Alexander Roberts and James Donaldson. Grand Rapids: Eerdmans, 1951.

Dix, Dom Gregory. *The Shape of the Liturgy*. London: Dacre, 1943.

Doolittle, Thomas. *A Treatise on the Lord's Supper* [1817]. In *The Worship of the American Puritans*, Horton Davies. Princeton, NJ: Center of Theological Inquiry, n.d.

Egyptian Canons LXXV. In *Eucharistic Origins*, edited by Paul F. Bradshaw. London: SPCK, 2004.

Eusebius. *The History of the Christian Church*. Harmondsworth: Penguin, 1967.

Every, George. *Basic Liturgy*. London: Faith, 1961.

Fenstanton Records. In *The Worship of the English Puritans*, Horton Davies, 205. Princeton: Soli Deo Gloria, 1997.

Fenwick, John. *The Eastern Orthodox Liturgy*. Bramcote: Grove, 1978.

Florovsky, George. *The Festal Menaion*. London: Faber & Faber, 1969.

Frith, John. *A Boke Made by John Frith*. In *The Lord's Supper from Wycliffe to Cranmer*, David B. Knox, 40. Exeter: Paternoster, 1983.

Gee, Henry. *The Elizabethan Prayer-Book and Ornaments*. London: Macmillan, 1902.

Gehardsson, Birger. *Memory and Manuscript: Oral Tradition and Written Transmission in Rabbinic Judaism and Early Christianity*. Livonia, MI: Dove, 1998.

Gerrish, Brian A. *Continuing the Reformation: Modern Religious Thought*. Chicago: University of Chicago Press, 1993.

Gibson, Edgar, E.C.S. *The First and Second Prayer Books of Edward VI*. London: J. M. Dent & Sons, 1932.

Gifford, Edward H., trans. *The Didache. The Nicene and Post-Nicene Fathers*, vol. 7, edited by Philip Schaff. New York: Christian Literature, 1984.

Goodwin, Thomas. *Works of Thomas Goodwin* [1861], 2 vols. In *The Lord's Supper in Early English Dissent*, Stephen Mayor, 91. London: Epworth, 1972.

Gould, David H. "Eucharistic Practice and the Risk of Infection." *Anglican Faith and Ministry*, 1–4. http://www.anglican.ca/faith/ministry/euc-practice-infection/.

Green, Michael. *Evangelism in the Early Church*. Grand Rapids: Eerdmans, 1970.

Gregory of Nyssa. *Sermon for the Day of Lights*. The Nicene and Post-Nicene Fathers, 2nd series, vol. 5, edited by Philip Schaff and Henry Wace. Grand Rapids: Eerdmans, 1956.

Grindal, Edmund. British Museum, Lansdowne MS 8, F.16. In *The Elizabethan Prayer-Book and Ornaments*. H. Gee, 165. London: Macmillan, 1902.

Grosart, Alexander Balloch, ed. *The Complete Works of Thomas Brooks*. Edinburgh: James Nicol, 1867.

Hardy, David, and David Ford. *Jubilate: Theology in Praise*. London: Darton, Longman & Todd, 1964.

Harper-Bill, Christopher. *The Pre-Reformation Church in England 1400–1530*. London: Longman, 1989.

Herbert, Charles. *The Lord's Supper: Uninspired Teaching*. London: Seeley, Jackson & Halliday, 1879.

Higgins, Angus J. B. *The Lord's Supper in the New Testament*. London: SCM, 1952.

Hippolytus. *Against all Heresies*. In *Fathers of the Third Century*, vol. 5, edited by Alexander Roberts and James Donaldson. Grand Rapids: Eerdmans, 1957.

———. *Apostolic Constitutions*. The Ante-Nicene Fathers, vol. 5, edited by Philip Schaff. Grand Rapids: Eerdmans, 1955.

———. *The Apostolic Tradition of Hippolytus*. The Ante-Nicene Fathers, vol. 7, edited by Philip Schaff and Henry Wace. Grand Rapids: Eerdmans, 1982.

———. "The Apostolic Tradition," 4. In *The Eucharist*, edited by Daniel J Sheerin, 355. Wilmington: Michael Glazier, 1986.

Hodge, Charles. *An Exposition of the First Epistle to the Corinthians*. London: The Banner of Truth Trust, 1959.

Hogg, Quentin. *The Door Wherein I Entered*. London: Collins, 1978.

Hughes, Philip E. *Theology of the English Reformers*. London: Hodder & Stoughton, 1965.

Hutton, William H. *William Laud*. London: Methuen, 1896.

Ignatius. *Letter to the Ephesians*. In *Early Christian Writings*, Andrew Louth. London: Penguin, 1968.

———. *Letter to the Philadelphians*. London: Penguin, 1987.

———. *Letter to the Smyrnaeans*. London: Penguin, 1987.

Inglis, Kenneth. S. "The Labour Church Movement." *International Review of Social History*, 3 (1958) 445–60.

Innocent III. *The Order of the Mass*. In *The Lord's Supper: Uninspired Teaching*, vol. 2, Charles Herbert, 126. London: Seeley, Jackson & Halliday, 1879.

Irenaeus. *Against Heresies*. The Ante-Nicene Fathers, vol. 1, edited by Philip Schaff and Henry Wace. Grand Rapids: Eerdmans, 1956.

Jacobi, Douglas. "Putting 'Supper' Back into the Lord's Supper." *Bible Gateway*, July 31, 2013.

Jeremias, Joachim. *The Eucharistic Words of Jesus*. Philadelphia: Fortress, 1977.

John of Damascus. *An Accurate Exposition of the Orthodox Faith*. In *The Eucharist*, edited by Daniel J. Sheerin. Wilmington, DE: Michael Glazier, 1986.

Johnson, Maxwell. *The Prayers of Serapion of Thmuis: A Literary, Liturgical and Theological Analysis*. Rome: Pontifical Oriental Institute, 1995.

Joorman, Jutta, et al. "Remembering the good, forgetting the bad: Intentional forgetting of emotional material in depression." *Journal of Abnormal Psychology*, 114 (2005) 4:610–48.

Jungmann, Josef A. *The Early Liturgy*. South Bend, IN: University of Notre Dame Press, 1959.

Justin. *Dialogue with Trypho. The Ante-Nicene Fathers*, vol. 1, edited by Alexander Roberts and James Donaldson. Grand Rapids: Eerdmans, 1956.

———. *First Apology. The Ante-Nicene Fathers*, vol. 1, edited by Alexander Roberts and James Donaldson. Grand Rapids: Eerdmans, 1956.

Kay, William B. *Apostolic Networks in Britain*. Milton Keynes: Paternoster, 2007.

Keating, John F. *The Agape and the Eucharist*. London: Methuen, 1901.

Keith, Khodadad E. *The Passover in the Time of Christ*. London: London Jews' Society, 1925.

Kelly, John N. D. *Early Christian Doctrines*. London: A & C Black, 1958.

Kendall, Holliday B. *History of Primitive Methodism*. London: Dalton, 1906.

Kirkpatrick, George D. "Anamnesis," *Liturgical Review* 5/1:35–40. In *Luther's Liturgical Criteria and his Reform of the Canon of the Mass*, edited by Brian Spinks. Bramcote: Grove, 1982.

Klawans, Jonathan. "Was Jesus' Last Supper a Seder?" *Bible Review* (October 2001) 1–29.

Knox, David B. *The Lord's Supper from Wycliffe to Cranmer*. Exeter: Paternoster, 1983.

Kreider, Eleanor. *Given for You: A Fresh Look at Communion*. Leicester: InterVarsity, 1998.

———. "The Lord's Supper." *Anabaptism Today* (February 1993) 1–14.

Kuhn, George. "The Lord's Supper and the Communal Meal at Qumran." In *The Scrolls in the New Testament*, edited by Krister Stendal, 25–93. New York: Harper Row, 1957.

Labour Prophet. August, 1893.

Lambert, John. *A Treatise made by John Lambert unto King Henry VIII*, fo. 23. In *The Lord's Supper from Wycliffe to Cranmer* by David B. Knox. Exeter: Paternoster, 1983.

Leaver, Robin, ed. *The Liturgy of the Frankfurt Exiles 1555*. Bramcote: Grove, 1984.

Lechford, Thomas. *Plaine-Dealing: Or, Newes from New England* [1642]. In *The Worship of the New England Puritans*, Horton Davies. Princeton: Center of Theological Inquiry, n.d.

Lee, Seong Hye, "The Psalter as an Anthology Designed to be Memorized." PhD diss., University of Bristol, 2011.

Leo, Pope. "Sermon 43/4." In *Leo the Great Sermons*. Washington DC: Catholic University Press of America, 1996.

———. "Sermon 58." In *Leo the Great Sermons*. Washington DC: Catholic University Press of America, 1996.

Lewis, C. S. *Letters to Malcolm Chiefly on Prayer*. New York: Harcourt Brace Jovanovich, 1970.

Lincoln, Abraham. *Collected Works*. Springfield: The Abraham Lincoln Association, 1953.

Lobdell, William. "Does the Communion Cup Runneth Over With Germs?" *Los Angeles Times*, January 1, 2005.

Louth, Andrew. *Early Christian Writings*. London: Penguin, 1968.

Loving, Anne LaGrange. "A Controlled Study on Intinction." *Journal of Environmental Health*, July, 1995, vol. 58, 5–10.

———. "The Effects of Receiving Holy Communion on Health." *Journal of Environmental Health* (July 1997) 15–18. http://www.thefreelibrary.com/The+effects+of+receiving+Holy+Communion+on+health.-a019736122.

Luff, Stanley G. F. *The Christian's Guide to Rome*. Tunbridge Wells: Burns & Oates, 1990.

Luther, Martin. "Admonition Concerning the Sacrament of the Body and Blood of Our Lord" [1530]. In Luther. *Works*, vol. 38: *Word and Sacrament: IV*. Philadelphia: Fortress, 1971.

———. "The Blessed Sacrament of the Holy and True Body of Christ, and the Brotherhood" [1519]. In Luther, *Works*, vol. 35: *Word and Sacrament*. Philadelphia: Muhlenberg, 1971.

Manangan, Lilia P., et al. "Risk of Infectious Disease Transmission from a Common Cup." *American Journal of Infection Control* 26 (October 1998), 5:538–39.

Maxwell, William D. *A History of Christian Worship: An Outline of Its Development and Form*. Grand Rapids: Baker, 1982.

Maxwell, William. *An Outline of Christian Worship*. Oxford: Oxford University Press, 1936.

Mayor, Stephen. *The Lord's Supper in Early English Dissent*. London: Epworth, 1972.

McGowan, Andrew. "Rethinking Agape and Eucharist in Early North African Christianity." *Studia Liturgica* (2004), 165–76.

McGowan, Anne. *Eucharistic Epicleses, Ancient and Modern*. London: SPCK, 2014.

McGrath, Patrick. *Papists and Puritans Under Elizabeth I*. New York: Blandford, 1967.

Melito of Sardis. *Concerning the Passover*. In *On Pascha and Fragments*, Melito of Sardis and Stuart G. Hall. Oxford: Oxford University Press, 1991.

Methodist Magazine, vol. 25, 1802.

Moule, Charles F. D. *Worship in the New Testament*. London: Lutterworth, 1961.

"The Necessity and Advantage of Frequent Communion." Tract 26, in *Tracts for the Times by Members of the University of Oxford*, John H. Newman. London: J.G.F. & J. Rivington, 1840.

Neil, Charles, and J.M. Willoughby. *The Tutorial Prayer Book*. London: Church Book Room, 1959.

Nolland, John. *Word Biblical Commentary: Luke*. London: Thomas Nelson, 1998.

O'Grady, Desmond. *The Victory of the Cross: A History of Early Christian Rome*. London: Harper Collins, 1992.

Origen. *Against Celsus. The Ante-Nicene Fathers*, vol. 4, edited by Alexander Roberts and James Donaldson. Grand Rapids: Eerdmans, 1956.

———. *Commentary on Romans 10:33. The Ante-Nicene Fathers*, vol. 4, edited by Alexander Roberts and James Donaldson. Grand Rapids: Eerdmans, 1956.

———. *Homily XI on Matthew Chapter 15. The Ante-Nicene Fathers*, vol. 4, edited by Alexander Roberts and James Donaldson. Grand Rapids: Eerdmans, 1956.

———. *Homily XIII on Exodus Chapter 35*. In *The Eucharist*, edited by Daniel J. Sheerin. Wilmington: Michael Glazier, 1986.

Owen, Robert, ed. "An Answer to Two Questions." In *The Works of John Owen DD*. New York: Robert Carter & Brothers, 1851.

Packer, James I. *Among God's Giants*. Eastbourne: Kingsway, 1997.

———. *A Quest for Godliness: The Puritan Vision of the Christian Life*. Wheaton, IL: Crossway, 1990.

Pecham, John. *Statute of the Province of Canterbury*. In *The Pre-Reformation Church in England 1400–1530*, edited by Christopher Harper-Bill. London: Longman, 1996.

Pitre, Brant. *Jesus and the Jewish Roots of the Eucharist*. New York: Double Day, 2011.

Pliny the Younger. "Letter to the Emperor Trajan." In *A New Eusebius*, edited by John Stevenson, 13–15. London: SPCK, 1977.

Potter, George R. *Huldrich Zwingli*. London: Edward Arnold, 1978.

———. *Ulrich Zwingli*. London: Historical Association, 1971.

Primitive Methodist Magazine, 1850.

Pugliese, Gina and Martin Favero. "Low Risk of Infection From Common Communion Cup." *Infection Control* (1999) 20:443.

Ratramnus. *De Corpore et Sanguine*. In *History of Christianity in the Middle Ages*, William R. Cannon, 99–100. New York: Abingdon, 1960.

Reardon, Bernard. *Religious Thought in the Reformation*. London: Longman, 1981.

Ridley, Nicholas. *Brief Declaration against Transubstantiation*. Cambridge: Parker Society, 1842.

Ridley, Nicholas, and Hugh Latimer. "Conferences between Nicholas Ridley and Hugh Latimer." In *The Works of Nicholas Ridley*. Cambridge: Parker Society, 1843.

Robinson, John A. T. *On Being the Church in the World*. London: Pelican, 1969.

Rosen, Ceil, and Moishe Rosen. *Christ in the Passover*. Chicago: Moody, 1978.

Rubin, Miri. *Corpus Christi: The Eucharist in Late Medieval Culture*. Cambridge: Cambridge University Press, 1991.

Savoy Declaration. In *The Lord's Supper in Early English Dissent*, Stephen Mayor. London: Epworth, 1972.

Scotland, Nigel A. D. *Evangelical Anglicans in a Revolutionary Age*. Carlisle: Paternoster, 2004.

———. *Good and Proper Men: Lord Palmerston and the Bench of Bishops*. Cambridge: James Clarke & Co, 2000.

———. *Rome City of Empire, Christendom and Culture*. Leominster: Day One, 2011.

Serapion. *Sacramentary*. In *The Shape of the Liturgy*, Dom Gregory Dix, 42. London: Dacre, 1943.

Sheerin, Daniel J. *The Eucharist*. Wilmintgon, DE: Michael Glazier, 1986.

Smyth, John. "The Bright Morning Star." *Works*, vol. 1, 190. In *The Lord's Supper in Early English Dissent*, Stephen Mayor. London: Epworth, 1972.

———. "Confession of Faith." *Works*, vol. 2, 745. In *The Lord's Supper in Early English Dissent*, Stephen Mayor, 71. London: Epworth, 1972.

Smythe, Charles H. *Cranmer and the Reformation under Edward VI*. London: SPCK, 1970.

Socrates. *Ecclesiastical History*. *The Post-Nicene Fathers*, 2nd Series, vol. 2, edited by Philip Schaff and Henry Wace. Grand Rapids: Eerdmans, 1957.

Sozomen. *Ecclesiastical History*. *The Post-Nicene Fathers*, 2nd series, vol. 2, edited by Philip Schaff and Henry Wace. Grand Rapids: Eerdmans, 1957.

Spinks, Brian. *Luther's Liturgical Criteria and his Reform of the Canon of the Mass*. Bramcote: Grove, 1982.

Spurgeon, Charles Haddon. *Lectures to My Students*. Grand Rapids: Zondervan, 1954.

———. *Treasury of David*. New York: Funk & Wagnalls, 1882.

Staniforth, M. *Early Christian Writings*. London: Penguin, 1968.

Stevenson, J. *A New Eusebius*. London: SPCK, 1977.

Stoughton, J. *Spiritual Heroes: Sketches of the Puritans*. New York: M. W. Dodd, 1848.

Stutzman, Paul. *Recovering the Love Feast*. Eugene, OR: Wipf and Stock, 2011.

Tertullian. *Ad Uxorem* [*To My Wife*]. *The Ante-Nicene Fathers*, vol. 3, edited by Philip Schaff. Grand Rapids: Eerdmans, 1957.

———. *De Corona* [*The Crown*]. *The Ante-Nicene Fathers*, vol. 3, edited by Alexander Roberts and James Donaldson. Grand Rapids: Eerdmans, 1957.

———. *De Cultu Feminarium* [*On Female Fashion*]. *The Ante-Nicene Fathers*, vol. 3, edited by Alexander Roberts and James Donaldson. Grand Rapids: Eerdmans, 1957.

Thomson, Andrew. *John Owen Prince of Puritans*. Tain: Christian Focus, 2004.

Tucker, Karen W. *American Methodist Worship*. Oxford: Oxford University Press, 2001.

Underwood, Alfred C. *A History of the English Baptists*. London: Kingsgate, 1947.

Vermigli, Peter Martyr. *The Oxford Treatise and Disputation on the Eucharist*. Kirksville, MO: Truman State University Press, 2001.

Wainwright, Geoffrey, and Karen Tucker. *The Oxford History of Christian Worship*. Oxford: Oxford University Press, 2005.

Walford, John. *Memoirs of the Late Venerable Hugh Bourne*, 2 vols. London: T. Kingswood & Co., 1856.

Werner, Julia. *The Primitive Methodist Connexion: Its Background and Early History*. Madison, WI: University of Wisconsin Press, 1984.

Wesley, John. *Hymns on the Lord's Supper* [1745]. In *Wesleyan and Tractarian Worship*, Trevor Dearing, 12. London: Epworth, 1966.

———. "Letter to a Friend on Public Worship, 20 September, 1757." In *The Works of The Rev. John Wesley in Ten Volumes*, vol. X, 232–34. New York: J & J Harper, 1826.

———. *Popery Calmly Considered*. In *Wesleyan and Tractarian Worship*, Trevor Dearing. London: Epworth, 1966.

Westminster Confession. Article VII. In *The Lord's Supper in Early English Dissent*, Stephen Mayor. London: Epworth, 1972.

Willard, Samuel. *Some Brief Sacramental Meditations Preparatory for Communion at the Great Ordinance of the Supper*. Boston: N.p., 1711.

Williams, Rowan, and John Sentamu. "Swine Flu: Archbishops' advice on Sharing of Communion." Church of England Website. https://www.churchofengland.org/media-centre/news/2009/07/swineflu230709.aspx.

Wyatt, Lucy. *Approaching Chaos: Can an Ancient Archtype Save 21st Century Civilization?* Winchester: O Books, 2010.

Zwingli, Ulrich. "Final Statement on the Eucharist" [July 1530]. In *Huldrich Zwingli*, George R. Potter. London: Edward Arnold, 1978.

———. "Letter to Thomas Watterbach" [June 15th, 1523]. In *Huldrich Zwingli*, George R. Potter. London: Edward Arnold, 1978.

———. *On the Lord's Supper*. London: Library of Christian Classics, SCM, 1953.

Index

Lightning Source UK Ltd.
Milton Keynes UK
UKHW012058290519

343529UK00004B/339/P